Illustrations by Boyoun Kim

Philip Jodidio

Rooftops

Islands in the Sky

TASCHEN

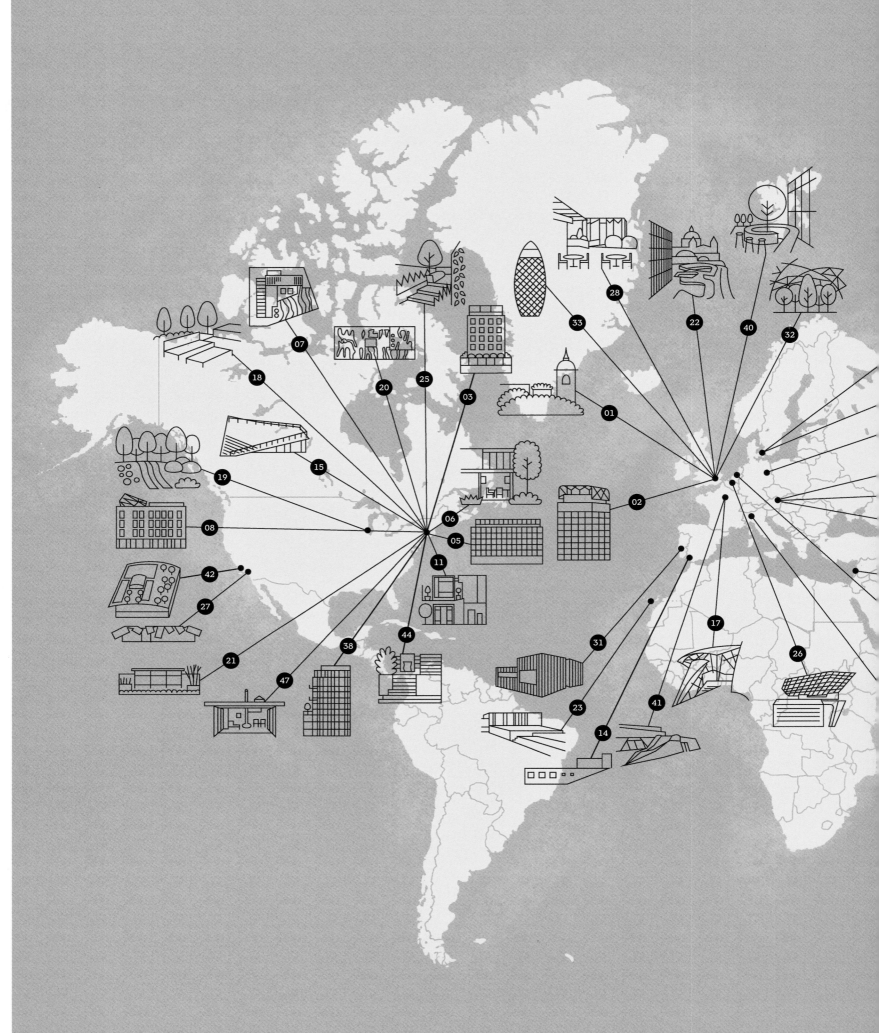

ISLANDS IN THE SKY

Then you will find your joy in the Lord, and I will cause you to ride in triumph on the heights of the land and to feast on the inheritance of your father Jacob. The mouth of the Lord has spoken.
Isaiah 58:14, Old Testament

But (as for) those who are careful of (their duty to) their Lord, they shall have high places, above them higher places, built (for them), beneath which flow rivers; (this is) the promise of Allah: Allah will not fail in (His) promise.
Surah Az-Zumar – Verse 20, Qur'an

And so the three religions of the book evoke the significance of high places with respect to piety and worthiness. The high place is more prosaically the one with the best view, a dominant location. This is surely a notion that dates back to the earliest times when seeing far could be a key to survival. From the strategic high placement of ancient fortresses to the more studied gardens of Le Nôtre—laying out a seemingly endless view of the king's domain—a view, and thus a high place, has been reserved to those who rule. More recently, a view has become a quintessential element of urban dwelling; rather than to be in the shadows of other tall buildings in New York, for example, the architects and promoters of Manhattan's new towers for the very rich place a particular emphasis on the penthouse, the uppermost pinnacle of viewing or, why not, dominating the city. The Old Testament Book of Isaiah does, indeed, equate triumph with the "heights of the land." Curiously though, the high places promised to the faithful in the Qur'an seem today reserved to the wealthy, who are not always the most pious. Without digression it could be asked if the biblical heights of the land are not now reserved to the acolytes of Mammon rather than to the servants of the Lord. Jesus made clear the contrast in the Sermon on the Mount: "You cannot serve God and mammon" (Matthew 6:19-24).

CLOSER TO GOD

The conquest of height in urban environments has taken on a global aspect since the hesitations engendered by the attacks on the World Trade Center in 2001. Towers of great height have risen from Shanghai to Dubai, from New York to London. Formerly symbols of business, these towers are now more and more often reserved to very expensive apartments, the higher the pricier. At the same time, urban density has also encouraged more and more frequent use of any rooftop for dining and viewing, or just for a garden in the midst of the concrete and steel of modernity. This book takes a look at different types of urban rooftops from around the world. Restaurants and bars have, of course, taken a place of honor in such cities as London, Bangkok, and Hong Kong. Penthouses are legion, but here an emphasis has been placed on the idea of adding such a residence above an existing building. The point is that rooftops have become a prime site for urban renovation and development, even beyond the phenomena of excessively high and expensive aeries in the sky. Here the attraction of the roof is double: views are of course best, but so, too, urban rooftops

have often been neglected and space in these locations can more easily be found and at a lower price than on the ground, where density rules. Curiously, though, the roof is at the top by definition, the most desirable and thus the most costly space in a city.

New York has seen considerable development of rooftops for purposes ranging from leisure to the display of art, as the regular exhibitions on the roof of the Metropolitan Museum of Art have demonstrated. Though rooftop spaces were not often exploited for New York museums in the past, a new facility such as Renzo Piano's Whitney Museum of American Art, located in the Lower Manhattan Meatpacking District, has several outdoor terraces, open to the public where sculptures are displayed. Older buildings like the Guggenheim by Frank Lloyd Wright or the original Whitney on Madison Avenue by Marcel Breuer did not seek to exploit such possibilities. Frank O. Gehry's Louis Vuitton Foundation in Paris (France, 2008-14; page 156) is a study in the use of the rooftop to expand and magnify the experience of visiting this cultural complex situated on the outskirts of the city. Visitors are invited to step out on numerous terraces where a relatively distant view of the towers of La Défense is available, but so too can they admire the architecture itself from various angles. In the case of the Louis Vuitton Foundation, roof terraces can almost be said to have been designed so that visitors can see Gehry's architecture from different angles and heights. Clearly rooftops are in fashion.

SUPPORTED BY A VIERENDEEL TRUSS

Apartments or even houses added to the top of existing buildings have also become an increasingly common solution to the creation of exceptional residences in an urban environment. Shigeru Ban's Cast Iron House (New York, USA, 2013-16; page 64) is a case in point. Here, at 67 Franklin in the Tribeca area of New York on lower Broadway, an 1881 building designed in the "Italianate cast-iron" style has been entirely restored to include a total of 13 duplex apartments. Beginning in the mid-19th century, cast-iron buildings, especially in Lower Manhattan, transformed the architectural aspect of the city, soon becoming the first structures to include elevators and large-pane bay windows. In terms of the content of this book though, the interesting aspect of this project has to do with the two cantilevered penthouses supported by a Vierendeel truss that Shigeru Ban designed for the rooftop. Expansive operable glass walls will give residents the impres-

SKYPARK (p. 006) → 286 | **CAST IRON HOUSE** → 64

sion that they are neither indoors nor outdoors, somehow floating over the city. "I wanted to articulate these penthouses as totally different from the existing building," says Ban.

While Ban has opted for a relatively sober rectilinear modernism for his Cast Iron House penthouses, other architects have taken the opportunity of such rooftop constructions to add fluid forms to earlier, more staid buildings. This is definitely the case of the Ray 1 House by the Austrian architects Delugan Meissl (Vienna, Austria, 2003; page 232). This residence seems to flow across the flat roof of a 1960s office building in Vienna. The architects willingly cite their desire to create a "clash of the static mass and the dynamic form of architecture in motion." The new rooftop thus redefines the building itself, and contributes a contemporary aspect to a structure that was more than 40 years old.

A NEW MODEL OF ADAPTIVE REUSE

Rooftop additions to older buildings can certainly take a number of different forms. The Diane von Furstenberg Studio HQ in New York by WORK Architecture Company (USA, 2005-07; page 86) actually involves far more than the rooftop penthouse. It includes a store, showroom, and offices, as well as the upper-level residence, for a total of over 3000 square meters of floor space. What was once a gap between the structures is now a concrete staircase that leads from the ground floor to the rooftop containing a living/work space and, above that, an 84-square-meter master suite with a terrace. The diamond-shaped penthouse juts out from the top of the pair of restored Victorian brick buildings in the Gansevoort Market historic district. New York's Landmarks Preservation Commission praised the project as a "new model of adaptive reuse for the city." Although the form of the glass and steel protrusion on the rooftop in New York is less emphatic, this aspect of the design does bring to mind the Falkestrasse Rooftop remodeling by Coop Himmelb(l)au (Vienna, Austria, 1988). The two young architects who are the principals of WORK AC sought with their rooftop protrusion to convince the very conservative officials in charge of the historic district that it was necessary to signal the new function of the Diane von Furstenberg buildings, and they succeeded, especially when lit at night it acts as a beacon in the district.

In Lisbon, the architects JAG have taken a different approach to the addition of a residence on top of an existing building. Their Roofbuilding-house is part of the renovation of a 1930s structure in the historic center of the Portuguese capital (Portugal, 2013-15; page 248). They imagined the new volumes as a kind of "tree house" that is also in willful contrast with the older structure. They explain: "This wood structure emerges from the rooftop, establishing its own space and defining its own spatial hierarchy, allowing a unique view, from the north to the south of the city." The Brussels architects JDS had a different take for their Hedonistic Rooftop Penthouses (2011; page 122) in Copenhagen. They added three penthouses in a densely populated part of the Danish capital. Inspiring themselves from Copenhagen garden typology, they explain: "The hedonistic rooftop is reflected in a playground with shock-absorbing surfaces and a playful suspension bridge, a green hill with varying accommodation backed by real grass and perennial vegetation, a viewing platform, an outdoor kitchen and barbecue, and a more quiet wooden deck."

JDS, who were also coauthors of the Mountain in Copenhagen (Denmark, 2006-08; page 328), conceived one of the more unusual rooftop viewing platforms seen in recent contemporary architecture. At the highest point of their dramatic Holmenkollen Ski Jump in Oslo (Norway, 2009-11; page 18), as the architects explain: "Atop the ski jump is a platform where visitors can take in some of the most breathtaking views of Oslo, the fjord, and the region beyond. It's a new form of public space, using an unlikely architectural form as its host, affording the same spectacular vantage point for everyone who comes to Holmenkollen." Viewing platforms at the top of tall buildings are of course nothing new, and often remain great tourist attractions, as is seen in the case of the Empire State Building in New York, where the Top Deck is situated on the 102nd floor. Together with a lower area on the 86th floor, these spaces receive more than four million visitors a year. This kind of figure may suffice to prove the democratic appeal of urban heights, but it also points to a contrast between the penthouses of the very rich and the viewing platforms for tourists.

Nor are spectacular rooftop apartments limited to the largest cities anymore. One case, not illustrated here because the promoters did not wish to publish computer-generated images, is the new penthouse atop the Odeon Tower in Monaco. Set in the top three floors of the 170-meter tower designed by the local architect Alexandre Giraldi, this 3500-square-meter

DIANE VON FURSTENBERG STUDIO HQ → 86

residence features a circular outdoor pool seemingly suspended in midair, and has been marketed for a reported £240 million, making it apparently the most expensive apartment in the world.[1] Monaco is known for its generous tax laws but, at this rate, it would seem that the price for being on top of the world has just gone up another notch.

INFINITELY DISCREET

The nature of rooftop additions can surely be related to the context of the existing buildings, but it is also a clear expression of architectural style, and undoubtedly the will of clients. Vladimir Djurovic, the Lebanese garden designer, shows just how effective his minimalist taste can be in his SST Building Private Rooftop in Beirut (Lebanon, 2008–13; page 302). Located not far from the Ramlet al-Baida beach at the southern end of the Corniche, this rooftop offers a nearly unrivaled view of the city and the shoreline. A panoramic bar, a cantilevered sunshade, and a long rectangular "infinity" pool blur the lines between the horizon and the rooftop hideaway. Indeed, an installation of this nature points also to a subsidiary benefit of being on top of a building. Especially when now higher structures look down on the space, such a rooftop is quite literally a hideaway, a place to be in the city while remaining discreet, or even invisible.

A project like Ban's Cast Iron House penthouses clearly is in the trend toward very expensive residences in New York, but other architects have made more modest efforts to occupy the highest points in existing buildings. The New York team of LOT-EK created the Guzman Penthouse (New York, USA; 1996; page 116) in the shadow of the Empire State Building using a six-meter aluminum truck container as a main element of the design. Even such elements as an external fire stair were used to connect the upper and lower levels of this much more modest residence, still situated in the heart of New York.

Rooftop gardens have also taken on new significance in New York, sometimes intended only to be viewed from above, removing something of the "gritty" aspect of city building tops as they have been known in the past. One of the most interesting examples of this trend was provided by the noted landscape designer Ken Smith with his MoMA Roof Garden in 2005 (USA; page 178) when the building was rebuilt by the Japanese architect

Yoshio Taniguchi. With a visual vocabulary inspired by military camouflage, Smith used such materials as recycled rubber chips, crushed glass and marble, artificial boulders and shrubs. The nature of this material palette had to do with the low load capacities of the roof where a "real" garden would have been impossible to install. Smith, though, also makes reference to the tradition of the Japanese "dry" garden where plants give way to stone or gravel. It is interesting to note that one real reason for the creation of this garden was to give residents of the neighboring Museum Tower Roof Garden (François de Menil; New York, USA, 2004–05; page 184) a nice view as they look down from their luxurious condominiums. Smith has recently completed another rooftop garden project in Lower Manhattan for the Conrad Hotel (New York, USA, 2011–12; page 80). The rooftop is partially intended to provide occupants of the neighboring office building a nice view, but Smith has carried out work in both structures. To quote the landscape architect: "This is a difficult urban site with three levels of roof landscape." The Conrad Hotel has street frontage on three sides and complex landscaping on multiple levels with green roof systems and vegetable garden plots. A midblock passage connects the hotel to the World Financial Center and Battery Park City. Cumulatively, these roof landscapes work as a unified whole while also functioning as a set of discreet spaces.

In New York and elsewhere, rooftop restaurants and bars have become a relatively standard feature of new hotels. This is the case for the Gansevoort Park Avenue Hotel by Stephen Jacobs and Andi Pepper, located on lower Park Avenue, where the top three floors of the 18-story building are open to the public, and include bars and lounges (New York, USA, 2011). The main rooftop measures 180 square meters and includes a pool with a view of the Empire State Building, which is located just five blocks further north on the corner of Fifth Avenue and 34th Street. The same hotel group has worked with Stephen Jacobs and Andi Pepper on its Gansevoort South Hotel in Miami Beach, Florida (USA, 2008; page 27). Here, the wood decking rooftop (1603 m²) includes an outdoor bar, palm trees, and cabanas. A ramp leads to the raised pool and deck at the center of the roof. Miami naturally seems to be a better place for outdoor spaces than Manhattan, if only for reasons of climate, but even in New York, the attraction of relatively private outdoor space above the streets of the city is making itself felt.

SYMBIOTIC RELATIONS

Other recent rooftop projects take on existing buildings in a much more robust way, thoroughly transforming them in the process. This will be the case of Zaha Hadid's Antwerp Port Authority Port House, now under construction (Belgium, 2009–; page 212). Here a 90-year-old fire station is surmounted by a signature Hadid structure intended to house 500 Port Authority employees. The angular addition conceived by the late London-based architect has a distinct appearance that seems in voluntary contradiction with the much more traditional base. Almost more than a rooftop structure, this is a symbiotic addition to an old building that transforms its appearance and very nature.

Another equally bold transformation is that conceived by the California architect Eric Owen Moss for his Pterodactyl building, which nearly envelops and totally alters a very standard 800-car parking garage built in 1998 (Culver City, California, USA, 2013–14; page 218). Eric Owen Moss is best known for his continuing transformation of the Culver City area of Los Angeles, mainly for the same real estate promoter-client. Here outdated buildings have been progressively replaced or fundamentally altered to create office space in particular, giving a rather run-down part of the city a new lease on life. In this instance, the garage rooftop itself is hardly the issue; it is, rather, a question of transforming an existing structure and giving it a new life, while in fact retaining the original parking function. The complex and apparently chaotic appearance of this project led the architect, when asked if he was trying to create a "modern day temple," to state: "It depends whether you believe that the world keeps getting different or that the world recycles. I saw it more like the mouth of the lion or the tiger—there's a piece hanging over you, which is showering you with flowers or could be a guillotine. You could probably make a case that both ideas have some truth to them. This building is complex because of the aggregate of simple components. The trick is how you put them together. For example, the western side of the building is, by intention, pulled past the edge of the garage to obviate the scale of the garage and to minimize the automobiles' context."[2] The California climate surely encourages the use of rooftops and the new Facebook headquarters by Frank O. Gehry is no exception. Known as MPK 20, the 40 000-square-meter headquarters of Facebook in Palo Alto (California, USA, 2015) boasts an open-plan office area large enough to seat 2800 people. The entire roof of the structure is occupied by a garden accessible via stairways, ramps, and elevators. Employees are encouraged to rest, walk, or even work on the roof.

LOST IN TRANSLATION

The use of rooftops for restaurants and bars is a fairly old tradition. New Yorkers and many tourists have fond memories of the Windows on the World restaurant and bar on the 106th and 107th floors of the former North Tower of the World Trade Center. The Rainbow Room on the 65th floor of the tower at 30 Rockefeller Center opened in 1934, and has reopened recently after a closure in 2009. In recent years there have been more and more such restaurants in spectacular locations, such as Searcy's, the club, restaurant, and bar located at the top of Norman Foster's former Swiss Re building in London's City (UK, 2001–04; page 260). Jean Nouvel, together with the Swiss artist Pipilotti Rist, signed the rooftop restaurant in his own Hotel Stephansdom in Vienna (Austria, 2007–10; page 150). Here the allure of work by a top artist and a noted architect combines with panoramic views of the city. This is obviously a winning combination when it comes to drawing in clients.

The urban environment takes on a scintillating new aspect, particularly at night when seen from on high. An example of the impact of this kind of view can be felt from the 52nd story of Kenzo Tange's Shinjuku Park Hyatt Hotel. Used as décor in the 2003 movie *Lost in Translation*, the New York Grill offers a sensational view of the urban vastness of Tokyo. Today, *Lost in Translation* tours are offered in Tokyo that take visitors to the bar of this famous venue. In a way, Tokyo is a city that can only begin to be understood from a high vantage point, and the New York Grill has an unbeatable panoramic view. Here the rooftop becomes a way to better understand the seeming chaos of the city itself.

One of the most successful rooftop restaurants in the world is surely Georges (France, 1999–2000; opposite page), set atop the Pompidou Center in Paris. Though the building itself was designed by Richard Rogers and Renzo Piano, Georges was the work of the younger Paris team Jakob + MacFarlane. This relatively early use of computer-driven design combines with a well-run restaurant and unbeatable views of the French capital. Despite the relatively amorphous shapes for the restaurant pavilions containing the kitchen or toilets and a bar, Georges fits in well with the more generally rectilinear and industrially inspired architecture of Piano & Rogers.

Georges has the advantage of occupying both indoor and outdoor dining spaces, a combination that works even better in warmer climates, as might be the case of the SEVVA Taste Bar in Hong Kong by Tsao & McKown (China, 2008; page 266), or the Sirocco Restaurant & Skybar in Bangkok by DWP (Thailand, 2004; page 272). But London, too, shares the growing taste for indoor-outdoor rooftops, as the Radio Rooftop Bar by Foster + Partners attests (UK, 2006–13; page 226). Even Londoners who know their city well almost discover a different urban configuration from an elevated vantage point.

FLY ME TO THE MOON

Nor are the uses of urban rooftops only "permanent": temporary structures or installations are also a frequent feature on the top of city buildings. This was certainly the case of the three-month installation of the restaurant Nomiya on the roof of the Palais de Tokyo in Paris in 2009. The artist Laurent Grasso and his brother Laurent Pascal, an architect, conceived of an easily transportable structure seating 12 diners. Built partially in the shipyards at Cherbourg, the 18-meter-long structure was brought to Paris in two pieces and assembled on the roof of the Palais de Tokyo. Instead, the American architect Jeffrey Inaba came up with a very different use for the rooftop of the former Dia Art Center in the Chelsea area of New York (USA, 2009; page 16). Using "pool noodles," which are long, cylindrical, foam, water floatation toys, he generated a 500-square-meter lounge area during the donation of the "No Soul for Sale" festival sponsored by X-Initiative in 2009. Ephemeral installations of this type of course facilitate the work of the architect, simplifying the otherwise complex permissions process.

In an interesting development, rooftop spaces are increasingly being used in urban environments to generate extra green areas, far above the ground. This type of use is apparent in a residential project in Copenhagen called the Mountain (BIG/JDS) where apartments with roof gardens are arrayed on top of a 10-story parking facility, combining two functions and also rendering the higher reaches of the project more attractive and surely economically viable (Denmark, 2006–08; page 328). Towers, too, have succumbed to the fashion of sky gardens. Jean Nouvel's One Central Park building in Sydney (Australia, 2010–14; page 204) involved collaboration with the botanist Patrick Blanc, well known for his vertical gardens—here called hydroponic walls. Combined with horizontal tubs, these walls allow the 34-story main tower to be increasingly covered with climbing plants and creepers. A panoramic terrace is situated on a monumental cantilevered plateau near the top of the building.

Toyo Ito's CapitaGreen building in Singapore has not only Sky Terraces but a Sky Forest, with trees that should eventually be 15 meters in height (2012–14; page 52). Combined with a Wind Catcher and set 245-meters above the ground, these installations of course emphasize the ecological awareness of the architect and the client, but they also point to an increasing trend in contemporary urban structures, where greenery and rooftop spaces have become much more the rule. Plants contribute to energy savings and also to a general feeling of well-being, either in office spaces like these or in residential buildings. It suffices to look at older skyscrapers anywhere in the world to be convinced that rooftop open spaces and even more so greenery were extremely rare above ground level.

Another example of "green" towers that include substantial roof space given over to planting is the Vertical Forest (Il Bosco Verticale) project carried forward by the architect Stefano Boeri in Milan (Italy, 2008–14; page 350). The two towers concerned are respectively 80 and 112 meters in height, and were inaugurated in 2014. The towers include 780 trees,

GEORGES RESTAURANT, POMPIDOU CENTER [Jakob & MacFarlane, Paris, France]

5000 shrubs, and 11000 perennial plants. The work by the architect and associated botanists is intended to create a sufficiently large green area to permit an enrichment of the local population of butterflies and birds. Planting on modern buildings can certainly be used to reduce heat gain and thus energy consumption. Contribution to the wider biosphere has also become an issue of concern. Given their usefulness in creating a heat shield, rooftop gardens are likely to become more and more frequent in contemporary architecture, even if such additions can create concerns about weight loads and potential leaks.

FLOATING PARK

The Marina Bay Sands complex by Moshe Safdie, located in Singapore takes the concept of the urban rooftop to new heights, both literally and figuratively (Skypark, 2010; page 286). Part of an enormous complex based on guidelines developed by the Urban Redevelopment Authority of Singapore for expansion of its downtown through reclamation of the bay front, Marina Bay Sands is anchored by three 55-story hotel towers. More unusual, a kind of airborne island unites these buildings. The 1.01-hectare Skypark connects the towers at a height of 190 meters, with a 65-meter cantilever at one end, the longest cantilever in a public building in the world. The Skypark can accommodate 3900 people at any one time. Its gardens include 250 trees and 650 plants, some up to eight meters tall. One of the signature amenities of the Skypark is the swimming area, which includes three linked 50-meter swimming pools and a 146-meter-long infinity edge overlooking the city. Safdie has long been known for a kind

of exuberance in his architecture that is not typical. With the climate and encouragement of Singapore, he has realized a building complex so exceptional that it has been reproduced all over the world. And what if rooftops were the place where an artificial version of nature might take hold as the level of the ground becomes too overcrowded and perhaps polluted for vegetation to survive. Lifting this island garden 190 meters in the air, Moshe Safdie certainly takes a step toward the kind of artificial nature that has long been posited by such figures as Toyo Ito in Japan.

Especially in an urban environment, rooftops are not always where they appear to be. Underground parking facilities have become common in many cities, and, above them, landscape architects have frequently been given the opportunity to create new green spaces. This is the case of Maggie Daley Park in Chicago (USA, 2002–15; page 172), a partial re-thinking of the city's well-known Grant Park located above a 4000-car underground parking garage adjacent to Millennium Park. Using geofoam (polystyrene in the form of large lightweight blocks) to create a "curvilinear, topographically dramatic, and relentlessly heterogeneous" new park area, Michael Van Valkenburgh Associates thus contributed to a broad recreational and cultural area that includes the Jay Pritzker Pavilion and BP Bridge by Frank O. Gehry and that is close to the Chicago Art Institute, with its Modern Wing designed by Renzo Piano. The geofoam was naturally employed to avoid overloading the roof of the parking garage, creating an interesting mixture of artificial and natural elements.

The Canary Wharf Crossrail project by Foster + Partners is a mixed-use scheme located above the new Canary Wharf Crossrail Station (London, UK, 2009–15; page 254). The complex includes four levels of retail, a roof garden, pavilions, and station entrances unified by a grid-shell timber

HYPAR PAVILION LAWN → 144

roof. The roof garden is accessible from ground level via two connecting bridges. The use of highly insulating ETFE cushions in the grid-shell roof helps to create a microclimate for the garden below, allowing the garden to be planted with some of the species that first entered Britain through the nearby docks. Here, as in other urban projects, roof space, be it in the actual buildings constructed above the Crossrail Station, or in such amenities as the rooftop garden, is being treated in a much more consequential and thought-out way than might ever have been the case in the past. Clearly most older urban rooftops are neglected—the sort of "junk space" that Rem Koolhaas has written about—but a combination of rising urban density, high land and construction costs, and interest in ecology have promoted and encouraged the use of areas, even when they are not visible from the ground. More and more, every inch of urban space is counted and used, thus the rooftop is a field of exploration that is not about to diminish: on the contrary, more and more existing urban roofs will be converted to new uses, and contemporary buildings are less and less likely to be without any roof features, even when it is clear that mechanical elements have to be provided for and set aside from decorative or more actively used spaces.

In New York, the architects Diller Scofidio + Renfro explored the use of a green roof on a relatively modest structure in the midst of Lincoln Center in Manhattan. Their Hypar Pavilion Lawn (USA, 2007; page 144) covers an area of just over 1000 square meters and can be occupied, creating what they call a form of "bucolic urbanism." Aside from creating unexpected leisure space, and a pleasant view from above, the Hypar Lawn once again clearly serves the requirements of increasingly energy-conscious clients. "The increased thermal mass of the grass roof dramatically reduces the mechanical loads of the restaurant below," they explain. "Water is drained through the structural columns underneath the lawn surface." It seems apparent that one of the most widespread new uses of rooftops is to reduce heat gain or loss, with a layer of soil and greenery.

ARTIFICIAL NATURE ON THE ROOF

It might be expected that Japan, with its very densely populated cities, would be the location of many interesting rooftop projects. The fact is that aside from numerous golf driving ranges set on top of buildings, gardens and outdoor spaces are relatively rare in Tokyo, for example, at least in the residential context, where tiny spaces and very small footprints are the rule. The talented architect Sou Fujimoto took a different approach than many of his colleagues to this issue. His House K located in Nishinomiya (Japan, 2011–12; page 128), between Osaka and Kobe, has a floor area of just 118 square meters. The diagonally sloped roof of the house has been conceived as a garden or even an extra outdoor room for the residence. Connections were established between the interior and the roof at all levels, and the architect compares this idea to that of a kind of natural topography. A small shed at the lower end of the sloped roof provides some shelter, but the rest of the roof is exposed to the elements, with a number of potted trees "floating" in the white surface. House K is an example of the pertinent exploration of the relationship between architecture, nature and

HOUSE K → 128

the city carried out by Japanese architects, ranging from Toyo Ito to Itsuko Hasegawa and even Tadao Ando, for whom the presence of sunlight inside a building establishes a rapport with nature. The codified or circumspect way that Fujimoto brings nature into his composition in the form of potted trees is a quite specific Japanese notion, where artificiality and nature coincide or cross through each other.

JUNK GOES GREEN

There may be as many ways to design and convert rooftops as there are buildings in modern cities. The attraction of the roof, the high place, is ancient, surely going further back in the human psyche than even the Old and New Testaments or the Qur'an. The high place is reserved to the virtuous, to the pious, to the powerful or finally, more recently, to the wealthy. Simply put, the roof offers a view, a place to contemplate the city, or to escape from its bustle and noise, at least for a time. The new intensity in the search for uses for urban rooftops has multiple reasons. First and foremost surely is the economic argument. Less space implies more interest in underused surfaces in the crowded contemporary city. What was "junk" in the parlance of Koolhaas, a left over area where air-conditioning units or cell phone repeaters were hidden, suddenly assumes a new value. Rooftops are cool; rooftops are coming to life. They are becoming bars and restaurants, apartments, and gardens. Beyond considerations of money and the use of space, new concerns such as ecology have made their weight felt in the rush to exploit the topmost level of the city. A layer of earth and a flourishing tree planted 200 meters off the ground protect and shelter interior spaces from devilish heat gain or loss. Again, the economy speaks, a green roof can be translated in terms of lower energy bills, sustainability being the ultimate goal of architects, promoters, and owners. Nor are rooftops at the end of their progression in the urban jungle, when the earth becomes too polluted, too congested. Then, perhaps, islands will be built far above the ground, in the image of Moshe Safdie's possibly visionary Marina Bay Sands complex in Singapore. An island of pleasures floating 190 meters from the earth, a pool suggesting the infinity of space, no longer trapped by a forest of towers, now open to the sky. Thus the top, the roof, is rooted in tradition and tied to the earth; the highest place is that of the just, the pious, and, oh yes, the wealthy. It is a place for new optimisim in the burgeoning global city, a refuge and a hope, an island in the sky from which to look down on the earth.

1   http://www.dailymail.co.uk/news/article-2729501/Inside-worlds-expensive-apartment-Penthouse-Monacos-new-Odeon-Tower-complete-water-slide-private-chauffeur-caterer-set-potential-owner-240MILLION.html, accessed on November 10, 2015.
2   Eric Owen Moss, interview, http://www.architectmagazine.com/project-gallery/pterodactyl_1, accessed on November 9, 2015.

HIMMELHOHE PARADIESE

Dann wirst du am Herrn deine Wonne haben, dann lasse ich dich über die Höhen der Erde dahinfahren und das Erbe deines Vaters Jakob genießen. Ja, der Mund des Herrn hat gesprochen.
Jesaja 58:14, Altes Testament

Vielmehr sind für die, die fürchten ihren Herrn, Obergemächer über Obergemächer erbaut, unterhalb derer Bäche fließen. Ein Versprechen Gottes, nicht bricht Gott sein Versprechen.[1]
Sure az-Zumar (Die Scharen) – Vers 20, Koran

So beschwören die drei Buchreligionen die Bedeutsamkeit des hohen Orts als Verweis auf Gottesfürchtigkeit und Verdienst. Prosaischer betrachtet ist der hohe Ort derjenige mit dem weitesten Blick, eine beherrschende Stellung. Dieses Bild wurzelt zweifellos in einer fernen Vergangenheit, als der Ausblick über das Land nicht selten überlebenswichtig war. Von der Ansiedlung alter Festungen auf strategischer Höhe bis zu den raffinierten Gärten Le Nôtres, die als scheinbar grenzenloser Blick über das Königreich konzipiert waren: Der weite Ausblick, die erhabene Lage blieb jenen vorbehalten, die das Zepter in der Hand hielten. In jüngster Zeit hat sich dieser Fernblick zu einer wesentlichen Komponente urbanen Wohnens entwickelt, und so rücken die Architekten und Projektträger der neuen Wohntürme für die Superreichen nun, um sich aus dem Schatten anderer Hochhäuser in Manhattan zu lösen, das Penthaus in den Mittelpunkt – den Gipfel, von dem aus sich die Stadt perfekt überblicken, um nicht zu sagen beherrschen lässt. Das alttestamentliche Buch Jesaja setzt tatsächlich Erfolg mit den „Höhen der Erde" gleich. Interessanterweise aber scheint diese erhabene Stellung, die auch der Koran den Gläubigen verspricht, heute den Reichen vorbehalten zu sein, die nicht immer zu den Frömmsten zählen. Die Frage, ob der biblische hohe Ort in unserer Zeit eher den Jüngern Mammons vorbehalten sei als den Dienern Gottes, hat eine gewisse Berechtigung. In der Bergpredigt stellte Jesus die Unvereinbarkeit klar heraus: „Ihr könnt nicht beiden dienen, Gott und dem Mammon." (Matthäus 6:24)

NÄHER ZU GOTT

Nach vorübergehendem Zögern infolge des Anschlags auf das World Trade Center 2001 ist inzwischen ein weltweiter Ansturm auf die Gipfellagen des urbanen Raums zu beobachten. Von Schanghai bis Dubai, von New York bis London erheben sich gewaltige neue Turmbauten. Einst Symbole der Wirtschaft, sind diese Hochhäuser nun immer häufiger exklusivem Wohnen vorbehalten – je höher hinauf, desto teurer. Gleichzeitig sorgt die Dichte der Innenstädte für die zunehmende Erschließung von Dachflächen zum Speisen mit Ausblick oder als Garten inmitten moderner Beton- und Stahlbauten. Dieses Buch wirft einen Blick auf unterschiedlich genutzte innerstädtische Dachflächen in aller Welt. In Metropolen wie London, Bangkok und Hongkong nehmen natürlich Restaurants und Bars einen Ehrenplatz ein. In der nahezu unüberschaubaren Kategorie Penthaus liegt das Haupt-

gewicht auf solchen Dachwohnungen, die einem Gebäude nachträglich aufgesetzt wurden. Über das Phänomen des ebenso hohen wie teuren Spitzenplatzes hinaus hat sich die Dachetage auch unter dem Aspekt der Stadterneuerung und -entwicklung als Premiumlage entpuppt. Der Reiz der Dachebene ist ein zweifacher, denn zu der unschlagbaren Aussicht gesellt sich die Tatsache, dass urbane Dachflächen über einen langen Zeitraum ignoriert wurden, deshalb sind freie Flächen leichter zu finden und kostengünstiger als unten am Boden, wo Dichte herrscht. Zugleich ist die Dachlage per definitionem die höchste, womit sie die begehrenswerteste und damit auch wertvollste Fläche der Stadt bleibt.

In New York City wurde inzwischen eine beträchtliche Zahl an Dachflächen auf unterschiedlichste Weise erschlossen. Die Nutzung reicht von Freizeitangeboten bis hin zur Kunstausstellung – auf dem Dach des Metropolitan Museum of Art werden beispielsweise regelmäßig Ausstellungen veranstaltet. Während die Museen New Yorks ihre Dachflächen in der Vergangenheit eher selten nutzten, präsentiert sich Renzo Pianos neues Whitney Museum of American Art im Meatpacking District von Lower Manhattan mit mehreren dem Publikumsverkehr geöffneten Freiflächen, auf denen Skulpturen ausgestellt sind. Ältere Bauten wie Frank Lloyd Wrights Guggenheim Museum und Marcel Breuers ursprüngliches Whitney Museum an der Madison Avenue strebten eine derartige Nutzung gar nicht erst an. Frank O. Gehrys am Pariser Stadtrand gelegenes Bauwerk für die Fondation Louis Vuitton (Paris, 2008–14; Seite 156) ist eine perfekte Fallstudie, wie sich das Besuchererlebnis durch die Einbeziehung von Dachflächen erweitern und steigern lässt. Der Besucher kann auf diverse Terrassen dieses Kulturtempels hinaustreten und seinen Blick bis zu der fernen Skyline von La Défense schweifen lassen; zugleich bietet sich die Gebäudearchitektur der Betrachtung aus unterschiedlichen Blickwinkeln dar. Es drängt sich der Gedanke auf, diese Dachterrassen seien explizit zu dem Zweck konzipiert, Gehrys Architektur auf verschiedenen Ebenen erlebbar zu machen – Dächer sind eindeutig im Trend.

VERLASS AUF DEN VIERENDEEL-FACHWERKBINDER

Inzwischen wird die Forderung nach außergewöhnlichem Wohnraum im urbanen Umfeld immer häufiger mit dem Aufsetzen von Wohnungen, teils sogar ganzen Häusern auf Bestandsgebäude erfüllt. Ein Beispiel dafür liefert Shigeru Bans Cast Iron House (New York, 2013–16; Seite 64). Das Ge-

RAY 1 HOUSE → 232

bäude in der Franklin Street 67 liegt in unmittelbarer Nähe des südlichen Broadway im New Yorker Stadtteil Tribeca; es wurde 1881 im Stil einer italianisierenden Gusseisen-Architektur errichtet und ist nun, nach gründlicher Restaurierung, in insgesamt 13 Maisonette-Wohnungen aufgeteilt. Ab Mitte des 19. Jahrhunderts verwandelten gusseiserne Fassaden vor allem in Lower Manhattan zunehmend das architektonische Gesicht der Stadt; bald waren die ersten dieser Bauten auch mit Aufzügen sowie mit großflächig verglasten Erkerfenstern versehen. Hier interessieren jedoch die beiden auskragenden, mit einem Vierendeel-Fachwerkbinder konstruierten Penthauseinheiten, die Shigeru Ban als Dachaufbau konzipierte. Dank großflächiger verschiebbarer Glaswände ergibt sich der Eindruck eines Zwischenraums, als befänden sich die Bewohner weder drinnen noch draußen – ein spannungsreicher Schwebezustand in luftiger Höhe. Ban erklärt dazu: „Ich wollte diesen Penthausaufbau von dem Bestandsbau als etwas völlig anders Geartetes absetzen."

Während Ban sich beim Cast Iron House für eine relativ nüchterne geradlinige Moderne entschied, nutzten andere Architekten den Dachaufbau als Gelegenheit, ältere, ruhige Gebäude mit fließenden Formen zu ergänzen. Definitiv der Fall ist dies beim Haus Ray 1 des österreichischen Architekturbüros Delugan Meissl (Wien, 2003; Seite 232). Die Privatwohnung auf einem Wiener Bürogebäude aus den 1960er-Jahren scheint sich förmlich über das Flachdach zu ergießen. Die Architekten verweisen freimütig auf ihren Wunsch, „die statische Masse mit der dynamisch

bewegten architektonischen Gestalt kollidieren" zu lassen. So definiert der Dachaufbau auch das Bestandsgebäude neu, das zum Zeitpunkt der Ausführung bereits über 40 Jahre alt war und durch den Eingriff einen modernen Zug gewann.

EIN NEUES MODELL FÜR FOLGENUTZUNGEN

Dachaufbauten auf älteren Gebäuden lassen sich auf diverse Weise realisieren. Der von der WORK Architecture Company gestaltete New Yorker Hauptsitz von Diane von Fürstenberg (2005-07; Seite 86) umfasst tatsächlich weit mehr als nur das Penthaus auf Dachebene. Zu dem Projekt gehören ein Ladenlokal, ein Vorführraum, diverse Büroräume sowie die auf oberster Ebene angesiedelte Privatwohnung – insgesamt über 3000 m² Nutzfläche. Eine frühere Gebäudelücke wird durch einen Treppenaufgang aus Beton geschlossen, der sich vom Parterre bis zum Dachgeschoss in einer einzigen Flucht durch den Wohn-/Arbeitsbereich zieht; den oberen Abschluss bildet die 84 m² große Mastersuite mit Terrasse. Wie ein geschliffener Diamant überragt das Penthaus die restaurierten viktorianischen Ziegelfassaden des historischen Gansevoort Market. Die New Yorker Denkmalschutz-Kommission würdigte das Projekt als „neues Modell für Folgenutzungen für diese Stadt". Der Dachauswuchs aus Stahl und Glas erinnert stark an den noch eindringlicheren Dachausbau Falkestra-

POOL NOODLE ROOFTOP [Inaba Williams, New York, USA]

ße von Coop Himmelb(l)au (Wien, 1988). Die beiden jungen Architekten an der Spitze von WORK AC wollten mit ihrem New Yorker Projekt die hochkonservativen Denkmalschützer des historischen Stadtviertels davon überzeugen, dass die neue Funktion der Gebäude von Diane von Fürstenberg zwingend sichtbar sein müsse. Ihr Erfolg zeigt sich vor allem nachts, wenn der beleuchtete Aufbau im Viertel weithin sichtbar strahlt.

Das Lissabonner Architekturbüro JAG verfolgte einen anderen Ansatz. Das Roofbuildinghouse, das die Architekten auf ein Bestandsgebäude setzten, entstand im Zuge der Renovierung eines Bauwerks aus den 1930er-Jahren im historischen Stadtkern der portugiesischen Hauptstadt (2013–15; Seite 248). Sie imaginierten das neue Raumgebilde als „Baumhaus", das zu dem älteren Bau in eigenwilligem Kontrast steht. Dazu erläutern sie: „Die Holzkonstruktion entwächst dem Dach, sie definiert einen eigenen Raum und eine eigene Raumhierarchie mit einem einzigartigen Blick über die Stadt, von Nord bis Süd."

Das Brüsseler Architekturbüro JDS verfolgte bei den Kopenhagener Hedonistic Rooftop Penthouses einen anderen Ansatz (2011; Seite 122). In einem dicht bevölkerten Bezirk der dänischen Hauptstadt realisierten sie drei Penthauseinheiten, wobei sie sich von der Kopenhagener Gartentypologie inspirieren ließen. Ihren Entwurf erläutern sie so: „Den Hedonismus der Dachfläche verkörpern ein Spielplatz mit trittdämpfenden Oberflächen sowie ein spielerischer Brückensteg, ein grüner Hügel mit unterschiedlichen Aufenthaltsorten vor einem Hintergrund aus echtem Rasen und mehrjährigem Grün, eine Aussichtsplattform, eine Grillküche und eine ruhiger gelegene Holzterrasse."

JDS, Miturheber des Kopenhagener Mountain (2006–08; Seite 328), zeichnet auch für das Konzept eines selbst für die neuere moderne Architektur ziemlich ausgefallenen Aussichtsdecks verantwortlich. Es nimmt den höchsten Punkt ihrer dramatischen Holmenkollen-Skischanze ein (Oslo, 2009–11; Seite 18), wozu die Architekten erklären: „Oben auf der Sprungschanze befindet sich eine Besucherplattform, die einen atemberaubenden Blick über Oslo, den Fjord und das weitere Umland bietet. Es ist eine neue Form des öffentlichen Raums auf einer ungewöhnlichen Architektur; jeder, der den Holmenkollen besucht, kommt so in den Ge-

nuss derselben spektakulären Aussicht." Aussichtsdecks auf Hochhäusern sind gewiss nichts Neues; etliche erfreuen sich bei Touristen ungebrochener Beliebtheit, wie beispielsweise das Top Deck auf der 102. Etage des Empire State Building in New York. Zusammen mit der Besucherplattform auf Höhe des 86. Stocks zählt es über vier Millionen Besucher pro Jahr. Eine Zahl dieser Größenordnung verdeutlicht die Anziehungskraft, die urbane Höhenluft auf alle Menschen ausübt, doch sie verweist auch auf den Kontrast zwischen dem Penthaus der Superreichen und der Aussichtsplattform für Touristen.

Spektakulärer Wohnraum auf Dachniveau findet sich inzwischen nicht mehr nur in Weltstädten. Ein Beispiel, das hier nicht gezeigt werden kann, weil die Projektträger computergenerierte Abbildungen ablehnten, ist das neue Penthaus des Odeon Tower in Monaco. Die Luxusresidenz mit einer Fläche von 3500 m² und einem kreisrunden Außenpool, der in der Luft zu schweben scheint, beansprucht die oberen drei Etagen des 170 m hohen Hochhauses, das der ortsansässige Architekt Alexandre Giraldi konzipierte; die angegebene Verkaufssumme von 240 Mio. Pfund macht diese Dachwohnung zur wohl teuersten der Welt.[2] Monaco ist für seine großzügige Steuergesetzgebung bekannt, doch wie es scheint, wurde das Preisniveau für einen solchen Platz an der Sonne gerade ein wenig höher geschraubt.

UNENDLICH DISKRET

Dachnutzungen lassen sich sicherlich in Bezug zum vorhandenen baulichen Kontext setzen, gleichzeitig jedoch bieten sie architektonische Ausdrucksmöglichkeiten, die die Ansprüche des Auftraggebers sichtbar machen. Der libanesische Gartengestalter Vladimir Djurovic stellt bei dem Private Rooftop auf dem SST Building in Beirut (Libanon, 2008–13; Seite 302) einen beeindruckenden Minimalismus zur Schau. Die oberste Etage dieses Bauwerks unweit des Strandes Ramlet al-Baida am Südende der Seepromenade von Beirut wartet mit einem unvergleichlichen Blick über die Hauptstadt und die Küstenlinie auf. Eine Panoramabar, eine

WEST VILLAGE PENTHOUSE → 358

auskragende Sonnenblende und ein langgestreckter Infinity Pool lassen die Grenzen zwischen dem Horizont und diesem Refugium auf Dachhöhe verschwimmen. Tatsächlich verweist eine derartige Umsetzung auf einen zusätzlichen Vorteil des hochgelegenen Standorts: Besonders wenn sie im Blickfeld noch höherer Bauten liegt, wird eine solchermaßen konzipierte Dachetage buchstäblich zum Versteck, zu einem verschwiegenen Ort, an dem man selbst inmitten der Stadt unsichtbar bleiben kann.

Ein Projekt wie Shigeru Bans Penthausetage für das Cast Iron House liegt eindeutig im New Yorker Trend zu exorbitant teurem Wohnraum; andere Architekten besetzen die Spitzenplätze auf Bestandsgebäuden mit bescheidenerem Aufwand. Für das im Schatten des Empire State Building gelegene Guzman Penthouse (1996; Seite 116) griff das New Yorker Architektur- und Designteam LOT-EK auf einen 6 m langen Lkw-Container aus Aluminium als zentrales Designelement zurück, ergänzt durch Komponenten wie eine Außenfeuertreppe, die das obere und untere Geschoss dieser ebenfalls im Herzen New Yorks gelegenen, wesentlich bescheideneren Bleibe miteinander verbindet.

Auch Dachgärten haben in New York eine neue Bedeutung erlangt; manchmal besteht ihr einziger Zweck darin, die bisher überwiegend garstige Anmutung eines Hochhausdachs, das im Blickfeld noch höherer Etagen liegt, zu verschönern. Ein hochinteressantes Beispiel für diesen Trend steuerte der prominente Landschaftsarchitekt Ken Smith 2005 mit seinem MoMA Roof Garden (New York; Seite 178) bei, der im Rahmen des Museumsumbaus durch den japanischen Architekten Yoshio Taniguchi entstand. Smiths von militärischer Tarnung inspiriertes visuelles Vokabular umfasst Materialien wie Recycling-Gummischnitzel, Glas- und Marmorschotter, künstliche Felsen und Sträucher. Grund für diese Materialwahl war die geringe Tragfähigkeit des Dachs, auf dem sich ein „echter" Garten nicht hätte realisieren lassen. Smith spielt zugleich auf die japanische Tradition des Trockenlandschaftsgartens an, in dem Felsen und Kies an die Stelle von Pflanzen treten. Den konkreten Anlass für diese Gartengestaltung lieferte interessanterweise der benachbarte Museum Tower Roof Garden (François de Menil; 2004–05; Seite 184), dessen Bewohner einen schönen Blick von ihren luxuriösen Eigentumswohnungen haben sollten. Vor Kurzem

stellte Smith in Lower Manhattan für das Conrad Hotel (2011–12; Seite 80) einen weiteren Dachgarten fertig. Er soll unter anderem den Beschäftigten im benachbarten Bürogebäude einen interessanten Anblick bieten. Der Landschaftsarchitekt, der an beiden Bauten tätig war, erklärt dazu: „Es handelt sich um eine schwierige urbane Situation mit einer Dachlandschaft auf drei Ebenen." Das Conrad Hotel ist auf drei Seiten von Straßen gesäumt und besitzt eine komplexe gestaffelte Dachlandschaft mit Dachbegrünung und Gemüseparzellen. Eine Passage quer durch den Häuserblock verbindet das Hotel mit dem World Financial Center und der Battery Park City. Die Teile der Dachlandschaft summieren sich zu einem geschlossenen Ganzen, funktionieren aber auch als Serie separater Räume.

Bei neu eröffneten Hotels in New York wie andernorts zählen Dachrestaurants und -bars inzwischen schon fast zum Standard. Ein Beispiel ist das von Stephen Jacobs und Andi Pepper konzipierte Gansevoort Park Avenue Hotel an der Lower Park Avenue. In den öffentlich zugänglichen drei oberen Etagen des 18-stöckigen Gebäudes sind diverse Bars und Lounges angeordnet (New York, 2011). Von dem Pool auf dem 180 m² großen Hauptdach hat man das Empire State Building im Blick, das nur fünf Blocks Richtung Norden an der Ecke Fifth Avenue/34th Street liegt. Auch für das Gansevoort South Hotel in Miami Beach (Florida, 2008; Seite 27) kooperierte die Hotelgruppe mit Stephen Jacobs und Andi Pepper. Hier wartet eine 1603 m² große, mit Holz belegte Dachterrasse mit einer Außenbar, Palmen und „Cabañas" auf. Eine Rampe führt auf das erhöhte Pooldeck im Zentrum der Fläche. Miami erscheint für Außengastronomie geeigneter als Manhattan, und sei es nur aufgrund des Klimas, und doch hat selbst in New York ein abgeschiedener Außenbereich hoch über den Straßen der Stadt eine nicht zu leugnende Attraktivität.

SYMBIOSEN

Andere neue Dachaufbauten nehmen einen deutlich handfesteren Eingriff in das Bestandsgebäude vor, was tiefgreifende Veränderungen zur Folge hat. Dies ist etwa bei Zaha Hadids derzeit im Bau befindlichen Port

HOLMENKOLLEN SKI JUMP [JDS, Oslo, Norway]

House für die Antwerpener Hafenbehörde der Fall (seit 2009; Seite 212). Hier wird ein 90-jähriges Feuerwehrhaus von einem typischen Hadid-Bau überragt, in dem einmal 500 Beschäftigte der Hafenbehörde arbeiten werden. Die Londoner Architektin konzipierte eine kantige Überbauung, deren markantes Erscheinungsbild bewusst im Kontrast zu der traditionellen Basis steht, eine symbiotische Ergänzung, die sich kaum noch als Dachaufbau klassifizieren lässt und das alte Bauwerk nicht nur in seiner Erscheinung, sondern in seinem ganzen Wesen verändert.

Eine andere, ebenso kühne Transformation erdachte der kalifornische Architekt Eric Owen Moss mit seinem Pterodactyl, einem Überbau, der ein 1998 errichtetes, ziemlich durchschnittliches Parkhaus mit 800 Stellplätzen nahezu vollständig umhüllt und grundlegend verändert (Culver City, Kalifornien, 2013-14; Seite 218). Eric Owen Moss ist vor allem für seine Umgestaltung der im Los Angeles County gelegenen Stadt Culver City bekannt, die er überwiegend im Auftrag eines bestimmten Immobilienentwicklers schrittweise voranbringt. Hier entstehen durch schrittweisen Neubau oder grundlegenden Umbau überalterter Gebäude vor allem Büroflächen, wodurch die Sanierung eines relativ verwahrlosten Stadtteils eingeläutet wurde. Im vorliegenden Fall ging es gar nicht so sehr um das Dach des Parkhauses, vielmehr sollte das vorhandene Bauwerk unter Erhaltung seiner Funktion durch die Umgestaltung „wiederbelebt" werden. Die Frage, ob er mit seinem Projekt einen „modernen Tempel" schaffen wolle, beantwortete der Architekt mit Blick auf die komplexe und scheinbar planlose Anmutung folgendermaßen: „Entscheidend ist, ob man glaubt, dass die Welt sich ständig weiter verändert, oder aber dass sie zyklisch geprägt ist. Für mich ist es eher ein Löwen- oder Tigerrachen – etwas hängt über meinem Kopf, es könnte mich mit Blumen überschütten oder ein Fallbeil herabsausen lassen. Wahrscheinlich ist an beiden Vorstellungen etwas dran. Die Komplexität des Bauwerks liegt in der Häufung einfacher Komponenten, der Trick besteht im Zusammenfügen. So wurde die Westfassade bewusst über die Parkhauskante hinausgezogen, um der Größe des Baus zu begegnen und den Fahrzeugkontext zu minimieren."[3] Auch das kalifornische Klima verleitet dazu, Dachflächen zu erschließen; Frank O. Gehrys neuer Facebook-Hauptsitz MPK 20 bildet keine Ausnahme. Das 40 000 m² Nutzfläche umfassende Gebäude in Palo Alto (Kalifornien, 2015) verfügt über ein Großraumbüro mit genügend Fläche für 2800 Arbeitsplätze. Das gesamte Dach ist als Park angelegt, der über Treppen, Rampen und Aufzüge zu erreichen ist. Die Beschäftigten werden angehalten, dort oben ihre Pausen zu verbringen, spazierenzugehen und sogar zu arbeiten.

LOST IN TRANSLATION

Die Einrichtung von Restaurants und Bars auf Dachflächen hat Tradition. Einheimischen wie Touristen ist das Windows on the World in guter Erinnerung, das New Yorker Restaurant mit Bar in der 106. und 107. Etage des Nordturms des früheren World Trade Center. Im 65. Stock des Hochhauses unter der Adresse Rockefeller Center 30 gab es bereits 1934 das Rainbow Room; nach der Schließung 2009 wurde es jüngst wiedereröffnet. Seit einigen Jahren suchen immer mehr Restaurants derart spektakuläre Lagen – ein Beispiel ist Searcy's, der Klub mit Restaurant und Bar hoch oben auf dem von Norman Foster ursprünglich für die Swiss Re errichteten Bauwerk in der Londoner City (2001-04; Seite 260). Jean Nouvel zeichnet gemeinsam mit der schweizerischen Künstlerin Pipilotti Rist für das Dachrestaurant in seinem Hotel Sofitel Vienna Stephansdom verantwortlich (2007-10; Seite 150). Zum Charme einer gemeinsamen Arbeit einer bedeutenden Künstlerin und eines bekannten Architekten gesellt sich der Panoramablick über die österreichische Hauptstadt – offenbar eine unschlagbar attraktive Kombination.

Nachts kleidet sich die Stadt in ein schillerndes neues Gewand, zu erleben vor allem beim Blick von oben. Welche Wirkung sich dann entfaltet, ist beispielsweise in der 52. Etage des von Kenzo Tange gestalteten Shinjuku Park Hyatt Hotel zu erleben. Der New York Grill, der 2003 als Location für die Dreharbeiten zu *Lost in Translation* diente, lockt mit einem grandiosen Blick über die unermessliche Hochhauslandschaft Tokios. Inzwischen werden *Lost in Translation*-Stadttouren angeboten, die den Besucher in die Bar des berühmten Lokals führen. Tokio ist eine Stadt, über die man tatsächlich nur dann einen Hauch von Überblick erhält, wenn man sie

PORT HOUSE → 212

aus der Höhe betrachtet; der New York Grill bietet dafür einen überragenden Panoramablick. Hier wird die Dachetage zur Verständnishilfe für alle, die das scheinbare Chaos der Metropole besser durchschauen wollen.

Eines der erfolgreichsten Dachrestaurants der Welt ist zweifellos das auf dem Pariser Centre Pompidou angesiedelte Georges (1999–2000; Seite 11). Während das Bauwerk selbst von Richard Rogers und Renzo Piano gestaltet wurde, ist das Georges das Werk des jüngeren Pariser Teams Jakob + MacFarlane. Dieses verhältnismäßig frühe Beispiel computergenerierten Designs lockt mit einem empfehlenswerten Restaurant und zugleich einem unschlagbaren Blick über die französische Metropole. Trotz der relativ amorphen Gestalt der Pavillons, in denen Küche, Bar und Waschräume untergebracht sind, bildet das Georges eine gute Ergänzung zu dem geradlinigen Industriedesign der Architektur von Piano & Rogers.

Das Georges hat den Vorzug, dass es sowohl über Freiflächen als auch über Innenräume verfügt – eine Kombination, deren Vorteile sich vor allem in wärmeren Klimazonen zeigen, so etwa bei Tsao & McKowns SEVVA Taste Bar in Hongkong (2008; Seite 266) und bei dem von DWP konzipierten Sirocco Restaurant & Skybar in Bangkok (Thailand, 2004; Seite 272). Doch auch in London begeistert man sich zunehmend für Indoor-/Outdoor-Dachlokale, es genügt ein Blick auf die Radio Rooftop Bar von Foster + Partners (2006–13; Seite 226). Selbst Londoner, die sich auskennen, können von einer solchen Warte eine neue Stadttopografie erleben.

FLY ME TO THE MOON

Urbane Dachflächen werden längst nicht nur dauerhaft erschlossen: Häufig finden sich auf den Dächern der städtischen Gebäude auch temporäre Einrichtungen. Eine solche war das Restaurant Nomiya, das im Jahr 2009 als dreimonatige Installation den Pariser Palais de Tokyo krönte. Der Künstler Laurent Grasso hatte zu diesem Zweck gemeinsam mit seinem Bruder, dem Architekten Pascal Grasso, einen leicht transportablen Aufbau mit Platz für zwölf Gäste konzipiert. Die 18 m lange, in der Werft von Cherbourg in zwei Teilen vorgefertigte Konstruktion ließen sie nach Paris bringen und

auf dem Dach des Palais de Tokyo zusammenfügen. Der amerikanische Architekt Jeffrey Inaba wiederum hatte eine völlig andere Eingebung für das Dach des ehemaligen Dia Art Center im New Yorker Stadtteil Chelsea (2009; Seite 16). Aus langen, zylindrischen Poolnudeln – Schwimmhilfen aus festem Schaumstoff – gestaltete er während des 2009 von der X-Initiative gesponserten Fundraiser-Festivals „No Soul for Sale" einen 500 m² großen Loungebereich. Derart vergängliche Installationen machen dem Architekten die Arbeit deutlich leichter, da sich der normalerweise komplexe Genehmigungsprozess dabei wesentlich einfacher gestaltet.

Eine interessante Entwicklung ist die zunehmende Nutzung urbaner Dachflächen als zusätzliche Grünflächen in luftiger Höhe. Ein Beispiel ist das Kopenhagener Wohnprojekt Mountain von BIG/JDS, ein Komplex, bei dem zahlreiche Wohneinheiten mit Dachgarten auf einem zehnstöckigen Parkhaus angeordnet sind. Dadurch werden gleich zwei Nutzungsarten miteinander kombiniert, und die erhöhte Lage ist attraktiver und zugleich bezahlbar (2006–08; Seite 328). Auch Hochhäuser beugen sich inzwischen der Mode des himmelhohen Gartens. Jean Nouvel kooperierte für die Adresse One Central Park in Sydney (Australien, 2010–14; Seite 204) mit dem Botaniker Patrick Blanc, der für seine Vertikalgärten – in diesem Fall als Hydrokulturwand bezeichnet – bekannt ist. Dank dieser mit horizontalen Trögen kombinierten Wände werden die 34 Stockwerke des Hauptgebäudes nach und nach von Kletterpflanzen erobert. Auf einer gewaltigen, von einem der oberen Stockwerke auskragenden Platte ist eine Panoramaterrasse eingerichtet.

Auf dem Dach von Toyo Itos CapitaGreen in Singapur befinden sich nicht nur sogenannte Sky Terraces, sondern sogar ein Wald, der Sky Forest, dessen Bäume einmal 15 m hoch werden sollen (2012–14; Seite 52). 245 m über dem Boden unterstreichen diese mit einem Windturm kombinierten Installationen das Umweltbewusstsein von Architekt und Auftraggeber; zugleich verweisen sie auf den wachsenden Trend zur Begrünung moderner urbaner Bauten sowie zur Nutzung ihrer Dächer. Pflanzen tragen zur Energieeinsparung bei und steigern das allgemeine Wohlbefinden, sei es bei Bürobauten wie diesem oder bei Wohngebäuden. Ein einziger Blick auf ältere Wolkenkratzer an einem beliebigen Ort der Welt macht klar, dass die Dachnutzung und erst recht Begrünungen oberhalb des Straßenniveaus früher extrem selten waren.

Ein weiteres Beispiel für ein „grünes" Hochhaus mit einem beträchtlichen Anteil an bepflanzter Außenfläche sind die Türme des Mailänder Vertical Forest (Il Bosco Verticale), ein Entwurf des Architekten Stefano Boeri (2008–14; Seite 350). Die beiden Hochhäuser mit einer Höhe von 80 bzw. 112 m wurden 2014 eingeweiht und sind mit 780 Bäumen, 5000 Sträuchern und 11000 Stauden besetzt. Die vom Architekten gemeinsam mit Botanikern konzipierte Anlage soll einmal so viel Grünfläche bereitstellen, dass die lokale Schmetterlings- und Vogelpopulation dadurch bereichert wird. Mit Pflanzen lässt sich bei neuen Gebäuden die Wärmeaufnahme und damit der Energieverbrauch reduzieren; ein weiterer Gesichtspunkt sind die Auswirkungen auf die Ökosphäre. Es ist davon auszugehen, dass Dachgärten trotz der mit ihnen einhergehenden Lasten und potenziellen Undichtigkeiten angesichts ihrer isolierenden Wirkung bei modernen Bauten zukünftig immer häufiger eingeplant werden.

SCHWEBENDER PARK

Marina Bay Sands ist ein von Moshe Safdie in Singapur errichtetes Resort, das das Konzept der urbanen Dachfläche im wörtlichen wie im übertragenen Sinn auf ein neues Niveau hebt (Skypark, 2010; Seite 286). Der gewaltige Komplex entstand nach den Richtlinien des Singapurer Amts für Stadterneuerung zur Vergrößerung des Downtown-Bezirks durch Auflandung der Uferzone; sein wichtigstes Bauwerk ist ein 55-stöckiges Trio von Hoteltürmen. Ungewöhnlicher als die Türme selbst ist die schwebende Insel, die sie verbindet. Der 1,01 ha große Skypark ruht in 190 m Höhe auf den drei Bauten, die er auf einer Seite um 67 m überragt – die weltweit größte Auskragung bei einem öffentlichen Gebäude. Der Skypark bietet 3900 Menschen gleichzeitig Platz; seine Gartenflächen beherbergen 250 Bäume und 650 weitere Pflanzen, einige davon 8 m hoch. Berühmt ist vor allem der Poolbereich, der über drei ineinander übergehende 50-Meter-Becken mit einer 146 m langen Infinity-Kante mit Blick über die Stadt verfügt. Safdie ist schon lange für seine ungewöhnlich überbordende Architektur bekannt. Angeregt durch das Klima und die Verwaltung von Singapur realisierte er hier einen beeindruckenden Gebäudekomplex, dessen Prinzip bereits weltweit kopiert wurde. Könnten Dächer tatsächlich zu einem Ort werden, an dem eine künstliche Natur Halt findet, wenn am Boden infolge von Übervölkerung und Umweltverschmutzung nichts mehr gedeiht? Moshe Safdie hob seinen Inselgarten 190 m in die Höhe und näherte sich damit deutlich einer künstlichen Natur, wie sie seit Langem von Persönlichkeiten wie Toyo Ito in Japan postuliert wird.

Vor allem im städtischen Raum befinden sich Dächer nicht immer dort, wo man sie vermuten würde. In vielen Städten sind Tiefgaragen üblich geworden, und nicht selten erhalten Landschaftsgestalter die Gelegenheit, darauf neuen Grünraum anzulegen. Dies ist zum Beispiel beim Maggie Daley Park in Chicago der Fall (2002–15; Seite 172), einem neu konzipierten Abschnitt des bekannten Grant Park, der neben dem Millennium Park auf einer Tiefgarage mit 4000 Stellplätzen angelegt ist. Mithilfe eines Unterbaus aus EPS-Leichtbaustoff schuf das Büro Michael Van Valkenburgh Associates hier einen „kurvenreichen, kompromisslos heterogenen" neuen Parkabschnitt „mit dramatischer Topografie" und trug damit zu der Vielfalt von Kultur- und Freizeitangeboten einer städtischen Parklandschaft bei, die auch den Jay Pritzker Pavilion und Frank O. Gehrys BP Bridge umfasst und in direkter Nachbarschaft zum Chicago Art Institute mit Renzo Pianos modernem Anbau liegt. Die Leichtbausteine wurden verwendet, um das Tiefgaragendach nicht zu überlasten; so entstand ein interessantes Miteinander künstlicher und natürlicher Elemente.

Crossrail Place, die von Foster + Partners projektierte Überbauung der Canary Wharf Station der neuen Crossrail-Linie, ist für eine Mischnutzung konzipiert (London, 2009–15; Seite 254). Der Komplex umfasst vier Etagen an Einzelhandelsflächen, einen Dachgarten, Pavillons und Bahnhofszugänge und wird von einer hölzernen Gitterschalenkonstruktion überspannt. Zwei Brücken verbinden den Dachgarten mit dem Straßenniveau. Hochisolierende ETFE-Folienkissen, die in die Gitterschale eingefügt sind, lassen ein Mikroklima entstehen, das es ermöglicht, den Garten mit solchen Spezies zu bepflanzen, die einst über die benachbarten Docks auf britischen Boden gelangten. Wie schon bei anderen Stadtentwicklungsprojekten ist sowohl bei den Neubauten, die über dem Crossrail-Bahnhof entstanden, als auch bei dem Dachgarten eine wesentlich stringentere und durchdachtere Dachflächennutzung zu beobachten, als sie früher je denkbar gewesen wäre. Zweifellos wird das Potenzial der meisten älteren Innenstadtdächer – Teil jenes „Junk Space", von dem Rem Koolhaas schrieb – bisher übersehen, doch die Verknüpfung von zunehmender Verdichtung, hohen Bau- und Grundstückskosten sowie wachsendem Umweltbewusstsein treibt die Nutzung selbst solcher Flächen voran, die vom Boden aus nicht zu sehen sind. Allmählich wird mit jedem Quadratdezimeter urbaner Fläche gerechnet. Das Dach stellt somit Neuland dar, das in absehbarer Zeit nicht weniger werden wird, im Gegenteil: Immer mehr städtische Dachflächen werden neuen Nutzungen zugeführt werden, und es wird immer weniger Neubauten geben, bei denen keine Dachnutzung eingeplant ist, auch wenn neben den dekorativ oder aktiv genutzten Flächen Platz für technische Komponenten vorzuhalten ist.

In New York erkundete das Architekturbüro Diller Scofidio + Renfro die Möglichkeiten eines Rasendachs auf einem relativ bescheidenen Gebäude inmitten des Lincoln Center for the Performing Arts in Manhattan. Der Hypar Pavilion Lawn (2007; Seite 144) mit einer Fläche von gut 1000 m² ist begehbar und wird von den Gestaltern als „urbane Idylle" beschrieben. Der Hypar Lawn bietet nicht nur überraschenden Erholungsraum und einen schönen Anblick von oben, sondern erfüllt die Ansprüche immer energiebewussterer Klienten. „Dank der gesteigerten Wärmespeicherkapazität des Grasdachs lässt sich die mechanische Belastung des Restaurants dramatisch reduzieren", heißt es. „Wasser wird durch die tragenden Säulen unter der Rasenfläche abgeführt." Offenbar besteht eine der häufigsten neuen Aufgaben solcher Dächer darin, mit Substrat- und Vegetationsschichten zur Verringerung der Wärmefluktuation beizutragen.

KÜNSTLICHE NATUR AUF DEM DACH

Japan, ein Land mit extremer Bevölkerungsdichte in den Städten, sollte eigentlich für eine Vielzahl interessanter Dacherschließungen prädestiniert sein. Tatsächlich aber finden sich beispielsweise in Tokio etliche Dachetagen mit Golfübungsanlagen, daneben aber relativ selten solche mit Gärten oder Freisitzen – zumindest nicht im Kontext der Wohnbebauung, die durch winzige Wohnungen und sehr kleine Grundstücke charakterisiert ist. Der talentierte Architekt Sou Fujimoto näherte sich diesem Thema anders als viele Kollegen. In Nishinomiya (2011–12; Seite 128), einem Ort zwischen Osaka und Kobe, errichtete er das Haus K mit einer Fläche von gerade mal 118 m². Das diagonal abfallende Dach des Wohnhauses ist als Garten oder sogar als zusätzlicher Raum im Freien konzipiert. Sämtliche Ebenen des umbauten Raums sind direkt mit dem Dach verbunden; der Architekt vergleicht sein Prinzip mit einer Art natürlicher Topografie. Ein Gartenhäuschen am unteren Ende der Dachschräge bietet einen gewissen Schutz vor der Witterung, während das übrige Dach den Elementen gänzlich ausgeliefert ist. Mehrere Bäume in Containern „schweben" über der weißen Oberfläche. Fujimotos Haus K ist ein Beispiel dafür, wie japanische Architekten, von Toyo Ito über Itsuko Hasegawa bis hin zu Tadao Ando, für den Sonnenlicht im Haus einen Bezug zur Natur herstellt, die Verbindung zwischen Architektur, Natur und Stadt ausloten. Die verhaltene, geradezu verschlüsselte Weise, auf die Fujimoto mit Bäumen in Containern die Natur in seine Komposition Einzug halten lässt, veranschaulicht die sehr japanische Vorstellung vom Nebeneinander bzw. der gegenseitigen Durchdringung von Künstlichkeit und Natur.

JUNK SPACE WIRD GRÜNRAUM

Es gibt wahrscheinlich ebenso viele Möglichkeiten, Dachflächen zu gestalten und umzunutzen, wie in modernen Städten Bauten stehen. Die Verlockung des Dachs, des hohen Orts, ist uralt, sie reicht in der menschlichen Psyche gewiss weiter zurück als das Alte und das Neue Testament und der

VERTICAL FOREST → 350

Koran. Der hohe Ort ist den Rechtschaffenen vorbehalten, den Frommen, den Mächtigen und schließlich, in jüngerer Zeit, den Wohlhabenden. Er lässt sich auf die einfache Formel des Fernblicks reduzieren, des Rundblicks über die Stadt oder der zumindest vorübergehenden Flucht vor ihrem Lärm und Getriebe. Die heute so intensiv betriebene Suche nach möglichen Nutzungen urbaner Dachflächen hat mehrere Gründe. An erster Stelle rangiert fraglos der wirtschaftliche Aspekt. Platzmangel impliziert gesteigertes Interesse an wenig genutzten Flächen im Gedränge der modernen Großstadt. Was Koolhaas dem „Junk Space" zurechnete – vernachlässigter Raum, auf dem Kühlanlagen und Mobilfunksender verborgen wurden –, gewinnt plötzlich einen neuen Wert. Dachflächen sind cool, Dachflächen lassen sich mit Leben füllen. Sie verwandeln sich in Bars und Restaurants, Wohnungen und Gärten.

Jenseits von Geld und Flächennutzung werden in der Eile, mit der die oberste Ebene der Stadt erobert wird, auch neue Bedenken wie die Sorge um die Umwelt spürbar. 200 m über dem Erdboden schützen eine Bodenschicht und ein grüner Baum Innenräume vor höllischem Wärmegewinn und -verlust. Und auch hier kommen ökonomische Überlegungen zu Wort, denn ein Gründach lässt sich in niedrigere Stromrechnungen übersetzen – Nachhaltigkeit ist das oberste Ziel der Architekten, Projektträger und Eigentümer. Dächer haben noch längst nicht die höchste Stufe ihrer Evolution im Stadtdschungel erreicht, wenn die Erde schließlich zu verschmutzt, zu übervölkert ist. Dann werden vielleicht Inseln hoch über dem Boden gebaut, nach dem Vorbild von Moshe Safdies womöglich visionärem Komplex Marina Bay Sands in Singapur. Eine Vergnügungsinsel,

die auf 190 m Höhe gehoben wurde, ein Pool, der die Unendlichkeit des Raums suggeriert, nicht mehr in einem Wald aus Hochhäusern eingesperrt, sondern hoch oben unter freiem Himmel. So bleibt der höchste Ort, das Dach, in der Tradition verwurzelt und erdverbunden; er ist ein Ort der Gerechten, der Frommen und – jawohl – der Reichen, ein Ort für neuen Optimismus in der blühenden Global City: Zuflucht und Hoffnung, eine schwebende Insel, von der wir auf die Erde herabblicken.

1   *Der Koran.* Hrsg. von Bernhard Uhle, übersetzt von Ahmad Milad Karimi. Herder, 2009.
2   http://www.dailymail.co.uk/news/article-2729501/Inside-worlds-expensive-apartment-Penthouse-Monacos-new-Odeon-Tower-complete-water-slide-private-chauffeur-caterer-set-potential-owner-240MILLION.html, Stand 10. November 2015.
3   Interview mit Eric Owen Moss, http://www.architectmagazine.com/project-gallery/pterodactyl_1, Stand 9. November 2015.

ÎLOTS DANS LE CIEL

Alors tu trouveras ta jouissance dans le Seigneur, je t'emmènerai en char sur les hauteurs de la Terre,
je te ferai savourer le patrimoine de Jacob, ton père. Oui, la bouche du Seigneur a parlé.
Ésaïe 58,14, Ancien Testament

Mais ceux qui auront craint leur Seigneur auront pour demeure des étages au-dessus desquels d'autres étages sont
construits et sous lesquels coulent les rivières. Promesse d'Allah ! Allah ne manque pas à Sa promesse.
Sourate Az-Zumar – verset 20, Coran

Les trois religions du livre soulignent l'importance des endroits élevés, associés à la piété et au mérite. Plus communément, il s'agit des emplacements où la vue est la meilleure, des positions pour ainsi dire dominantes. La notion remonte probablement aux temps les plus anciens, lorsque voir de loin pouvait véritablement être une question de vie ou de mort. Par la suite, la vue, et donc la position en hauteur, a souvent été dévolue aux gouvernants – depuis les emplacements en hauteur stratégiques des anciennes forteresses jusqu'aux jardins plus étudiés de Le Nôtre, affichant une perspective en apparence interminable du domaine royal. Plus récemment, la vue est devenue un élément essentiel de l'habitat urbain ; les architectes et promoteurs des nouvelles tours de Manhattan destinées aux très riches, plutôt que d'être à l'ombre des autres gratte-ciel de New York, mettent particulièrement l'accent sur les « penthouses », des appartements de grand standing, sommet absolu pour voir ou, pourquoi pas, dominer la ville. Le livre d'Ésaïe, dans l'Ancien Testament, assimile lui aussi les « hauteurs de la Terre » au triomphe. Curieusement cependant, les étages promis aux croyants par le Coran semblent aujourd'hui surtout réservés aux plus fortunés – qui ne sont pas toujours les plus pieux. Il pourrait donc paraître opportun de se demander si les « hauteurs de la Terre » bibliques ne sont pas aujourd'hui destinées plus aux adeptes de Mammon qu'aux serviteurs du Seigneur ? C'est bien le contraire, pourtant, que Jésus a voulu faire comprendre dans son Sermon sur la montagne : « Vous ne pouvez servir Dieu et l'argent » (Matthieu VI, 19-24).

PLUS PRÈS DE DIEU

Après les hésitations qui ont suivi les attaques du World Trade Center en 2001, la conquête des sommets dans les environnements urbains a gagné le monde entier et on a vu des tours s'élever toujours plus hautes, de Shanghai à Dubaï ou de New York à Londres. D'abord symboles de grandes sociétés, elles sont aujourd'hui de plus en plus souvent occupées par des appartements de très grand prix, les plus hauts étant les plus chers. En même temps, la densité urbaine a favorisé l'usage des toits pour dîner ou admirer la vue, ou simplement pour un jardin au milieu du béton et de l'acier. Le livre qui suit examine plusieurs types de toitures urbaines dans le monde entier. Si les restaurants et les bars occupent, bien sûr, la place d'honneur dans des villes telles que Londres, Bangkok et Hong Kong, les appartements de luxe sont eux aussi légion, mais l'accent est surtout mis sur l'idée même d'ajouter ce type de domicile au-dessus d'une construction existante. Il faut dire que les toits sont devenus un emplacement de tout premier choix pour les rénovateurs et développeurs urbains, au-delà même du phénomène des nids d'aigles en plein ciel, excessivement élevés et onéreux. L'attraction est double : la vue, bien sûr, est meilleure, mais les toits ont souvent aussi été négligés et on y trouve plus facilement de l'espace à un prix moindre qu'au niveau du sol où la densité impose sa loi. Aussi curieux que cela paraisse, les toits, sommets par nature, sont donc aujourd'hui les espaces les plus convoités, et donc les plus coûteux, de nos villes.

New York a ainsi vu ses toits massivement exploités à des fins allant des simples loisirs à la présentation d'art, comme en témoignent les expositions organisées régulièrement en haut du Metropolitan Museum of Art. En effet, si les musées new-yorkais n'ont guère tiré profit de leurs toits par le passé, l'un des plus récents, le Whitney Museum of American Art, construit par Renzo Piano dans le Meatpacking District du Sud de Manhattan, possède plusieurs terrasses ouvertes au public sur lesquelles sont exposées des sculptures. Des bâtiments plus anciens comme le Guggenheim de Frank Lloyd Wright ou le Whitney d'origine sur Madison Avenue, par Marcel Breuer, n'ont pas cherché à exploiter ces possibilités. À Paris, la Fondation Louis Vuitton (France, 2008-2014 ; page 156) par Frank O. Gehry est l'archétype du toit utilisé pour élargir et amplifier l'expérience vécue par les visiteurs du centre culturel en périphérie de la ville. Ces derniers sont invités à sortir sur l'une des nombreuses terrasses pour admirer la vue sur les tours de La Défense, pas très éloignées, mais aussi pour contempler l'architecture de différents points de vue. On peut presque dire que les terrasses du toit ont été ici spécialement conçues pour permettre aux visiteurs de voir l'œuvre de Gehry sous différents angles et depuis différentes hauteurs. Les toits sont décidément à la mode.

UNE POUTRE-ÉCHELLE COMME BASE

Les appartements, ou même les maisons, ajoutés au-dessus de constructions existantes sont aussi une solution de plus en plus souvent adoptée aujourd'hui pour créer des résidences d'exception en milieu urbain. La Maison de fonte (Cast Iron House, New York, 2013-2016 ; page 64) de Shigeru Ban est un exemple typique. Située 67 Franklin Street, dans le

FACEBOOK HEADQUARTERS ROOFTOP [Frank O. Gehry, Palo Alto, California]

quartier Tribeca du Sud de Broadway, elle comprend la restauration complète d'un immeuble de 1881 à façade en fonte de style « italianisant » pour y ajouter treize appartements en duplex. Dès le milieu du XIXᵉ siècle, ces bâtiments ont transformé l'architecture de la ville, surtout dans le Sud de Manhattan, et sont vite devenus les premiers à être dotés d'ascenseurs et de bow-windows généreusement vitrés. Mais ce qui nous intéresse ici, ce sont les deux appartements de luxe en encorbellement portés par une poutre-échelle que Shigeru Ban a créés sur le toit. De vastes parois vitrées s'ouvrent et donnent l'impression de n'être ni à l'intérieur, ni à l'extérieur, mais de flotter en quelque sorte au-dessus de la ville. « Je voulais trouver une expression qui diffère totalement du bâtiment existant », explique Ban.

S'il a opté pour un modernisme rectiligne et plutôt sobre, d'autres architectes ont, au contraire, profité de l'occasion pour ajouter des formes fluides à des immeubles plus anciens et ordinaires. C'est notamment le cas de la maison Ray 1 des architectes autrichiens Delugan Meissl (Haus Ray 1, Vienne, 2003 ; page 232) qui semble couler en travers du toit en terrasse d'un immeuble de bureaux viennois des années 1960. Les auteurs évoquent leur désir conscient de faire « se heurter la masse statique et la forme dynamique d'une architecture en mouvement ». Le nouveau toit redéfinit le bâtiment et confère un aspect presque contemporain à un ensemble vieux de plus de quarante ans.

UN NOUVEAU MODÈLE DE RÉUTILISATION ADAPTATIVE

Les constructions ajoutées sur le toit de bâtiments plus anciens peuvent revêtir des formes extrêmement diverses. Le siège du studio de Diane von Fürstenberg à New York par WORK Architecture Company (Diane von Furstenberg Studio HQ, États-Unis, 2005–2007 ; page 86) est ainsi bien plus qu'un appartement de luxe. Il comporte un magasin, un espace d'exposition et des bureaux, en plus du logement de l'étage supérieur, le tout sur une superficie totale de plus de 3000 mètres carrés. Là où une brèche s'ouvrait entre les différentes structures, une cage d'escalier en béton mène aujourd'hui du rez-de-chaussée au toit où se trouve un espace de vie et de travail surmonté d'un appartement de maître de 84 mètres carrés avec terrasse. En forme de diamant, il dépasse au sommet de deux immeubles victoriens en briques restaurés dans le quartier historique de Gansevoort Market. La Commission de conservation des monuments de la Ville de New York a loué le projet, qualifié de « nouveau modèle de réutilisation adaptative pour la ville ». Bien que moins ambitieux, la forme de ce surplomb de verre et d'acier sur les toits de New York fait forcément penser à celui de la Falkestrasse réaménagé par Coop Himmelb(l)au (Rooftop Remodeling Falkestrasse, Vienne, 1988). Les deux jeunes architectes à la tête de WORK AC ont ici cherché à convaincre les fonctionnaires très

MUSEUM OF MODERN ART ROOF GARDEN → 178

conservateurs chargés du quartier historique de la nécessité de signaler la nouvelle fonction de l'immeuble de Diane von Fürstenberg, et ils y sont parvenus, surtout la nuit lorsque leur œuvre est illuminée tel un phare.

À Lisbonne, les architectes JAG ont adopté une approche différente pour ajouter un logement au sommet d'un immeuble existant. Leur Maison sur le toit fait partie de la rénovation d'un complexe des années 1930 dans le centre historique de la capitale portugaise (2013-2015 ; page 248). Ils en ont imaginé les nouveaux volumes comme une sorte de «maison dans les arbres» qui contraste délibérément avec l'ensemble plus ancien. Ils expliquent que «la structure en bois émerge au sommet du toit, créant son propre espace et définissant sa propre échelle spatiale en offrant une vue unique du nord au sud de la ville». Les architectes bruxellois JDS, eux, avaient encore un autre point de vue lorsqu'ils ont créé leurs appartements hédonistes (Hedonistic Rooftop Penthouses, Copenhague, 2011 ; page 122) à Copenhague, ajoutant trois logements de standing à une zone très densément peuplée de la capitale danoise. Ils expliquent s'être inspirés de la typologie des jardins de Copenhague : «Le toit hédoniste fait écho à un terrain de jeu au revêtement de surface antichoc, doté d'un amusant pont suspendu, une colline verte comportant différents logements recouverts d'herbe véritable et de plantes vivaces, une plate-forme d'observation, une cuisine extérieure avec barbecue et un pont en bois plus tranquille.»

JDS, qui sont également coauteurs de la Montagne, à Copenhague, ont aussi imaginé l'une des plates-formes d'observation les plus originales de l'architecture contemporaine récente. Située tout en haut du spectaculaire tremplin de saut à ski d'Holmenkollen, à Oslo (Holmenkollen Ski Jump, Norvège, 2009-2011 ; page 18), les architectes la décrivent ainsi : «Tout en haut du tremplin, une plate-forme permet aux visiteurs de profiter de l'une des vues les plus extraordinaires sur Oslo, le fjord et la région tout autour. C'est une nouvelle forme d'espace public, hébergée par une

forme improbable d'architecture, qui offre la même position avantageuse à tous ceux qui viennent à Holmenkollen.» Bien sûr, les plates-formes d'observation au sommet des bâtiments les plus élevés n'ont rien de nouveau et restent pour la plupart des attractions touristiques très fréquentées, comme celle du niveau supérieur (*Top Deck*) de l'Empire State Building, située au 102e niveau. Avec l'espace inférieur du 86e niveau, elle accueille plus de quatre millions de visiteurs par an. Ce chiffre à lui seul suffit à démontrer la démocratisation des hauteurs urbaines, mais il attire aussi l'attention sur le contraste entre les appartements de luxe des très riches et les plates-formes d'observation pour touristes.

Les premiers ne sont par ailleurs plus limités aux grandes métropoles désormais. À titre d'exemple – non illustré ici car les promoteurs ne souhaitaient pas publier des images générées par ordinateur –, le nouveau «penthouse» au sommet de la tour Odéon, à Monaco. Cette résidence de 3500 mètres carrés occupe les trois derniers étages de la tour de 170 mètres conçue par l'architecte local Alexandre Giraldi et comprend notamment une piscine circulaire qui donne l'impression d'être suspendue en plein ciel ; l'ensemble aurait été commercialisé pour plus de 300 millions d'euros, ce qui en ferait l'appartement le plus cher du monde[1]. Monaco est, certes, connu pour sa législation fiscale généreuse, mais à ce niveau, il semblerait que le prix pour dominer le monde soit encore monté d'un cran.

UNE DISCRÉTION INFINIE

La nature des constructions ajoutées sur les toits, si elle est souvent en lien avec celle du bâtiment existant, est aussi l'expression d'un style architectural et, incontestablement, de la volonté des clients. Vladimir Djurovic, le créateur de jardins libanais, montre par exemple à quel point son goût

OFFICES FOR THE JUNTA DE CASTILLA Y LEÓN [Alberto Campo Baeza, Zamora, Spain]

minimaliste peut faire preuve d'efficacité avec le toit privé de l'immeuble SST à Beyrouth (SST Building Private Rooftop, Liban, 2008-2013 ; page 302). Situé non loin de la plage de Ramlet al-Baïda, à l'extrémité sud de la Corniche, il offre une vue incomparable sur la ville et le littoral. Un bar panoramique, un pare-soleil en porte-à-faux et une longue piscine à débordement rectangulaire brouillent les limites entre l'horizon et le renfoncement sous la toiture. Un tel espace ainsi aménagé met en évidence l'un des avantages secondaires d'être au sommet, surtout lorsque des constructions plus hautes ont vue sur lui : ce toit est véritablement une cachette, un lieu pour être dans la ville tout en restant discret, voire invisible.

Si un projet comme la Cast Iron House de Ban incarne clairement la tendance vers des résidences de très grand prix à New York, d'autres architectes ont tenté plus modestement d'occuper les sommets de bâtiments existants. L'équipe new-yorkaise de LOT-EK a notamment créé l'appartement Guzman (Guzman Penthouse, New York, 1996 ; page 116) à l'ombre de l'Empire State Building à partir d'un conteneur de camion en aluminium de six mètres qui constitue l'un des éléments principaux du design. D'autres éléments semblables, tels qu'un escalier de secours extérieur, ont été utilisés pour relier le niveau supérieur et le niveau inférieur de cette résidence bien plus modeste, même si elle est elle aussi située en plein cœur de New York.

Les jardins sur les toits ont aussi pris une grande importance à New York, parfois dans le seul but d'être vus d'en haut, pour rendre la vue des toits moins « graveleuse », comme on disait autrefois. L'un des exemples les plus intéressants est l'œuvre de l'architecte-paysagiste de renom Ken Smith, qui a créé le jardin-terrasse du MoMA (Museum of Modern Art Roof Garden, États-Unis ; page 178) en 2005 lors de la reconstruction du bâtiment par l'architecte japonais Yoshio Taniguchi. Usant d'un vocabulaire inspiré du camouflage militaire, Smith a eu recours à des matériaux tels que copeaux de caoutchouc récupéré, verre et marbre pilé, rochers arti-

ficiels et arbrisseaux – toute une palette dont la nature correspondait à la faible capacité de charge du toit où il aurait été impossible d'installer un « vrai » jardin. C'est aussi une référence à la tradition des jardins japonais « secs » dans lesquels la végétation fait place aux pierres ou graviers. Il est intéressant de noter que la véritable raison de la création de ce jardin par François de Menil était d'offrir une vue agréable aux habitants de la tour Museum Tower voisine (Museum Tower Roof Garden, New York, 2004-2005 ; page 184) lorsqu'ils baissent les yeux depuis leurs luxueux appartements. Smith vient aussi d'achever un autre projet de jardin sur un toit pour l'hôtel Conrad (New York, 2011-2012 ; page 80), dans le Sud de Manhattan. Si l'aménagement du toit a lui aussi en partie pour objectif de fournir une vue agréable aux occupants de l'immeuble de bureaux voisin, Smith n'a pas ménagé ses efforts pour autant, ni dans l'une ni dans l'autre des deux réalisations. Il explique notamment que « c'est un site urbain difficile, avec trois niveaux de toits paysagés. L'hôtel Conrad est bordé par des rues sur trois côtés et présente un aménagement complexe de toitures à plusieurs niveaux avec des toits végétalisés et des parcelles de jardin potager. Un passage entre deux pâtés de maisons relie l'hôtel au World Financial Center et au Battery Park City. Dans leur ensemble, ces toits paysagés fonctionnent comme un tout unifié, tout en formant plusieurs espaces secrets ».

À New York et ailleurs, les restaurants et bars sur le toit sont aujourd'hui de rigueur dans presque tous les nouveaux hôtels. C'est le cas du Gansevoort Park Avenue Hotel de Stephen Jacobs et Andi Pepper, en bas de Park Avenue, un immeuble de 18 niveaux dont les trois derniers sont ouverts au public et comprennent des bars et lieux de détente (New York, 2011) Le toit principal a une superficie de 180 mètres carrés et sa piscine a vue sur l'Empire State Building, cinq blocs plus au nord, au coin de la Cinquième Avenue et de la 34e Rue. Stephen Jacobs et Andi Pepper ont travaillé avec le même groupe hôtelier au Gansevoort South Hotel de

Miami Beach, en Floride (États-Unis, 2008 ; page ci-contre). Le pont en bois du toit (1603 m²) y comporte un bar, des palmiers et des « cabañas ». Une rampe mène à la piscine surélevée et au ponton qui occupent le centre du toit. Miami semble a priori un endroit plus approprié pour les extérieurs aménagés que Manhattan, avant tout pour des raisons climatiques, mais même à New York, l'attrait des espaces un tant soit peu personnels au-dessus des rues se fait sentir.

EN SYMBIOSE

D'autres projets récents s'emparent plus fermement des bâtiments existants et les transforment entièrement. C'est le cas de la Maison du port de Zaha Hadid pour les autorités portuaires d'Anvers, actuellement en construction (Port House, Belgique, 2009- ; page 212). Une caserne de pompiers vieille de quatre-vingt-dix ans y sera surmontée d'une structure portant la signature de Hadid destinée à accueillir cinq cents employés portuaires. La forme anguleuse de l'ajout imaginé par l'architecte originaire de Londres récemment disparue présente un caractère spécifique qui semble délibérément contraster avec la base plus classique. Plus qu'une structure sur le toit, c'est une extension symbiotique en ce sens qu'elle transforme l'apparence et la nature même d'une construction ancienne.

Parmi les autres transformations tout aussi osées, le « Ptérodactyle » imaginé par l'architecte californien Eric Owen Moss recouvre presque entièrement et modifie totalement un parking couvert de huit cents places très ordinaire, construit en 1998 (Pterodactyl, Culver City, Californie, 2013-2014 ; page 218). Eric Owen Moss est surtout connu pour les changements constants apportés à Culver City, à Los Angeles, la plupart pour le même promoteur immobilier. Des bâtiments démodés y ont été progressivement remplacés ou modifiés en profondeur pour créer des espaces de bureaux, donnant une nouvelle jeunesse à un quartier plutôt délabré. Dans cet exemple, ce n'est pas le toit du garage en soi qui importe, il s'agit plutôt de métamorphoser une structure existante pour lui redonner vie, mais en conservant sa fonction première de parking. L'aspect complexe et en apparence chaotique du projet a fait dire à l'architecte, en réponse à la question de savoir s'il avait tenté de créer un « temple des temps modernes » : « Tout dépend de si l'on croit que le monde ne cesse de changer ou qu'il recycle. Personnellement, j'y ai plutôt vu la gueule du lion ou du tigre – l'un des éléments suspendus déverse une pluie de fleurs ou pourrait être une guillotine. On pourrait sans doute argumenter que les deux idées ont une part de vérité. Ce bâtiment est complexe car il est composé d'une accumulation d'éléments simples. Son intérêt vient de la manière dont ils sont assemblés. Le côté ouest, par exemple, est volontairement tiré au-delà de l'extrémité du parking pour en réduire l'ampleur et minimiser le contexte "automobile²". » Le climat californien incite certes à l'usage de toitures-terrasses et le nouveau siège de Facebook par Frank O. Gehry ne fait pas exception. Appelé MPK 20, le site de Facebook de 40000 mètres carrés à Palo Alto (Californie, 2015) possède une zone de bureaux à espace décloisonné assez vaste pour accueillir 2800 personnes. La toiture de la structure est intégralement occupée par un jardin accessible via des escaliers, des rampes et des ascenseurs. Les employés sont incités à se reposer, se promener, voire même à travailler sur le toit.

LOST IN TRANSLATION

L'utilisation des toits pour des bars et restaurants est une tradition déjà ancienne. Les New-Yorkais et de nombreux touristes se souviennent avec émotion du restaurant et bar Windows on the World aux 106ᵉ et 107ᵉ niveaux de l'ancienne tour Nord du World Trade Center. De même, la Rainbow Room au 65ᵉ niveau de la tour du 30 Rockefeller Center a ouvert en 1934, et rouvert récemment, après avoir fermé en 2009. Depuis quelques années, de plus en plus de restaurants ont ainsi été créés dans des lieux d'exception, tels le club, restaurant et bar Searcy's en haut de l'ancien bâtiment construit pour la Swiss Re par Norman Foster dans la city de Londres (Searcy's, 30 St. Mary Axe, 2001-2004 ; page 260). Jean Nouvel a lui aussi signé, avec l'artiste suisse Pipilotti Rist, le Loft Restaurant sur le toit de son hôtel Stephansdom à Vienne (Autriche, 2007-2010 ; page 150) qui associe l'œuvre d'un grand artiste et d'un célèbre architecte à des vues panoramiques sur la ville – une combinaison visiblement gagnante pour attirer les clients.

C'est tout l'environnement urbain qui brille alors d'un nouvel éclat, surtout la nuit vu de haut. Le 52ᵉ niveau de l'hôtel Park Hyatt de Shinjuku, construit par Kenzo Tange, constitue un autre exemple de l'effet produit par ce genre de vue. Décor du film *Lost in Translation* de 2003, le New York Grill offre une vue exceptionnelle sur l'immensité urbaine de Tokyo. Des circuits Lost in Translation emmènent aujourd'hui les visiteurs au célèbre bar. En un sens, on ne peut commencer à comprendre la ville de Tokyo que depuis une position avantageuse en hauteur, et la vue panoramique du New York Grill est imbattable. Le toit devient ici un moyen de mieux comprendre le chaos apparent de la ville.

Georges (France, 1999-2000 ; page 11), situé tout en haut du Centre Pompidou à Paris, est certainement l'un des restaurants sur le toit les plus populaires. Le bâtiment lui-même a été conçu par Richard Rogers et Renzo Piano, mais Georges est l'œuvre de la jeune équipe parisienne de Jakob + MacFarlane. Le recours assez récent à l'informatique pour le design est ici associé à un restaurant très fréquenté et à des vues incomparables sur la capitale française. Malgré le caractère plutôt amorphe des pavillons qui abritent la cuisine, les toilettes et un bar, Georges s'intègre bien à l'architecture plus généralement rectiligne et d'inspiration industrielle de Piano & Rogers.

Le restaurant présente l'avantage de disposer d'espaces à la fois intérieurs et extérieurs, une association qui fonctionne mieux sous des climats plus chauds, comme sans doute au bar SEVVA de Hong Kong, par Tsao & McKown (Chine, 2008 ; page 266), ou au restaurant & skybar Sirocco de Bangkok, par DWP (Thaïlande, 2004 ; page 272). Mais Londres aussi partage ce goût croissant pour les toits mêlant intérieur et extérieur, comme en témoigne le Radio Rooftop Bar de Foster + Partners (RU, 2006-2013 ; page 226) – et même les Londoniens qui connaissent le mieux leur ville découvrent une configuration urbaine différente lorsqu'elle est vue d'en haut.

FLY ME TO THE MOON

Les constructions sur les toits des villes ne sont pas non plus toujours permanentes : les structures temporaires ou installations y sont fréquentes. C'était notamment le cas du restaurant Nomiya, installé pour trois mois sur le toit du Palais de Tokyo en 2009. L'artiste Laurent Grasso et son frère, l'architecte Pascal Grasso, ont conçu une structure de douze places facile à transporter. Construit en partie sur les chantiers navals de Cherbourg, l'ensemble de 18 mètres de long a été transporté jusqu'à Paris en deux morceaux et assemblé sur le toit du Palais de Tokyo. L'architecte américain Inaba Williams, lui, a trouvé un usage très différent au toit de l'ancien Dia Art Center, dans le quartier new-yorkais de Chelsea (Pool Noodle Rooftop, États-Unis, 2009 ; page 16) : à partir de « frites de piscine », des jouets flottants en mousse longs et cylindriques, il a créé un espace de détente de 500 mètres carrés pour le festival « No Soul for Sale » parrainé par X-Initiative en 2009. Ce type d'installation éphémère facilite, bien sûr, le travail de l'architecte en simplifiant les démarches sinon complexes pour obtenir les autorisations nécessaires.

Un autre développement intéressant auquel on assiste consiste à exploiter les espaces sur les toits pour créer des espaces verts supplémentaires en milieu urbain, loin au-dessus du sol. C'est notamment apparent dans le projet résidentiel baptisé La Montagne (BIG/JDS) à Copenhague, où des appartements aux toits surmontés de jardins sont disposés au-dessus d'un parking couvert de dix niveaux, associant deux fonctions et conférant un attrait supplémentaire aux régions supérieures de l'ensemble, qui en devient aussi plus viable économiquement (The Mountain, Danemark, 2006-2008 ; page 328). Les tours elles aussi ont cédé à la mode des jardins en plein ciel. L'ensemble One Central Park de Jean Nouvel à Sydney (Australie, 2010-2014 ; page 204) a été construit en collaboration avec le botaniste Patrick Blanc, connu pour ses jardins verticaux – ou murs hydroponiques. Associés à des bacs horizontaux, ils doivent couvrir progressivement

GANSEVOORT SOUTH [Stephen B. Jacobs, Andi Pepper, Miami Beach, Florida, USA]

de plantes grimpantes et rampantes la tour principale de 34 niveaux. Près du toit, un immense plateau en porte-à-faux porte une terrasse panoramique.

Le gratte-ciel CapitaGreen de Toyo Ito à Singapour dispose, lui, en plus des terrasses, d'une forêt en plein ciel dont les arbres devraient atteindre 15 mètres de haut (2012-2014 ; page 52). Associée à un récepteur de vent et plantée à 245 mètres au-dessus du sol, elle met en avant la conscience écologique de l'architecte et de son client, mais pointe aussi du doigt une tendance en hausse dans les constructions urbaines contemporaines où la verdure et l'utilisation des espaces sur le toit deviennent de plus en plus la règle. En effet, la végétation permet des économies d'énergie et contribue à un sentiment général de bien-être, dans les bureaux comme ici ou dans les immeubles résidentiels. Or, il suffit de regarder les gratte-ciel plus anciens partout dans le monde pour se rendre compte à quel point les espaces découverts sur les toits, et plus encore la végétation, étaient rares.

Parmi les autres exemples de tours « vertes » dont le toit comporte un vaste espace dédié à la végétation, le projet de Forêt verticale de Milan (Il Bosco Verticale, Italie, 2008-2014 ; page 350) est l'œuvre de l'architecte Stefano Boeri. Les deux tours qui le composent sont hautes de 80 et de 112 mètres, elles ont été inaugurées en 2014 et sont plantées de 780 arbres, 5000 arbustes et 11 000 plantes vivaces. L'architecte et les botanistes associés ont voulu créer un espace vert suffisamment grand pour permettre aux populations locales de papillons et d'oiseaux de se diversifier. Par ailleurs, les plantations d'immeubles modernes contribuent sans aucun doute à réduire les gains de chaleur, et donc la consommation d'énergie. La question de l'élargissement des réserves de biosphère elle aussi est devenue un sujet de préoccupation. Étant donné leur utilité en tant que bouclier thermique, les jardins sur les toits sont donc appelés à se multiplier dans l'architecture contemporaine, et ce malgré les inquiétudes en matière de poids et de fuites éventuelles.

UN PARC FLOTTANT

L'ensemble de Marina Bay Sands créé par Moshe Safdie à Singapour incarne un nouveau sommet dans le concept de toiture urbaine, au sens propre comme au sens figuré (Skypark, 2010 ; page 286). Il appartient à un immense complexe construit sur la base de directives élaborées par les services de rénovation urbaine de Singapour pour agrandir le centre-ville en mettant en valeur le front de mer. Marina Bay Sands est ancré par les trois tours de 55 niveaux d'un hôtel. Son originalité vient de l'« île » aéroportée qui les réunit. Le Skypark de 1,01 hectares relie les tours à 190 mètres de haut, l'avancée de 65 mètres qui prolonge l'une de ses extrémités est le plus long porte-à-faux construit sur un bâtiment public au monde. Il peut accueillir 3900 personnes en même temps. Ses jardins comptent 250 arbres et 650 plantes, pour certains hauts de huit mètres. Parmi les aménagements les plus marquants du Skypark, l'espace de baignade comprend trois bassins de 50 mètres en enfilade et une piscine à débordement de 146 mètres de long qui domine la ville. Safdie est connu depuis longtemps pour une certaine exubérance qui caractérise son architecture originale. Sous le climat de Singapour, et grâce aux soutiens qu'il y a trouvés, il a réalisé un ensemble exceptionnel au point d'être reproduit partout dans le monde. Et si les toits étaient le lieu par excellence où une version artificielle de la nature peut s'imposer au fur et à mesure que le plancher des vaches devient trop surpeuplé, et peut-être trop pollué, pour permettre à la végétation de survivre ? En élevant son île de jardins à 190 mètres dans les airs, Moshe Safdie a sans aucun doute franchi un pas vers la nature artificielle du type de celle postulée depuis longtemps par des personnalités telles que Toyo Ito au Japon.

Les toits ne sont pas toujours là où on les attend, surtout en milieu urbain. Les parkings souterrains sont aujourd'hui courants dans beaucoup

ONE CENTRAL PARK → 204

de villes et leurs toitures ont souvent donné à des architectes paysagistes l'opportunité de créer de nouveaux espaces verts. C'est le cas du Maggie Daley Park de Chicago (États-Unis, 2002-2015 ; page 172), qui renouvelle en partie le Grant Park bien connu, situé au-dessus d'un parking souterrain de 4000 places adjacent au Millennium Park. En utilisant la géomousse (polystyrène expansé en forme de gros blocs légers) pour créer un nouveau parc « curviligne, à la topographie spectaculaire et absolument hétérogène », Michael Van Valkenburgh Associates a contribué à une vaste zone de loisirs et de culture qui comprend notamment le pavillon Jay Pritzker et la passerelle BP de Frank O. Gehry, proche du Chicago Art Institute dont l'aile moderne a été conçue par Renzo Piano. La géomousse a permis d'éviter naturellement de surcharger le toit du parking, ce qui donne lieu à un mélange intéressant d'éléments artificiels et naturels.

Le projet Crossrail Place de Foster + Partners est un exemple d'usage mixte, situé au-dessus de la nouvelle gare de Canary Wharf du réseau express londonien Crossrail (Canary Wharf, Londres, 2009-2015 ; page 254). L'ensemble comprend quatre niveaux de commerces, un jardin sur le toit, des pavillons et les entrées de la gare, tous réunis sous un toit en grid shell de bois. Le jardin est accessible depuis le rez-de-chaussée par deux passerelles communicantes. Le choix de coussins en ETFE très isolant pour le grid shell a permis de créer un microclimat pour le jardin par dessous, afin de le planter de certaines espèces qui ont pénétré pour la première fois en Grande-Bretagne par les docks voisins. Là comme dans d'autres projets urbains, l'espace du toit, qu'il s'agisse des bâtiments construits au-dessus de la gare ou d'aménagements comme le jardin, a été pris en compte de manière beaucoup plus conséquente et réfléchie que jamais auparavant. Bien sûr, la plupart des toitures urbaines plus anciennes sont négligées – et forment le « junk space » sur lequel Rem Koolhaas a écrit – mais l'addition de plusieurs facteurs tels que la densité urbaine croissante, les prix élevés du terrain et de la construction et l'intérêt pour les questions écologiques ont favorisé et fait progresser l'utilisation de ces endroits, même lorsqu'ils sont invisibles depuis le sol. De

plus en plus, chaque pouce d'espace urbain est comptabilisé et exploité, de sorte que le toit représente un domaine d'exploration qui n'est pas prêt de s'épuiser : au contraire, les toits des villes vont être de plus en plus souvent reconvertis pour de nouveaux usages et les bâtiments contemporains de plus en plus souvent dotés de toits aménagés, même lorsqu'il est évident que cela implique des éléments mécaniques distincts d'autres espaces ornementaux ou plus intensivement exploités.

À New York, les architectes Diller Scofidio + Renfro ont testé le toit végétalisé dans une structure relativement modeste au cœur du Lincoln Center de Manhattan. Leur pelouse du pavillon Hypar (Hypar Pavilion Lawn, 2007 ; page 144) couvre une surface d'à peine plus de 1000 mètres carrés et peut être occupée pour créer une forme de ce qu'ils qualifient d'« urbanisme bucolique ». En plus d'un espace de loisir inattendu et d'une vue agréable depuis le haut, l'espace obtenu répond lui aussi clairement à la demande d'une clientèle de plus en plus consciente des problèmes énergétiques. « La masse thermique accrue du toit en pelouse réduit considérablement les charges mécaniques du restaurant en dessous, expliquent les architectes. L'eau est drainée dans les colonnes structurales sous la surface de l'herbe. » L'un des nouveaux usages les plus répandus des toits semble donc visiblement la réduction du gain ou des pertes de chaleur au moyen d'une couche de terre et de végétation.

LA NATURE ARTIFICIELLE DU TOIT

On pouvait s'attendre à voir le Japon, avec ses villes aux populations si denses, accueillir de nombreux et intéressants projets en toiture. Or, à part les multiples practices, les jardins et espaces découverts sont plutôt rares à Tokyo, du moins dans les zones résidentielles où les espaces minuscules et les surfaces d'encombrement très réduites sont de rigueur. L'architecte de talent Sou Fujimoto a cependant adopté une approche qui diffère de bon nombre de ses collègues. Sa Maison K de Nishinomiya (House K, Japon,

SKYHABITAT → 278

2011–2012 ; page 128), entre Osaka et Kobe, a une surface de plancher de seulement 118 mètres carrés, mais le toit pentu en diagonale en a été conçu comme un jardin, ou encore une pièce extérieure supplémentaire. Il est accessible de l'intérieur à tous les niveaux et l'architecte compare le tout à une topographie naturelle. Une petite remise en bas du toit offre un abri mais le reste est exposé aux intempéries avec ses arbres en pots qui « flottent » à sa surface blanche. La Maison K est un exemple de l'exploration pertinente du lien entre architecture, nature et ville à laquelle se livrent les architectes japonais, de Toyo Ito à Itsuko Hasegawa ou même Tadao Ando pour qui la présence de la lumière du soleil à l'intérieur d'un bâtiment constitue déjà un contact avec la nature. La manière codifiée, ou circonspecte, dont Fujimoto introduit la nature dans son concept, sous forme d'arbres en pots, correspond à une notion assez spécifiquement japonaise où naturel et artificiel soit coïncident, soit s'interpénètrent.

JUNK ET VERT

Il y a sans doute autant de possibilités de concevoir et de reconvertir les toits que de toits eux-mêmes dans les villes modernes. L'attrait qu'ils exercent sur l'âme humaine, en tant qu'endroits élevés, est très ancien et remonte sûrement plus loin que l'Ancien et le Nouveau Testament, ou le Coran. Les emplacements les plus hauts sont réservés aux plus vertueux, aux plus pieux, aux plus puissants ou, en fin de compte, depuis peu, aux plus riches. Pour dire les choses simplement, le toit permet la vue, c'est un lieu où contempler la ville en contrebas, où échapper à son agitation et au bruit, au moins un instant. Plusieurs raisons expliquent l'intensification actuelle de la recherche de nouveaux usages pour les toits. Tout d'abord et avant tout, l'argument économique. La raréfaction de l'espace suscite un intérêt accru pour les surfaces sous-exploitées dans les villes modernes surpeuplées. Le « junk » dans le langage de Koolhaas, une zone à l'abandon où les climatiseurs et les amplificateurs de téléphones cellulaires seraient

cachés, acquiert tout d'un coup une nouvelle valeur. Les toits sont cool, les toits s'éveillent à la vie. Ils se transforment en bars et restaurants, en appartements et jardins. Au-delà des questions d'argent et d'exploitation de l'espace, d'autres inquiétudes d'ordre notamment écologique ont pesé de tout leur poids dans la course vers les plus hauts sommets urbains. Une couche de terreau et un arbre planté à 200 mètres au-dessus du sol protègent et abritent les espaces intérieurs des pernicieux gains ou pertes de chaleur. Là encore, c'est l'économie qui tranche, un toit végétalisé peut se traduire par des factures d'énergie moins importantes, la durabilité étant le but ultime de tout architecte, promoteur et propriétaire. Les toits n'ont pas encore fini d'évoluer dans la jungle urbaine, alors que la pollution et la congestion progressent sur la terre. Peut-être des îles finiront-elles par être construites très haut au-dessus du sol, à l'instar du complexe sans doute visionnaire de Marina Bay Sands qu'a édifié Moshe Safdie à Singapour. Une île dédiée au plaisir qui flotte à 190 mètres au-dessus de la terre, une piscine qui évoque l'espace infini, non plus enfermé dans une forêt de tours, mais ouvert sur le ciel. Le sommet, le toit, se trouve ainsi ancré dans la tradition et relié à la terre, l'endroit le plus haut est celui dévolu aux justes, aux pieux et, bien sûr, aux riches. C'est le lieu d'un nouvel optimisme dans la cité mondiale en train d'éclore, un refuge et un espoir, une île en plein ciel d'où regarder la terre en bas.

1 http://www.dailymail.co.uk/news/article-2729501/Inside-worlds-expensive-apartment-Penthouse-Monacos-new-Odeon-Tower-complete-water-slide-private-chauffeur-caterer-set-potential-owner-240MILLION.html, consulté le 10 novembre 2015.
2 Eric Owen Moss, interview, http://www.architectmagazine.com/project-gallery/pterodactyl_1, consulté le 9 novembre 2015.

FLETCHER PRIEST
London [UK]
2007-09

1 Angel Lane

Address: 1 Angel Lane, London EC4R 3 AB, UK, +44 20 71 02 10 00, www.nomura.com
Area: 70 000 m² (internal) + 2000 m² (terraces) | Client: Oxford Properties / UBS
Cost: £175 million (construction of building) | Collaboration: Townsend Landscape Architects

In the City of London, 1 Angel Lane is the headquarters for the Japanese bank Nomura. It includes 50 725 square meters on 11 floors that are used as space for 1800 traders. The two roof terraces, respectively measuring 2000 square meters and 500 square meters overlooking the River Thames, are the largest in the City of London. Part of the terrace is used for a vegetable plot where ingredients for Nomura's dining rooms are grown. A bee colony located on a normally inaccessible roof produces honey for the café. The whole of the building, which has a five-story timber shading structure and timber louvers, was specifically designed to have a low carbon footprint, to which the roof terraces naturally contribute. The largest of the rooftop gardens has pools and cascades. Iroko timber was used by the landscape architects for planters and seating elements. Herbaceous perennial planting and evergreen hedging offer notes of color throughout the year. Part of both terraces is finished in York stone paving to provide space for corporate events, and there is a lawn for use in the summer months.

An der Adresse Angel Lane 1 in der City of London befindet sich der Hauptsitz der japanischen Nomura-Bank. Auf elf Etagen mit 50 725 m² Bürofläche sind dort 1800 Wertpapierhändler tätig. Die beiden mit Blick auf die Themse gelegenen Dachterrassen sind mit ihrer Fläche von 2000 m² bzw. 500 m² die größten der City. Ein Teil der Dachfläche wird zum Gemüseanbau genutzt, dort werden Küchenzutaten für die Speiseräume der Bank gezogen; Bienenstöcke auf einem üblicherweise unzugänglichen Dachabschnitt produzieren Honig für das Café. Holzjalousien sowie über fünf Etagen reichende, aus Holz konstruierte Sonnenblenden beschatten das Gebäude, das im Hinblick auf eine niedrige CO_2-Bilanz geplant wurde, wozu auch die Dachterrassen auf natürliche Weise beitragen. Der größere der Dachgärten ist mit Zierbecken und Wasserkaskaden gestaltet. Bei den Pflanzkästen und Sitzgelegenheiten entschieden sich die Landschaftsarchitekten für Iroko-Holz; Staudenflächen und immergrüne Hecken sorgen ganzjährig für Farbe. Beide Dachterrassen sind zum Teil mit Sandstein aus York gepflastert und bieten Raum für Firmenevents; in den Sommermonaten kann außerdem eine Rasenfläche genutzt werden.

Le 1 Angel Lane, dans la city de Londres, est le siège de la banque japonaise Nomura. L'ensemble compte 50 725 m² répartis sur 11 niveaux occupés par 1800 traders. Les deux terrasses du toit qui surplombent la Tamise, aux surfaces respectives de 2000 m² et 500 m², sont les plus grandes de la City. Une partie sert de potager où sont cultivés les légumes servis dans les salles de restaurant de l'entreprise. Une colonie d'abeilles, sur un toit inaccessible en temps normal, produit le miel servi dans le café. Le bâtiment tout entier, doté notamment d'une structure brise-soleil en bois d'œuvre sur cinq étages et de persiennes également en bois, a été spécialement conçu pour laisser une faible empreinte carbone, les terrasses du toit y contribuant naturellement. Le plus grand des jardins comporte plusieurs bassins et cascades. Les paysagistes ont utilisé du bois d'iroko pour les jardinières et les sièges. Des plantations d'herbes vivaces et des haies à feuilles persistantes donnent des notes de couleur toute l'année. Les deux terrasses sont partiellement couvertes d'un dallage en Yorkstone qui fournit un espace pour les évènements organisés par l'entreprise et pendant les mois d'été, une pelouse peut être utilisée.

Situated on the Thames not far from St. Paul's
Cathedral, the complex has green elements visible
in these images and in the rendering above.

Sowohl auf den Fotos als auch in der gerenderten
Darstellung (oben) sind die grünen Elemente zu
erkennen, die diesen unweit der St. Paul's Cathedral
an der Themse angesiedelten Komplex auszeichnen.

La verdure du complexe au bord de la Tamise et
à proximité de la cathédrale St. Paul est visible sur
les photos et le rendu ci-dessus.

Herbaceous perennials cover
roof areas and bring the presence
of nature into the heart of the
City. Right, Iroko timber planters
contribute to the natural appearance of the garden.

Großflächige Staudenbeete auf der
Dachfläche bringen Natur ins Herz
der City. Pflanzbehältnisse aus
Iroko-Holz verstärken die natürliche
Anmutung des Gartens (rechts).

Des plantes herbacées vivaces
recouvrent les toits et apportent la
présence de la nature au cœur de
la City. À droite, les jardinières
en bois d'iroko contribuent au caractère naturel du jardin.

Right, a plan of the rooftop spaces
with the Thames at the bottom
of the image. The building is composed of three linked buildings
and has three terraces on two different levels.

Rechts: Grundriss der Dachflächen,
im unteren Bereich die Themse.
Der Komplex besteht aus drei
miteinander verbundenen Bauten;
auf zwei verschiedenen Etagen
sind drei Terrassen angesiedelt.

À droite, plan des toits aménagés
avec la Tamise en bas. L'ensemble
est composé de trois bâtiments
reliés les uns aux autres avec trois
terrasses à deux niveaux différents.

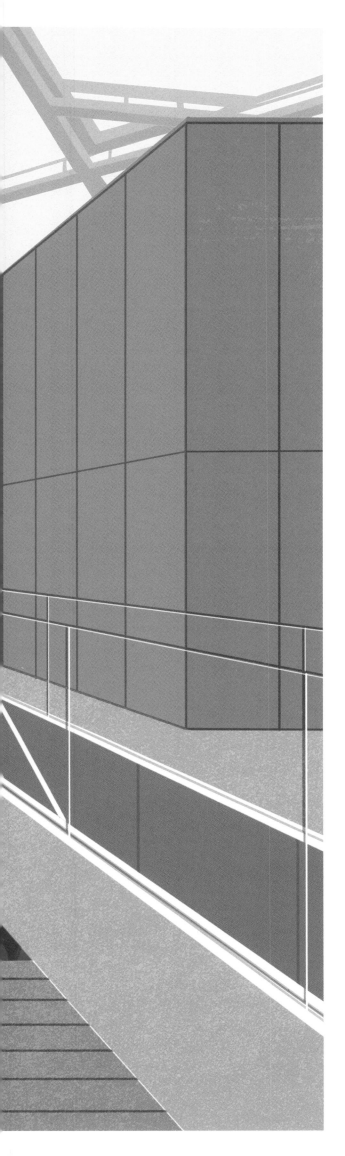

FLETCHER PRIEST
London [UK]
2012–14

6 Bevis Marks

Address: 6 Bevis Marks, Bury Court, London EC3A 7BA, UK, www.6bevismarks.com
Area: 21 750 m² (internal), 1100 m² (roof gardens) | Client: AXA, BlackRock, Wells Fargo
and CORE | Cost: £50 million (approximate total construction cost) | Collaboration:
Jonathan Hodge, Christina Stellmacher, Anne Schroeder, Townsend Landscape Architects

6 Bevis Marks is a new 16-story building in the City of London, near Norman Foster's 30 St. Mary Axe tower (see p. 268) and the Heron Tower (see p. 316). Roof gardens were designed by Fletcher Priest and Townsend Landscape Architects on the 11th, 15th, and 16th floors. According to Townsend: "The design incorporates Sedum species and wildflower mixes, as well as insect habitats and bird boxes, all of which aim to enhance biodiversity in the City." A protected, open roof garden offers year-round access and spectacular views. An ETFE roof together with the high-level gardens and terraces introduce a range of possibilities for social interaction. As the architects explain: "Materially the exterior pays homage to the glazed terracotta of Holland House and the expressed dia-grid steelwork of the neighboring towers." This steel work is in evidence on the main rooftop garden ETFE area. The dramatic and sculptural structure is significantly lighter and stronger than traditional roofing materials, while the high level of light transmission through the inflated cushions benefits the lush vegetation below. A lift with an electric-current-charged crystal glass door links the reception area directly to the roof garden on the 16th floor.

An der Adresse Bevis Marks 6 in der City of London, unmittelbar neben Norman Fosters Hochhaus (St. Mary Axe 30, Seite 268) und dem Heron Tower (Seite 316), befindet sich ein neues 16-stöckiges Gebäude. Hier plante das Architekturbüro Fletcher Priest mit Townsend Landscape Architects Dachgärten für die 11., 15. und 16. Etage. Townsend kommentiert: „Sedum-Arten und Wiesenblumenmischungen als Teil der Gestaltung sowie Insektenhotels und Nistkästen zielen darauf ab, die Biodiversität in der City zu erhöhen." Ein geschützter offener Dachgarten mit spektakulärem Ausblick ist ganzjährig zugänglich. Die hochgelegenen Beet- und Terrassenflächen eröffnen zusammen mit einer ETFE-Überdachung vielfältige Möglichkeiten für soziales Miteinander. Die Architekten: „Das Material der Außenhülle erweist der glasierten Baukeramik des Holland House sowie dem freiliegenden Stahl-Diagonalraster der benachbarten Türme seine Reverenz." Solche Stahlstrukturen prägen auch die ETFE-überdachte Fläche des größeren Dachgartens. Diese dramatische, skulpturale Konstruktion ist bedeutend leichter und fester als traditionelle Dachkonstruktionen, und die üppige Bepflanzung profitiert von der hohen Lichtdurchlässigkeit der Folienkissen. Ein Fahrstuhl mit einer Tür aus elektrochromem Glas verbindet die Lobby mit dem Dachgarten in der 16. Etage.

Le 6 Bevis Marks est un nouvel immeuble de 16 niveaux situé dans la City de Londres, à côté de la tour du 30 St. Mary's Axe de Norman Foster (voir p. 316) et de la Heron Tower (voir p. 392). Les jardins sur le toit des 10ᵉ, 14ᵉ et 15ᵉ étages ont été conçus par Fletcher Priest et Townsend Landscape Architects. Townsend explique: «Le concept comprend des variétés de *sedum* et des mélanges de fleurs sauvages, ainsi que des habitats pour insectes et des nichoirs à oiseaux, le tout dans le but d'accroître la biodiversité de la City.» Un jardin sous toit ouvert permet l'accès toute l'année et offre un magnifique panorama. La toiture en ETFE et la hauteur des jardins et terrasses ouvrent de multiples possibilités d'échanges et de vie sociale. Les architectes expliquent que «sur le plan matériel, l'extérieur est un hommage à la terre cuite vitrifiée de Holland House et aux triangles d'acier de la structure "diagrid" des tours voisines». L'ossature en acier apparaît surtout au-dessus du jardin principal sous le toit en ETFE. La remarquable structure au caractère sculptural est beaucoup plus légère et solide que les toitures traditionnelles, et la transmission lumineuse élevée des coussins gonflables profite à la végétation luxuriante en dessous. Un ascenseur à porte en verre cristallin électrochrome relie directement la zone de réception au jardin sur le toit du 15ᵉ étage.

The roof garden is available to occupiers of the building and can be booked by tenants for their own events.

Der Dachgarten steht allen Gebäudenutzern zur Verfügung; von den Mietparteien kann er für eigene Veranstaltungen gebucht werden.

Le jardin sur le toit est accessible aux occupants de l'immeuble qui peuvent le réserver pour y organiser des manifestations diverses.

A shuttle lift can be programmed to take guests directly from reception. Right, a plan of the garden spaces on the roof.

Ein Aufzug lässt sich zu einem Shuttle programmieren, um Gäste vom Eingangsbereich direkt nach oben zu transportieren. Rechts: Plan der Dachgartenbereiche.

Un ascenseur-navette peut être programmé pour amener les invités directement depuis la réception. À droite, plan des jardins.

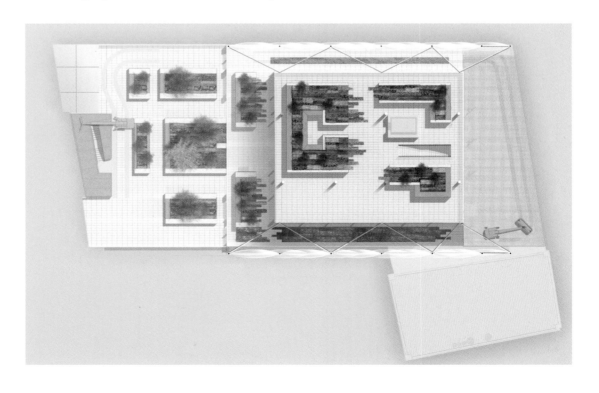

ANNABELLE SELLDORF
New York, New York [USA]
2013–18

21 East 12th Street

*Address: 21 East 12th Street, New York, New York, USA, +1 212 982 2112,
www.21east12.com | Area: 10 758 m² | Client: William Macklowe Company
Cost: not disclosed | Collaboration: Sara Lopergolo (Partner in Charge),
Anna Barretto (Project Manager), SLCE Architects (Architect of Record),
Future Green (Landscape Consultant)*

This is a mixed-use project situated in Greenwich Village in Manhattan. The two lower floors are devoted to retail space. Twenty floors of apartments rise above this base, somewhat "set back to maximize the amount of sunlight that reaches the adjacent sidewalks and provide generous rooftop gardens." Light-colored cast stone and punched windows were chosen "to resonate with the neighborhood's classic prewar limestone apartments." Usable rooftop space begins above the second floor where two "townhomes" with double-height volumes and private gardens are located. Garden spaces wrap around the corner of 12th Street and University Place where the building is located. Two duplex penthouses have large terraces located adjacent to the main living spaces, as well as private balconies at the uppermost level. Selldorf's mixture of modernity and respect for neighborhood architecture fits well with the numerous renovation projects she has worked on, such as the Neue Gallerie and Luma Arles.

Dieses projektierte Gebäude für Mischnutzung wird in Greenwich Village in Manhattan realisiert. Die beiden untersten Etagen sind Verkaufsflächen vorbehalten. Über diesem Sockel erhebt sich ein 20-stöckiger Wohnbau, „dessen Versatz nach hinten zum einen den maximalen Einfall von Tageslicht auf die angrenzenden Fußverkehrsflächen und zum anderen die Anlage großzügiger Dachgartenflächen gestattet". Die Lochfassade aus hellem Betonstein „harmoniert mit den diesen Stadtteil charakterisierenden, in Kalkstein ausgeführten klassischen Wohnbauten aus den ersten Jahrzehnten des 20. Jahrhunderts". Bewohnbare Dachfläche steht unter anderem oberhalb der 2. Etage zur Verfügung, beispielsweise als Privatgarten der zwei Maisonette-Wohnungen. Die Gartenflächen begleiten die Straßenfronten zu 12th Street und University Place, an deren Kreuzung das Gebäude sich erhebt. Zwei Maisonette-Penthouse-Wohnungen verfügen über geräumige Terrassenflächen, die den Hauptwohnbereich ergänzen, sowie über nicht einsehbare Austritte in der oberen Etage. Selldorfs zeitgemäße, die stadtteiltypische Architektur respektierende Gestaltung passt zu ihren zahlreichen Renovierungen, etwa jener der Neuen Galerie New York und der Bauten von Luma Arles.

Le projet à usage mixte est situé à Greenwich Village, Manhattan. Les deux étages inférieurs sont occupés par des espaces de vente. Ils sont surmontés de vingt étages de logements, placés quelque peu «en retrait pour un ensoleillement optimal des trottoirs adjacents et pour faire place à de vastes jardins sur le toit.» La pierre reconstituée de couleur claire et les découpures des fenêtres ont été choisies «pour faire écho au calcaire des appartements classiques d'avant-guerre du voisinage.» L'espace du toit est utilisé dès le deuxième étage avec deux «rangées» aux volumes double hauteur et des jardins particuliers. Les jardins tournent au coin de la 12ᵉ Rue et d'University Place où l'immeuble est situé. Deux duplex de luxe au dernier étage possèdent de vastes terrasses qui jouxtent les principaux espaces de séjour et des balcons privés. Selldorf affiche ici un mélange de modernité et de respect pour l'architecture environnante parfaitement adapté aux nombreux projets de rénovation auxquels elle a travaillé, notamment la Neue Gallery et le Luma d'Arles.

Above, a view of the penthouse kitchen and the outdoor terrace space on the rooftop. Opposite, a general view of the building in its neighborhood with the third-floor "maisonnette" terraces visible. Further rooftop images on the following two double pages.

Oben: Blick durch die Penthouse-Küche auf die Terrassen der Dachetage. Rechts: Gesamtansicht des Gebäudes in seinem Kontext, mit Blick auf die Dachgärten der Maisonette-Wohnungen in der dritten Etage. Weitere Ansichten von Dachflächen auf den folgenden Doppelseiten.

Ci-dessus, vue de la cuisine et de la terrasse de l'appartement « penthouse » sur le toit. Ci-contre, vue d'ensemble de l'immeuble et des bâtiments voisins avec les terrasses « en duplex » du troisième étage. Deux double-pages suivantes : autres vues du toit.

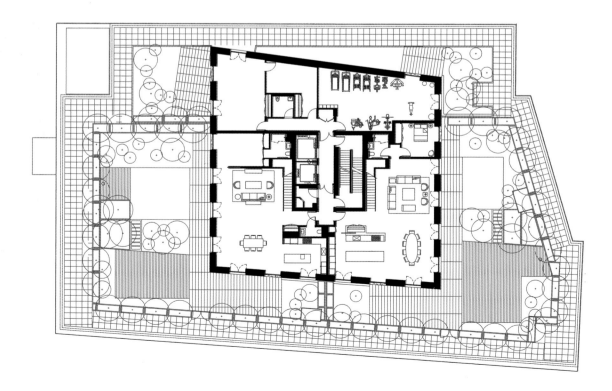

TOYO ITO
Singapore [SINGAPORE]
2012–14

CapitaGreen

*Address: 138 Market Street, Singapore 048946, Singapore, www.cct.com.sg/
our-properties/singapore/capitagreen | Area: 82 003 m² | Client: CapitaLand,
CapitaLand Commercial Trust, Mitsubishi Estate Asia | Cost: not disclosed
Collaboration: RSP, TAKENAKA Corporation*

This 245-meter-high tower is located in the central business district of Singapore. The building was designed with two façades, an "urban façade" and a "green façade," as the architects explain: "The 'green façade' that covers 55% of the entire façade's surface area is formed by plants, providing visual relaxation as well as softly diffusing the strong Singaporean sun. The 'green façade,' symbolizing the lush greenery that once covered the face of the earth, continues to extend toward the Sky Terraces and Sky Forest." The rooftop Sky Forest is planted with 40 different types of trees and shrubs that are expected to grow to a height of 15 meters. The Sky Forest includes a 45-meter-high Wind Catcher that captures cool fresh air 245 meters above ground, distributing it to each office floor via a "cool void" that penetrates the entire building. Toyo Ito explains that the CapitaGreen Tower "brings back the abundance of nature within the homogeneous office environment, providing a comfortable work space that also promotes energy conservation."

Standort dieses 245 m hohen Turms ist das Stadtzentrum von Singapur. Die Architekten erläutern, das Bauwerk sei mit zwei Fassaden konzipiert, einer „City-Fassade" und einer „grünen Fassade": „Pflanzen bilden die ‚grüne Fassade', die 55 % der gesamten Oberfläche ausmacht; sie bringen dem Auge Entspannung und streuen zugleich sanft das grelle Sonnenlicht Singapurs. Als Symbol für das üppige Grün, das einst die ganze Erde bedeckte, setzt sich die ‚grüne Fassade' bis zu den Sky Terraces und dem Sky Forest fort." Der Sky Forest auf dem Dach besteht aus 40 verschiedenen Gehölzarten, die einmal bis zu 15 m hoch werden sollen. Hier befindet sich zudem ein 45 m hoher Windturm, der 245 m über dem Boden frische, kühle Luft aufnimmt und diese über einen „Kälteschacht", der das Gebäude in voller Höhe durchzieht, in alle Büroetagen schickt. Toyo Ito erklärt: „[Der CapitaGreen Tower] bringt die Fülle der Natur in die gleichförmige Büroumgebung und schafft einen angenehmen Arbeitsraum, der zugleich eine Energieersparnis ermöglicht."

La tour de 245 m est située au cœur du quartier des affaires de Singapour. Elle a été conçue avec deux façades, l'une «urbaine» et l'autre «verte», expliquent les architectes: «La "façade verte" couvre 55 % de la surface totale de la façade; elle est constituée de végétation qui repose l'œil tout en tamisant le fort soleil de Singapour. Elle symbolise la verdure luxuriante qui couvrait autrefois la surface de la Terre et monte jusqu'aux Sky Terraces et la Sky Forest.» La Sky Forest du toit est plantée de quarante arbres et arbrisseaux différents qui devraient grandir et atteindre 15 m de haut. La forêt comprend un capteur de vent haut de 45 m qui canalise l'air frais à 245 m au-dessus du sol pour le répartir à tous les étages de bureaux par l'intermédiaire d'un «puits de fraîcheur» qui traverse tout le bâtiment. Toyo Ito explique que la tour CapitaGreen «réintègre la nature dans toute son abondance au sein d'un environnement de bureaux homogène, créant un espace de travail agréable tout en favorisant les économies d'énergie».

Greenery accompanies the tower as it rises, with intermediate planted areas and open spaces, such as the one above, that become the location of elevated gardens. Below, left, a plan of the 14th-story terrace roof and, right, a plan of the 40th-story Sky Forest.

Grün begleitet den Turm über alle Etagen, mit eingeschobenen grünen Öffnungen wie dem oben gezeigten Bereich, in dem luftige Etagengärten angesiedelt sind. Unten: Pläne des Terrassendachs im 14. Stock (links) und des Sky Forest auf der 40. Etage (rechts).

La verdure accompagne la tour dans son ascension avec des zones intermédiaires plantées et des espaces ouverts, comme celui-ci-dessus, qui accueillent des jardins suspendus. Ci-dessous, à gauche, plan de la terrasse du 13ᵉ étage et à droite, plan de la Sky Forest du 39ᵉ étage.

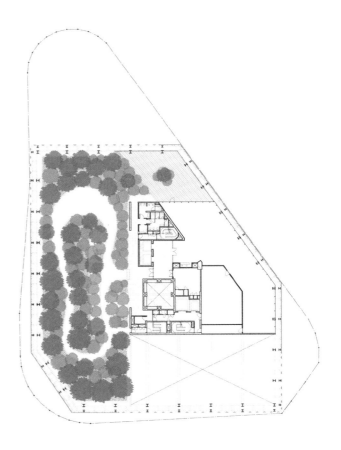

Left and above, views of the 40th-story Sky Forest with its pathways and large trees, surrounded by a steel and glass grid that follows logically from the tower's design.

Links und oben: Ein Glas-und-Stahl-Raster, das sich logisch aus der Konstruktion des Hochhauses ergibt, umhüllt den auf der 40. Etage angesiedelten Sky Forest mit seinen Wegen und großen Bäumen.

À gauche et ci-dessus, vues de la Sky Forest du 39ᵉ étage avec ses allées et ses grands arbres, entourés d'un réseau d'acier et de verre logiquement inspiré du design de la tour.

Despite being 40 floors above ground level, the garden very much gives the impression of being planted in the earth.

Obwohl dieser Garten in der 40. Etage liegt, wirkt er, als sei er mit dem Boden verwurzelt.

Bien que situé au 39ᵉ étage, le jardin donne vraiment l'impression d'être planté dans la terre.

The Sky Forest with its unusual
45-meter-high Wind Catcher that
captures cool air 245 meters above
the ground and distributes it to
the office level via a "cool void" in
the heart of the tower.

Der ungewöhnliche, 45 m hohe
Windturm im Sky Forest fängt
in 245 m Höhe kühle Luft ein, um
sie über einen „Kälteschacht"
ins Innere des Hochhauses zu
transportieren.

La Sky Forest et son étrange
capteur de vent haut de 45 m
qui canalise l'air frais à 245 m
au-dessus du sol pour le répartir
à tous les étages de bureaux par
l'intermédiaire d'un «puits de
fraîcheur» au cœur du bâtiment.

SHIGERU BAN
New York, New York [USA]
2013–16

Cast Iron House

Address: 361 Broadway, New York, NY, 10013, USA, www.castironhouse.com
Area: 5029 m² | Client: Knightsbridge Properties | Cost: not disclosed
Collaboration: Hayes Davidson (Renderer)

Located on Broadway at the corner of Franklin Street near Leonard Street, where Herzog & de Meuron are building a 57-story residential building in the Tribeca district of Manhattan, the Cast Iron House contains 11 duplex loft residences and two cantilevered penthouses. A Vierendeel truss system is used to support the penthouses. The whole structure is built on top of an 1881 building restored by the client that is considered to be one of the most significant examples of Italianate cast-iron architecture in Manhattan. At a time when new construction has appeared all over New York, this project was granted unanimous approval from the city's Landmark Preservation Commission in May 2012. Seen here in the form of renderings, because it was not yet complete at the time that this book went to press, this structure is Shigeru Ban's second residential project in New York after his Metal Shutter House (2010).

Das Cast Iron House in Manhattans Stadtteil Tribeca liegt an der Einmündung der Franklin Street in den Broadway, ganz in der Nähe der Leonard Street, wo Herzog & de Meuron gerade einen 57 Stockwerke zählenden Wohnturm errichten. Es umfasst elf Maisonette-Lofts und zwei Penthauseinheiten, bei denen Vierendeel-Fachwerkbinder als tragendes Element dienen. Die Konstruktion ist einem vom Auftraggeber restaurierten Gebäude aus dem Jahr 1881 aufgesetzt, das als eines der bedeutendsten Beispiele in Manhattan für Gusseisen-Architektur im italienischen Stil gilt. Während gleichzeitig überall in New York Neubauten entstanden, erhielt dieses Projekt im Mai 2012 die einstimmige Genehmigung der städtischen Denkmalschutz-Kommission. Die Abbildungen sind Renderings, da der Bau zur Zeit der Drucklegung noch nicht fertiggestellt war. Nach dem Metal Shutter House (2010) ist dieser Dachaufbau Shigeru Bans zweites Wohnprojekt in New York.

Située à Broadway, à l'angle de Franklin Street et tout près de Leonard Street où Herzog & de Meuron construisent un immeuble résidentiel de 57 niveaux dans le quartier Tribeca de Manhattan, la Cast Iron House abrite onze lofts en duplex et deux appartements de luxe en encorbellement, portés par un système de poutre échelle. La structure est construite au sommet d'un immeuble de 1881 restauré par le client et considéré comme l'un des exemples les plus significatifs d'architecture italianisante en fonte de Manhattan. Édifié à un moment où les nouvelles constructions surgissaient partout dans New York, le projet a été unanimement approuvé par la Commission de conservation des monuments de la ville en mai 2012. Seules des images de synthèse peuvent être présentées ici car il était encore inachevé au moment de la mise sous presse du livre. C'est le deuxième projet résidentiel de Shigeru Ban à New York après la Metal Shutter House (2010).

A rendering shows how Shigeru Ban has added two extra levels to the old, renovated building, allowing the creation of luxury rooftop apartments.

Diese Darstellung zeigt die beiden zusätzlichen Etagen mit luxuriösen Penthauswohnungen, die Shigeru Ban dem alten, renovierten Bauwerk aufsetzte.

Le rendu montre comment Shigeru Ban a ajouté deux niveaux supplémentaires à l'immeuble ancien rénové pour y créer des appartements de luxe.

Another rendering with the added apartments and roof terrace visible: the architect's strict lines echo those of the old building, but remain decidedly contemporary.

In dieser Darstellung der neuen Wohnungen ist auch die Dachterrasse zu sehen. In den strengen Linien des Architekten klingt noch die Linienführung des Bestandsgebäudes an, doch sie sind entschieden modern.

Autre rendu avec les appartements ajoutés et la terrasse : les lignes sévères de l'architecture font écho à celles du bâtiment ancien mais restent néanmoins résolument contemporaines.

Thirteen duplex residences were created within the volumes of the existing building, with ceilings exceeding 7.5 meters in height.

Im Bestandsgebäude entstanden 13 Maisonette-Wohnungen mit Deckenhöhen von teilweise mehr als 7,50 m.

Treize logements en duplex ont été créés dans les volumes du bâtiment existant avec des hauteurs de plafonds de plus de 7,5 m.

Above, another of the double-height living spaces within the Cast Iron House. Right, an axonometric drawing shows the added apartments on the roof-top of the older building.

Oben: Eine weitere Wohnung im Cast Iron House mit doppelter Deckenhöhe. Rechts: Die axonometrische Projektion zeigt die neuen Wohnungen auf dem Dach des älteren Bauwerks.

Ci-dessus, un autre salon double hauteur dans la Cast Iron House. À droite, un schéma axonométrique montre les appartements qui ont été ajoutés sur le toit de l'immeuble ancien.

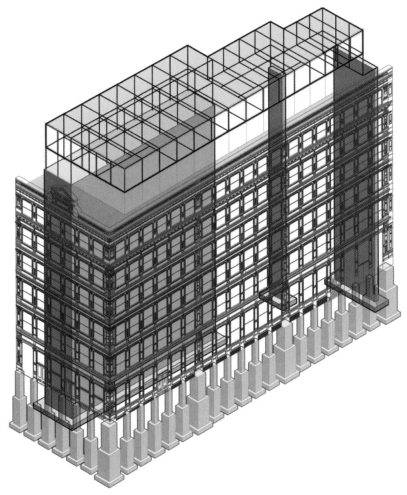

GUNN LANDSCAPE ARCHITECTURE
New York, New York [USA]
2012–13

Central Park West Residence

Address: not disclosed | Area: 40 m² | Client: Josh Sapan | Cost: not disclosed
Collaboration: Foley Fiore Architecture (Architect), Vert Gardens, Inc.
(Installation and Maintenance)

Central Park West runs along the side of Central Park on New York's Upper West Side. The landscape architects describe their intervention here as being in a "romantic style" for a small rooftop garden. The materials used include Ipe wood, cedar, and zinc. As they describe the installation: "Showy and rare white buds from an eastern redbud tree and the flowers from a dogwood make a dramatic appearance in the spring, and branches evolve to leafy shade canopies thereafter. A Japanese black pine is a bonsai-like form within a flourishing wall of climbing greenery. A custom-built fountain carries the sound of running water from its louvered wall and lightning rods impart more charm into the scene, welcomed as pieces of antique sculpture from the owners' collection." The central part of the garden is a paved seating area that the surrounding greenery transforms into a peaceful haven in the city.

Central Park West verläuft am Central Park in der Upper West Side von New York. Die Landschaftsarchitekten beschreiben ihre dortige Intervention als kleinen Dachgarten „im romantischen Stil". Verwendete Materialien sind unter anderem Ipe-Holz, Zeder und Zink. Die Gestaltung kommentieren sie folgendermaßen: „Im Frühjahr sorgen die auffallenden, seltenen weißen Knospen des Kanadischen Judasbaums und die Blüten eines Hartriegels für eine effektvolle Erscheinung, danach treibt das Geäst zu einem grünen Schattendach aus. Eine japanische Mädchenkiefer präsentiert sich wie ein Bonsai vor einem Hintergrund aus üppigen grünen Ranken. Eine eigens angefertigte Wasserwand betört mit dem Geräusch fließenden Wassers, und Blitzableiter steuern dekorative Akzente bei und sind ebenso willkommen wie antike Skulpturen aus der Sammlung des Eigentümers." Den Mittelpunkt des Gartens bildet ein gepflasterter Sitzbereich, der durch den grünen Rahmen in einen friedlichen Zufluchtsort inmitten der Großstadt verwandelt wird.

Central Park West longe Central Park dans le quartier de l'Upper West Side, à New York. Les architectes paysagistes qualifient de «romantique» leur intervention visant à créer un petit jardin sur un toit. Les matériaux utilisés comprennent notamment du bois d'ipé, du cèdre et du zinc. Ils décrivent l'ensemble en ces termes: «Les bourgeons blancs éclatants et rares d'un gainier du Canada et les fleurs d'un cornouiller font une apparition spectaculaire au printemps, tandis que leurs branches s'apprêtent à se transformer en voûtes de feuillage dispensatrices d'ombre. La silhouette de bonsaï d'un pin noir du Japon se détache sur un mur couvert de plantes grimpantes en fleurs. Une fontaine créée sur mesure fait entendre le son de l'eau courante depuis son mur à claire-voie et des paratonnerres ajoutent au charme du tableau où ils trouvent place au même titre que les sculptures antiques de la collection des propriétaires.» La partie centrale du jardin est pavée et occupée par des sièges que la verdure environnante transforme en un havre de paix en pleine ville.

The modest dimensions of the terrace (40 m²) have been arranged to create a sense of enclosed intimacy.

Der Grundriss der mit 40 m² eher bescheiden dimensionierten Terrasse lässt den Eindruck von geschützter Intimität entstehen.

Les dimensions modestes de la terrasse (40 m²) ont été aménagées pour lui donner un caractère intime et clos.

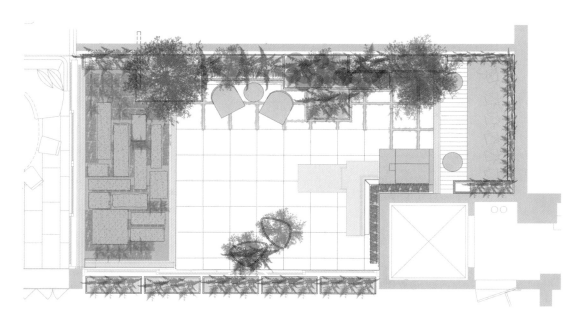

The terrace seems to continue the green environment of nearby Central Park.

Die Terrasse erscheint wie eine Fortsetzung des nahegelegenen grünen Central Park.

La végétation de la terrasse semble prolonger celle de Central Park tout proche.

KEN SMITH
New York, New York [USA]
2011–12

Conrad Hotel

Address: 102 North End Avenue, New York, NY 10282, USA, +1 212 945 0100,
www.conradnewyork.com | Area: 5989 m² | Client: not disclosed | Cost: not disclosed
Collaboration: Kohn Pederson Fox Associates

The rooftop gardens designed by Ken Smith for the recently renovated Conrad Hotel, located near the World Trade Center, are new proof of his impact on New York's roofscape. To quote the landscape architect: "This is a difficult urban site with three levels of roof landscape." The Conrad Hotel has street frontage on three sides and complex landscaping on multiple levels with green roof systems and vegetable garden plots. A midblock passage connects the hotel to the World Financial Center and Battery Park City. Cumulatively, these roof landscapes work as a unified whole while also functioning as a set of discreet spaces.

Die Dachgärten, die Ken Smith für das jüngst renovierte Conrad Hotel in der Nähe des World Trade Center gestaltete, bestätigen erneut seinen Einfluss auf die Dachlandschaft New Yorks. Der Landschaftsarchitekt erklärt dazu: „Es handelt sich um eine schwierige urbane Situation mit einer Dachlandschaft auf drei Ebenen." Das Conrad Hotel ist auf drei Seiten von Straßen gesäumt und besitzt komplexe gestaffelte Dachflächen mit Begrünung und Gemüseparzellen. Eine quer durch den Häuserblock verlaufende Passage verbindet das Hotel mit dem World Financial Center und der Battery Park City. Die Dachlandschaften lassen sich in Summe als Einheit betrachten, funktionieren aber auch als mehrere separate Räume.

Les jardins créés par Ken Smith pour l'hôtel Conrad récemment rénové, à proximité du World Trade Center, apposent une fois de plus sa marque sur les toits de New York. Pour citer l'architecte paysagiste : « C'est un site urbain complexe avec trois niveaux de toits paysagés. L'hôtel Conrad est bordé par des rues sur trois côtés et présente un aménagement complexe de toiture à plusieurs niveaux avec des toits végétalisés et des parcelles de jardin potager. Un passage entre deux pâtés de maisons le relie au World Financial Center et à Battery Park City. Dans leur ensemble, ces toits paysagés fonctionnent comme un tout unifié, tout en formant plusieurs espaces secrets. »

The landscape is composed of paint, sedum plantings, inorganic ground covers, and raised vegetable beds for use in the hotel restaurant.

Die Dachlandschaft ist aus Farbflächen, Sedum-Anpflanzungen, mineralischen Bodenabdeckungen und Hochbeeten mit Gemüse für die Hotelküche komponiert.

Le décor est constitué de surfaces colorées, plantations de sedum, couvertures inorganiques et plates-bandes surélevées où sont cultivés les légumes destinés au restaurant de l'hôtel.

To unify the composition, a system of lightweight serpentine headers divides the roof into zones of different landscape treatment.

Der gestalterische Zusammenhang verdankt sich einem System leichter Steinkanten, die sich über die Dachfläche schlängeln und die unterschiedlich behandelten Bereiche voneinander trennen.

Pour une composition unifiée, un réseau sinueux de tracés légers en pierre délimite le toit en zones aux traitements différents.

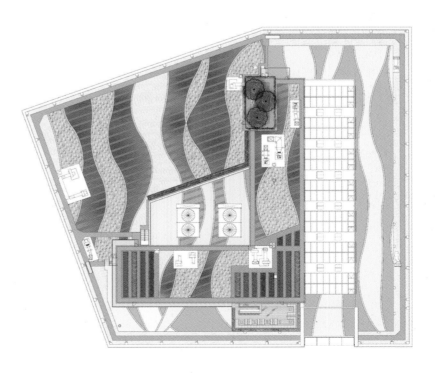

Diane von Fursten-berg Studio HQ

Address: 440 West 14th Street New York, NY 10002, USA, www.dvf.com (only retail accessible) | Area: 3252 m² | Client: Diane von Furstenberg | Cost: not disclosed

Built in two adjacent historic buildings in the Meatpacking district of Manhattan, the headquarters for the fashion designer Diane von Furstenberg accommodates a store, lobby, showroom, offices, and a private residence. The landmark façades were retained, but a new six-story building was created inside of these walls. An inhabitable "stairdelier," conceived as a cross between a stair and a chandelier, crosses the building diagonally to bring in natural light with the aid of heliostat mirrors. This aspect of the project is expressed on the roof in the form of the diamond-shaped penthouse studio, which serves during the day and at night to signal the presence of Diane von Furstenberg's building.

Der Hauptsitz der Modedesignerin Diane von Fürstenberg beherbergt ein Ladengeschäft, eine Lobby, einen Vorführraum, Büroflächen sowie privaten Wohnraum; untergebracht ist er in zwei direkt benachbarten historischen Gebäuden im Meatpacking District Manhattans. Die denkmalgeschützten Fassaden wurden erhalten, hinter den Mauern jedoch entstand ein sechsstöckiger Neubau. Ein bewohnbarer „Treppenlüster", als Synthese aus Treppe und Lichtquelle konzipiert, durchquert das Gebäude diagonal und reflektiert mithilfe von Heliostat-Spiegeln Tageslicht in den Innenraum. Diesen Aspekt des Projekts greift auf dem Dach das Penthausstudio mit einer leuchtenden Kristallform auf, die den Hauptsitz von Diane von Fürstenberg bei Tag und Nacht unübersehbar macht.

Construit sur deux bâtiments historiques adjacents du Meatpacking district de Manhattan, le siège de la styliste Diane von Fürstenberg abrite un magasin, un hall, un espace d'exposition, des bureaux et un logement privé. Les façades représentatives ont été conservées mais un nouvel immeuble de six étages a été créé à l'intérieur des murs. Un « stairdelier » fonctionnel, conçu comme un croisement entre un escalier (stair) et un lustre (chandelier), traverse le bâtiment en diagonale pour y faire entrer la lumière du jour à l'aide des miroirs d'un héliostat. Cet aspect du projet trouve une autre expression sur le toit avec le studio de luxe en forme de diamant qui signale la présence de l'immeuble de Diane von Fürstenberg de jour comme de nuit.

The architects have woven two brick structures together and above all created a rooftop penthouse and terrace, visible on the left page.

Die Architekten verbanden zwei Ziegelbauten zu einem und setzten darauf ein Penthaus mit Terrasse, links auf dem Foto zu sehen.

Les architectes ont entretissé deux structures de briques et créé par-dessus le tout un appartement de luxe et une terrasse au sommet du toit, visibles sur la photo de la page de gauche.

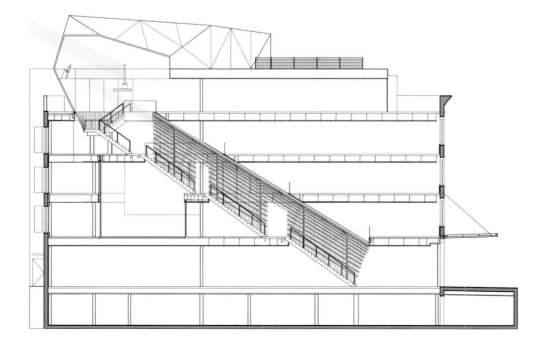

To the left, a section drawing shows the "stairdelier" that brings light into the building with the use of heliostat mirrors. The crystalline form of the upper-level penthouse is visible both in the drawing and in the photo above.

Der Schnitt links zeigt den „Treppenlüster", der mithilfe von Heliostat-Spiegeln Licht in das Bauwerk lenkt. Das kristallförmige Penthouse auf der obersten Ebene ist sowohl auf der Zeichnung als auch auf dem Foto oben zu sehen.

À gauche, un schéma en coupe montre le « stairdelier » qui fait entrer la lumière à l'intérieur à l'aide des miroirs d'un héliostat. La forme de cristal de l'appartement du dernier étage est parfaitement visible sur le schéma et la photo ci-dessus.

The uppermost level combines triangular and rectangular glass surfaces with a light metal framework. The brick of the original structures is visible below, and a panorama of downtown buildings appears beyond the garden.

Die oberste Ebene kombiniert dreieckige und rechteckige Glasflächen mit einem leichten Metallfachwerk. In der Aufnahme unten ist der Ziegel der ursprünglichen Gebäude zu sehen; über den Garten hinweg reicht der Blick bis zum Innenstadt-Panorama.

Le niveau le plus élevé associe les surfaces vitrées triangulaires et rectangulaires à un cadre métallique léger. La brique des constructions d'origine apparaît sur la photo ci-dessous, et un panorama du centre de New York surgit derrière le jardin.

The almost fully glazed penthouse can be shaded with large curtains (below). Right page, the top of the "stairdelier" and the mirror system that brings light to the levels below.

Das fast vollständig verglaste Penthaus lässt sich mit Vorhängen verschatten (unten). Rechts: Das obere Ende des „Treppenlüsters" und das Spiegelsystem, das Licht bis zu den unteren Ebenen lenkt.

L'appartement presque entièrement vitré peut être occulté par d'immenses rideaux (ci-dessous). Page de droite, le haut du «stairdelier» et le système de miroirs qui achemine la lumière vers les niveaux inférieurs.

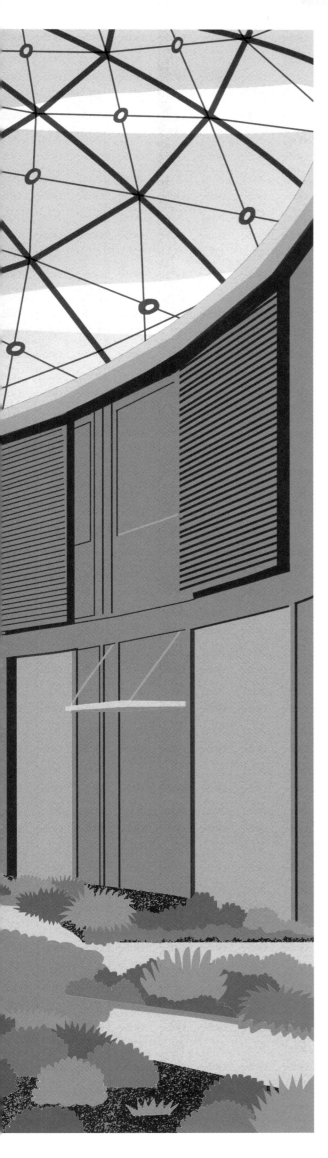

Fichtebunker

Address: Fichtestr. 6, 10967 Berlin, Germany | Area: 2500 m²
Client: Speicherwerk GmbH | Cost: not disclosed
Collaboration: Ingenbleek Architekten

The Fichtebunker was built in 1876 as a gasometer (gasholder) to supply the lanterns of Berlin. This is the only surviving structure of its type in Berlin, built out of bricks. Fifty-six meters in diameter and 21 meters in height, the structure was converted into an air-raid shelter during World War II. A total of 13 houses surrounded by as many gardens were built on the roof of the Fichtebunker. Dagmar Heitmann used the round plan of the building and the steel dome of the gasholder as her inspiration to create round or radial gardens. The materials employed include Corten steel, gravel, black slate, dark colored bricks, wood, and plants selected specifically for rooftop growing. The Corten steel is employed for containers for the plants and to provide some privacy to garden owners. Brick similar to that used for the façades of the original building creates paths and dark gravel is employed in the planting beds. High trees and climbing plants could not be used in this listed building in order to protect the cupola. This project is unique in Berlin.

Der Fichtebunker wurde 1876 als Gasometer zur Versorgung der Berliner Straßenlaternen errichtet. Die Ziegelkonstruktion ist das einzige erhaltene derartige Bauwerk Berlins. Während des Zweiten Weltkriegs wurde der 21 m hohe Rundbau mit einem Durchmesser von 56 m zu einem Luftschutzbunker ausgebaut. Auf dem Dach entstanden nun insgesamt 13 Häuser mit ebenso vielen Gärten. Dagmar Heitmann ließ sich von dem kreisförmigen Gebäudegrundriss und der Stahlkuppel des Gasometers zu kreis- und strahlenförmigen Gärten inspirieren. Als Materialien kamen unter anderem Cortenstahl, Kies, schwarzer Schiefer, dunkler Ziegel, Holz und gründachgeeignete Pflanzen zum Einsatz. Der Cortenstahl wurde bei den Pflanzcontainern und dem Sichtschutz für die Gartenbesitzer verwendet. Als Belag für die Wege wurde Pflasterziegel verlegt, der dem Mauerstein der original erhaltenen Fassade ähnelt; die Beete sind mit dunklem Kies bedeckt. Hohe Bäume und Kletterpflanzen konnten bei dem denkmalgeschützten Bau nicht verwendet werden, da die Kuppel unter Schutz steht. Dieses Projekt ist einzigartig in Berlin.

Le Fichtebunker est un gazomètre bâti en 1876 pour alimenter les becs de gaz berlinois. Construite en briques, c'est la seule structure de ce type qui subsiste encore à Berlin. Avec son diamètre de 56 m et sa hauteur de 21 m, elle a servi d'abri antiaérien pendant la Deuxième Guerre mondiale. Treize maisons entourées d'autant de jardins ont été construites sur son toit. Dagmar Heitmann s'est inspirée du plan circulaire et du dôme en acier pour créer des jardins ronds ou en étoile. Les matériaux utilisés comprennent de l'acier Corten, des graviers, de l'ardoise noire, des briques aux teintes sombres, du bois et des végétaux spécialement sélectionnés pour être cultivés sur un toit. L'acier Corten sert aux bacs à plantes et à assurer une certaine intimité aux propriétaires. Des briques semblables à celles des façades d'origine forment des sentiers, tandis que des graviers sombres emplissent les plates-bandes. Les arbres trop hauts et les plantes grimpantes ont été proscrits afin de préserver la coupole du bâtiment classé. Le projet est unique à Berlin.

An aerial view shows the circular design of the rooftop apartments and gardens situated on top of the original 1876 gasometer.

Eine Luftaufnahme zeigt das kreisrunde Konzept der Dachwohnungen und -gärten, die auf dem original erhaltenen Gasometer von 1876 angelegt sind.

Une vue aérienne montre la configuration circulaire des appartements et jardins au sommet du gazomètre original de 1876.

The original steel dome of the structure inspired the radial design of the new apartments and gardens.

Die historische Stahlkuppel des Bauwerks inspirierte die strahlenförmig angelegten neuen Wohnungen und Gärten.

La coupole en acier du bâtiment d'origine a inspiré la disposition en étoile des nouveaux appartements et jardins.

A plan of the rooftop (below) and a view of garden space (above) show how an otherwise unused structure has been transformed into an unusual and convivial living environment.

Der Plan der Dachfläche (unten) und eine Ansicht des Gartenraums (oben) zeigen, wie dieser ungenutzte Bau in eine ungewöhnliche, gastliche Wohnumgebung verwandelt wurde.

Un plan du toit (ci-dessous) et une vue du jardin (ci-dessus) montrent comment une structure inutilisée a été transformée en un cadre de vie inhabituel et convivial.

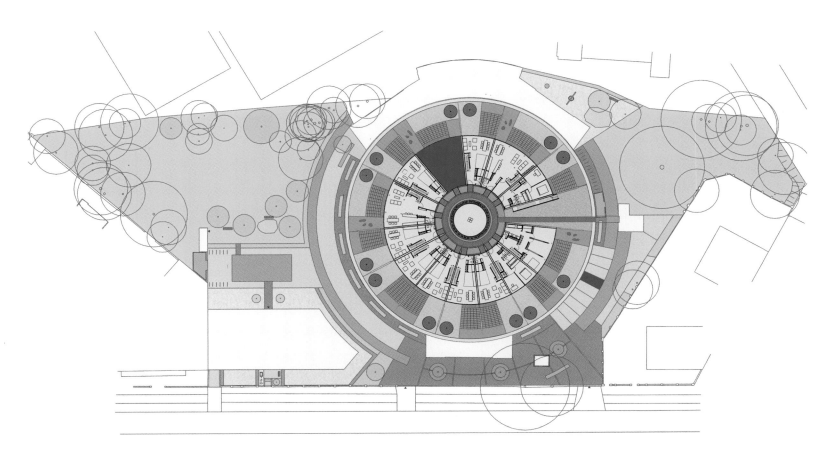

Corten-steel planters and greenery transform what might have been a hard industrial-era environment into modern and welcoming spaces.

Pflanzgefäße aus Cortenstahl und reichlich Grün verwandeln eine vom Industriezeitalter geprägte Umgebung in ein modernes, einladendes Ambiente.

Les bacs à plantes en acier Corten et la verdure transforment en espaces modernes et accueillants ce qui aurait pu être un décor inhospitalier de l'époque industrielle.

RYUE NISHIZAWA
Tokyo [JAPAN]
2010–11

Garden & House

Address: not disclosed | Area: 66 m² | Client: not disclosed
Cost: not disclosed | Collaboration: Teako Nakatsubo, Alan Burden, Hiroki Osanai,
Hachiro Horigome, Kim Daehwan, Takehito Sano, Akiko Sano

Located in a dense urban zone with condominium and office buildings rising above 30 meters, this house for two women is built on an 8 × 4-meter site, and includes an office, a common living space, a private room for each, and a guest room. "Suspecting that a building with regular frame walls would result in reducing the already narrow usable space of the site," states Nishizawa, "my final scheme consisted of a layering of horizontal slabs to create a building without walls. A garden and a room are distributed as a pair on each floor—every room, whether it is the living room, private room or the bathroom, has a garden of its own so that the residents may go outside to feel the breeze, read a book, or cool off in the evening..." The rooftop is a logical extension of this house, acceded to by a ladder, and with a round hole opening to the garden on the level below. Though this Tokyo rooftop may have no view to speak of, it allows access to light and air.

Auf einem 8 × 4 m großen Grundstück in einem dicht bebauten urbanen Bezirk mit wenigstens 30 m hoch aufragenden Wohn- und Bürogebäuden steht dieses für zwei Bewohnerinnen konzipierte Haus mit einem Arbeitsbereich, einem gemeinsamen Wohnbereich, zwei Privaträumen und einem Gästezimmer. „Ich fand, dass ein auf die übliche Weise errichtetes Haus zu viel der knappen Nutzfläche für Wände beanspruchen würde; so entschied ich mich letztlich für eine wandlose Konstruktion aus horizontal geschichteten Platten. In jedem Stockwerk ist ein Garten mit einem Zimmer verbunden – jeder Raum, der Wohnbereich ebenso wie die Privaträume und das Bad, verfügt über einen eigenen Garten, in den die Bewohnerinnen hinaustreten können, um den Wind zu spüren, zu lesen oder die Abendkühle zu genießen." Die Dachterrasse ist die logische Fortführung dieses Hauses; über eine Stiege gelangt man hinauf, und ein runder Bodenausschnitt stellt die Verbindung zum darunter gelegenen Garten her. Dieses Tokioter Dach bietet zwar keinen beeindruckenden Rundblick, doch den Bewohnerinnen schenkt es Licht und Luft.

Située dans une zone urbaine très dense où les immeubles en copropriété et les tours de bureaux se dressent à plus de 30 mètres, cette maison construite pour deux femmes occupe un espace de 8 × 4 m et comprend un bureau, un séjour commun, une chambre pour chacune et une chambre d'hôtes. «Je me doutais qu'un bâtiment encadré de murs aux formes régulières ne ferait que réduire encore plus l'espace utilisable du terrain déjà étroit», explique Nishizawa, «j'ai finalement conçu un empilement de dalles horizontales qui créent une maison sans murs. Chaque étage comporte un jardin et une pièce et chaque pièce, qu'il s'agisse du salon, des chambres ou de la salle de bains, possède son propre jardin qui permet aux habitantes de sortir pour sentir le vent, lire ou se rafraîchir le soir...» Le toit est une extension logique de la maison à laquelle on accède par une échelle, avec une ouverture circulaire vers le jardin au-dessus. Même si ce toit de Tokyo n'a aucune vue digne de ce nom, il donne accès à la lumière et à l'air libre.

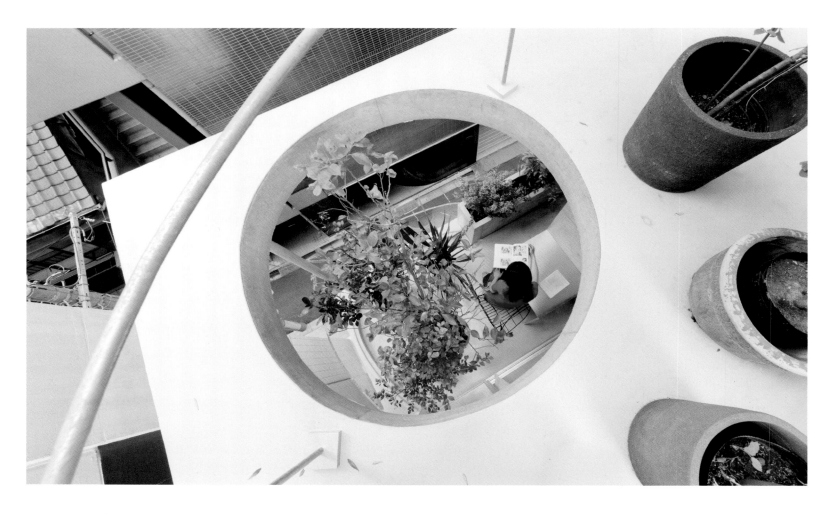

The Garden & House is tiny, but offers not only terraces but also a rooftop space, seen above. Access to the different floor levels is via a spiral staircase (below), and openings in the floors open the entire space to light and air.

Oben: Das winzige Garden & House bietet neben den Etagengärten auch eine Dachterrasse. Unten: Eine Wendeltreppe verbindet die Geschosse miteinander. Die Deckendurchlässe sorgen für lichtdurchflutete, luftige Räume.

La Garden & House est minuscule mais dispose de terrasses et d'un espace sur le toit, vu ci-dessus. Un escalier en colimaçon (ci-dessous) donne accès aux différents niveaux, tandis que des ouvertures dans les sols font entrer l'air et la lumière dans tout l'espace.

Left, a view of the spiral staircase. Greenery and terraces give the occupants a sense of communion with nature despite the very urban setting. Below, plans from the ground floor up to the roof (last drawing on the right).

Links: Die Wendeltreppe im Fokus. Durch das Grün und die Terrassenflächen scheint trotz der innerstädtischen Lage der Kontakt zur Natur gegeben. Unten, von links nach rechts: Die Grundrisse vom Erdgeschoss bis zur Dachebene.

À gauche, vue de l'escalier en colimaçon. La verdure et les terrasses donnent aux habitantes une impression de communion avec la nature malgré le cadre très urbanisé. Ci-dessous, plans des différents niveaux, du rez-de-chaussée au toit (le dernier à droite).

   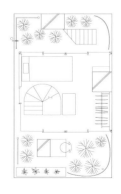 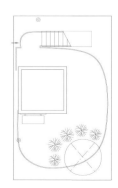

Looking down on the Garden & House, the outdoor terraces and greenery are visible at each level, with a large unexpected circular hole on the roof connecting this space to the rest of the house.

Beim Blick von oben sieht man auf jeder Etage die grünen Außenterrassen; die Dachterrasse kommuniziert über einen großen, unvermuteten Kreisausschnitt mit den übrigen Etagen.

Vue d'en haut, les terrasses et les espaces verts sont visibles à tous les étages, un vaste et surprenant trou circulaire dans le toit relie cet espace au reste de la maison.

LOT-EK
New York, New York [USA]
1996

Guzman Penthouse

Address: 31st Street, New York, NY, USA | Area: 186 m²
Client: Connie Hansen and Russell Peacock | Cost: not disclosed

The Guzman Penthouse was created by the transformation of a mechanical room and the addition of a compact bedroom with a patio on top of it, the whole on a roof just below the Empire State Building on 31st Street in Manhattan. The architects list their materials for this project as "truck containers, refrigerators, and newspaper dispensers." The master bedroom was made with a yellow aluminum six-meter-long truck container added to the existing structure. The bed is designed to move in and out of a closet on tracks, while an internal, steel, fire-escape ladder connects the bedroom to the living room. The interior of the existing structure houses the living/dining/kitchen area as well as a child's bedroom, the whole rendered with exposed steel pipes and beams. The refrigerators and newspaper dispensers were used to create small windows on the longitudinal wall. Sound and video systems are installed in the refrigerators as well.

Das Guzman Penthouse entstand durch den Ausbau eines Betriebsraums, dem ein kompakter Schlafraum mit Terrassenfläche aufgepflanzt wurde, das Ganze auf dem Dach eines Gebäudes an der 31st Street in Manhattan in unmittelbarer Nähe des Empire State Building. Die Materialliste der Architekten verzeichnet für dieses Projekt „Lkw-Container, Kühlschränke und Zeitungsautomaten". Das größere Schlafzimmer wurde in einem 6 m langen, gelben Lkw-Alucontainer eingerichtet, der dem vorhandenen Baukörper aufgesetzt wurde. Das Bett lässt sich auf Schienen unter einen Schrank verschieben; eine innen montierte Stahlfeuerleiter verbindet den Schlafraum mit dem Wohnbereich. Der vorhandene Baukörper beherbergt den Wohn-/Ess-/Kochbereich sowie ein Kinderzimmer; Stahlrohre und Stützen liegen mit Absicht offen. Die Kühlschränke und Zeitungsautomaten wurden verwendet, um entlang der Längswand kleine Fensteröffnungen zu schaffen. Hifi- und Videotechnik sind ebenfalls in den Kühlschränken untergebracht.

L'appartement «penthouse» Guzman est né de la transformation d'un local technique auquel a été ajoutée une chambre à coucher compacte surmontée d'un patio, le tout sur un toit de la 31ᵉ Rue de Manhattan, juste en dessous de l'Empire State Building. La liste des matériaux utilisés par les architectes comprend «des conteneurs de camion, des réfrigérateurs et des présentoirs à journaux». La chambre à coucher est faite d'un conteneur en aluminium jaune de six mètres de long qui a été ajouté à la structure existante. Le lit est conçu pour pouvoir entrer et sortir d'un placard sur des rails, tandis qu'une échelle d'incendie en acier relie la chambre au séjour à l'intérieur. La structure existante abrite l'espace séjour/salle à manger/cuisine et une chambre d'enfant, le tout réinterprété à l'aide de tuyaux et de poutres en acier apparents. Les réfrigérateurs et présentoirs de journaux ont permis d'ouvrir de petites fenêtres dans le mur longitudinal. Les équipements audio et vidéo ont également été placés dans les réfrigérateurs.

The penthouse is inserted into a typical older New York roofscape including a water tank, as seen in the pictures here.

Auf den Fotos erkennt man die typische ältere New Yorker Dachlandschaft mitsamt Zisterne, neben der das Penthaus seinen Platz fand.

L'appartement de standing s'intègre à un décor de toitures anciennes typiquement new-yorkais, avec notamment un réservoir d'eau..

Exposed pipes and rough finishing characterize
the penthouse, making its décor fit in perfectly with its
intensely urban location.

Offenliegende Rohre und eine grobe Oberflächen-
behandlung sind für dieses Penthaus charakteristisch –
eine passende Gestaltung in dieser entschieden
urbanen Umgebung.

L'appartement est caractérisé par ses tuyaux
apparents et ses finitions brutes, parfaitement adaptés
à la densité de son environnement urbain.

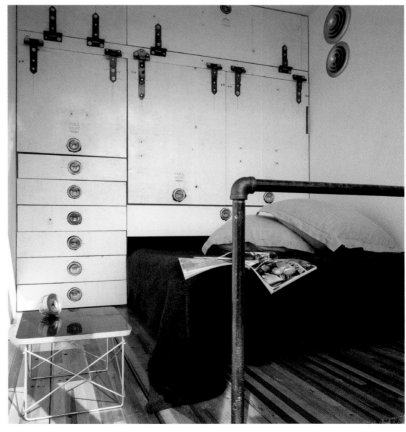

JDS
Copenhagen [DENMARK]
2011

Hedonistic Rooftop Penthouses

Address: not disclosed | Area: 900 m² | Client: A/B Birkegade | Cost: €950 000

The architects were asked to add three penthouses in the densely populated Birkegade/ Egegade/Elmegade block of the Danish capital. Given the lack of courtyard space, JDS conceived the addition as a kind of "missing garden" for the inhabitants of the block. In order to define this "missing garden," the architects looked at Copenhagen garden typology, which characteristically has an associated functional aspect. They state: "The hedonistic rooftop is reflected in a playground with shock-absorbing surfaces and a playful suspension bridge, a green hill with varying accommodation backed by real grass and perennial vegetation, a viewing platform, an outdoor kitchen and barbecue, and a more quiet wooden deck."

Der Auftrag an die Architekten lautete, dem eng bebauten Block zwischen Birkegade, Egegade und Elmegade in der dänischen Hauptstadt drei Penthauseinheiten aufzusetzen. Angesichts des Mangels an Freifläche konzipierte JDS den Aufbau als eine Art „Gartenersatz" für die Bewohner. Um diesen „fehlenden Garten" zu definieren, orientierten sich die Architekten an der Kopenhagener Gartentypologie, die mit einem Garten üblicherweise eine konkrete Funktion verbindet. Dazu erklären sie: „Den Hedonismus der Dachfläche verkörpern ein Spielplatz mit trittdämpfenden Oberflächen sowie ein spielerischer Brückensteg, ein grüner Hügel mit unterschiedlichen Aufenthaltsorten vor einem Hintergrund aus echtem Rasen und mehrjährigem Grün, eine Aussichtsplattform, eine Grillküche und eine ruhiger gelegene Holzterrasse."

Les architectes devaient ajouter trois logements de standing au quartier Birkegade/ Egegade/Elmegade de la capitale danoise, très densément peuplé. Étant donné l'absence d'espace disponible pour créer une cour, JDS a conçu l'ajout comme un « jardin manquant ». Pour le définir, les architectes ont observé la typologie des jardins de Copenhague, caractérisée notamment par son aspect fonctionnel. Ils expliquent : « L'image du toit hédoniste est celle d'un terrain de jeu au revêtement de surface antichoc et à l'amusant pont suspendu, d'une colline verte comportant différents logements recouverts d'herbe véritable et de plantes vivaces, d'une plate-forme d'observation, d'une cuisine extérieure avec barbecue et d'une terrasse en bois plus tranquille. »

The unusual rooftop configuration, with its artificial hill and greenery, stands out from its more ordinary neighbors and illustrates the ways that the tops of buildings can become an integral part of a city.

Die ungewöhnliche Dachgestaltung mit künstlichem Hügel und Begrünung setzt sich deutlich von der gewöhnlicheren Nachbarschaft ab und veranschaulicht, wie sich Hausdächer als städtischer Raum interpretieren lassen.

La configuration originale du toit avec sa colline artificielle et sa verdure contraste avec les immeubles voisins plus ordinaires et illustre la manière dont les sommets des bâtiments peuvent devenir une partie intégrante de la ville.

The architects state: "Usually a roof defines a final measure of any construction. We imagine cities where people will be the (ultimate) measure of the environment."

Die Architekten meinen dazu: „Normalerweise definiert das Dach den Abschluss einer Baumaßnahme. Wir träumen von Städten, in denen der Mensch das (endgültige) Maß des Raums sein wird."

Les architectes déclarent : « Un toit définit habituellement la mesure finale d'une construction. Nous imaginons des villes où les gens seront la mesure (ultime) de l'environnement. »

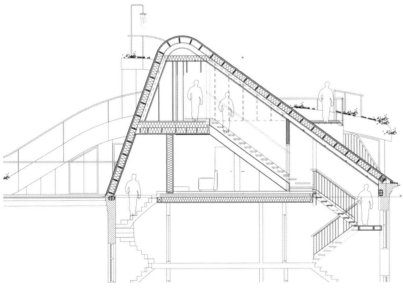

Right, a floor plan shows part of the rooftop area (top of drawing).
Above, a section drawing shows the sharply curved red roof visible in
the images above and on the left page.

*Rechts: Auf dem Grundriss ist ein Teil der Dachfläche sichtbar (oberer
Teil der Zeichnung). Oben: Der Schnitt ist durch das steil geschwungene
rote Dach geführt, das man auf den Fotos oben und links sieht.*

*À droite, plan de niveau qui montre une partie du toit (en haut du
schéma). Ci-dessus, schéma en coupe qui montre la forte pente du toit
rouge qu'on voit sur les photos ci-dessus et page de gauche.*

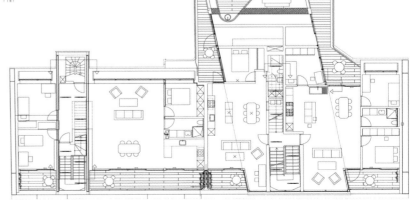

SOU FUJIMOTO
Nishinomiya-shi, Hyogo [JAPAN]
2011–12

House K

Address: not disclosed | Area: 118 m² | Client: not disclosed
Cost: not disclosed

Located in a calm residential area of Nishinomiya-shi, between Osaka and Kobe, this house was conceived with an open line of sight toward woods located to the west. The concept of a roof garden was extended here in a diagonal form. Dotted with potted trees that look as though they are "floating" on the roof, the garden is described alternatively as "semi-natural" or "semi-artificial." There are three interior floor levels, with kitchen and living space on the ground level. Windows were added in a random pattern, creating a variety of different views, accentuated by the diagonal rise of the house. An important part of the design involved creating connections between the interior and the roof garden at all levels so that the residence assumed a kind of natural "topography." A hut or shed was placed on the roof, like a "small villa."

Dieses Haus in einer ruhigen Wohngegend von Nishinomiya-shi, zwischen Osaka und Kobe gelegen, wurde mit freiem Blick auf ein im Westen anschließendes Waldstück geplant. Das Konzept des Dachgartens wurde hier in der Diagonalen umgesetzt. Einzelne Bäume in Containern scheinen auf dem Dach zu „schweben"; der Gartenraum lässt sich entweder als „halb natürlich" oder als „halb künstlich" beschreiben. Der Innenraum erstreckt sich über drei Ebenen; Küche und Wohnbereich sind im Parterre angesiedelt. Die wie zufällig angeordneten Fenster schaffen ganz unterschiedliche Ausblicke, die durch die ansteigende Decke zusätzlich hervorgehoben werden. Ein wichtiger Aspekt des Konzepts war es, auf allen Ebenen Bezüge zwischen Innenraum und Dachgarten zu schaffen, was dem Wohnhaus eine Art „natürliche Topografie" verleiht. Auf dem Dach wurde eine Hütte wie eine „kleine Villa" platziert.

Située dans un quartier résidentiel calme de Nishinomiya-shi, entre Osaka et Kōbe, cette maison a été conçue pour avoir une vue dégagée sur les bois à l'ouest. Le concept de jardin sur le toit prend ici une forme diagonale. Ponctué par des arbres en pots qui semblent « flotter » sur le toit, le jardin est décrit alternativement comme « semi-naturel » ou « semi-artificiel ». L'intérieur compte trois niveaux, la cuisine et le salon occupant celui du bas. Les fenêtres ont été créées de manière aléatoire et ouvrent sur différentes vues, accentuées par la pente. Le design a cherché pour l'essentiel à créer des liens entre l'intérieur et le jardin sur le toit à tous les niveaux afin de conférer une sorte de « topographie » naturelle à l'ensemble. Une cabane ou resserre a été placée sur le toit telle une « petite villa ».

Above, the slanted roof becomes another part of the usable area of the house, with trees in planters and a bench.

Oben: Das schräge Dach wird zu einer ebenfalls nutzbaren Fläche des Hauses, mit Bäumen in Containern und einer Bank.

Ci-dessus, le toit en pente devient une partie habitable de la maison avec des arbres en pots et un banc.

Right, a rooftop window allows views into the residence from above, while of course admitting natural light.

Rechts: Durch ein Dachfenster fällt der Blick ins Haus; gleichzeitig gelangt dadurch reichlich Tageslicht hinein.

À droite, une fenêtre dans le toit permet de voir l'intérieur depuis le haut et, bien sûr, fait entrer la lumière du jour.

The architect compares the rooftop structure visible both above and in the image below to a "small villa."

Der Architekt vergleicht den Dachaufbau, der auf diesen beiden Fotos zu sehen ist, mit einem „kleinen Landhaus".

L'architecte compare la construction sur le toit qu'on voit sur la photo du haut et celle du bas à une «petite villa».

A large, rooftop window opens, allowing residents to go in and out of the house. Right page, interior space is open and not strictly defined in terms of use and precise level.

Durch ein großes Dachfenster können die Bewohner ins Freie bzw. zurück ins Haus gelangen. Rechts: Der Innenraum ist offen gestaltet, ohne präzise Zuordnung zu Zweck und Etage.

La vaste fenêtre dans le toit peut être ouverte pour permettre aux habitants de la maison d'entrer et de sortir. Page de droite, l'espace intérieur est ouvert et n'est pas défini précisément en termes d'usage et de niveau.

Below, a short ladder permits movement between the interior and the exterior, almost as though it had become possible to climb up into the sky (or at least the rooftop terrace).

Unten: Eine Leiter verbindet drinnen und draußen, fast als sei es von hier aus möglich, in den Himmel hinaufzusteigen (zumindest jedoch auf die Dachterrasse).

Ci-dessous, une échelle fait le lien entre l'intérieur et l'extérieur, presque comme s'il était possible de grimper dans le ciel (ou au moins sur la terrasse).

House of the Infinite

Address: not disclosed | Area: 900 m² | Client: not disclosed
Cost: not disclosed | Collaboration: Tomás Carranza, Javier Montero, Alejandro Cervilla

Also called the VT House, this residence is located on a beach near the city of Cádiz. The architect, who is given to a minimalist form of expression, states: "We have built the most radical house we have ever made, an infinite plane facing the infinite sea." The volume is clad in Roman travertine and the roof is one of its most important spaces. Set on an inclined site, the house quite naturally allows residents to use the roof, as an experience of integration with the natural setting. Space for the house itself was excavated out of solid rock to create two floors. The simplicity of the design, which is a 20 × 36-meter box, allows Alberto Campo Baeza to refer to "this resounding horizontal plane, bare and denuded..." He also refers to the presence in the past of the Romans near here, and to the idea of a temple, or to the Greek temenos, "a meeting-place, where, according to mythology, humans and gods come together." The architect's more recent references include Mies van der Rohe and the Casa Malaparte (Adalberto Libera, Capri, Italy, 1937). The city and the house face the Atlantic Ocean to the west, and the setting sun.

Die Casa VT – VT House – liegt am Strand unweit der andalusischen Stadt Cádiz. Der Architekt, der minimalistisches Design bevorzugt, kommentiert: „Dies ist das radikalste Haus, das wir je gebaut haben, eine grenzenlose Fläche, die die grenzenlose See überblickt." Der Baukörper ist mit römischem Travertin verkleidet; der Dachfläche als Raum kommt eine wichtige Rolle zu. Der Bewohner nutzt ganz selbstverständlich die Dachebene des in den Hang gefügten Bauwerks, so sehr ist dieses mit seiner natürlichen Umgebung verwachsen. Für den Wohnbau wurde der gewachsene Fels so weit ausgehöhlt, dass zwei Gebäudeetagen Platz fanden. Das schlichte Design besteht aus einem 20 × 36 m großen Quader, den Alberto Campo Baeza als „überwältigende horizontale Fläche, nackt und bloß" beschreibt. Er verweist darauf, dass hier einst die Römer herrschten, und zieht einen Vergleich mit dem heiligen Tempelbezirk, griechisch Temenos, der „Versammlungsstätte, da der Sage nach Menschen und Götter aufeinandertrafen". Auch auf jüngere Architekturen verweist der Architekt, darunter die Arbeiten von Mies van der Rohe sowie die Casa Malaparte (Adalberto Libera, Capri, Italien, 1937). Sowohl die Stadt als auch das Haus blicken nach Westen auf den Atlantik, in Richtung der untergehenden Sonne.

Aussi appelée Maison VT, cette résidence a été construite sur une plage proche de Cadix. L'architecte, adepte d'une forme d'expression minimaliste, explique : « C'est la maison la plus radicale que nous ayons jamais construite, un plan infini face à l'infini de la mer. » Le volume est revêtu de travertin romain et le toit constitue l'un des principaux espaces. Bâtie sur un terrain en pente, la construction permet assez naturellement aux résidents d'utiliser le toit qui leur offre une intégration totale au décor naturel. L'espace pour la maison a été creusé dans la roche afin de créer deux étages. La simplicité de la conception, un simple cube de 20 × 36 m, se traduit pour Alberto Campo Baeza par « un retentissant plan horizontal, nu et dépouillé... » Il rappelle aussi l'ancienne présence romaine à proximité et l'idée d'un temple, ou du grec temenos, « un lieu de rencontre où, dans la mythologie, les humains et les dieux se retrouvaient. » Parmi ses références plus récentes figurent Mies van der Rohe et la Casa Malaparte (Adalberto Libera, Capri, Italie, 1937). La ville et la maison font face à l'océan Atlantique á l'ouest, et au soleil couchant.

This large house sits in minimalist splendor on a beachside site. The insertion of the rectangular volume into the slope is seen in the drawings below, in particular the elevation at the bottom of the page.

Dieses geräumige, minimalistisch-beeindruckende Bauwerk liegt direkt am Strand. Die untenstehenden Zeichnungen, insbesondere der Aufriss unten, verdeutlichen, wie der quaderförmige Bau in den Hang eingelassen ist.

La grande maison dans toute sa splendeur minimaliste est située sur une plage. Les schémas ci-dessous montrent l'insertion du volume rectangulaire dans la pente, notamment la vue en élévation tout en bas.

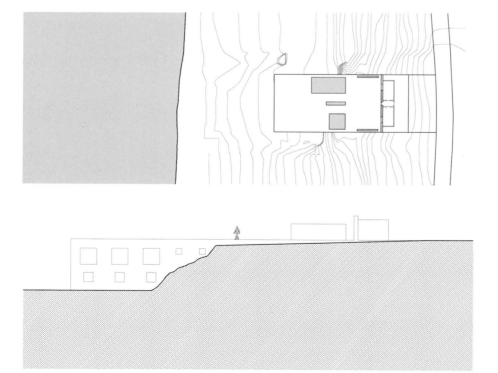

Opposite page: Alberto Campo Baeza contrasts the smooth white purity, here the rooftop, with the colors and textures of the landscape and the Atlantic Ocean.

Gegenüber: Alberto Campo Baeza kontrastiert glatte weiße puristische Flächen – hier die Dachterrasse – mit den Farben und Texturen der Landschaft und des Atlantiks.

Page ci-contre : Alberto Campo Baeza oppose la pureté lisse et blanche, ici celle du toit, aux couleurs et textures du paysage et de l'océan Atlantique.

The house features a rectangular pool etched out of the marble surface of the rooftop, with an uninterrupted view of the ocean. The lack of railings on the roof accentuates the impression of "infinity" sought by the architect.

Ein rechteckiges Schwimmbecken ist in die Travertinfläche eingesenkt; von hier geht der Blick weit über den Ozean. Das gänzliche Fehlen von Brüstungen unterstreicht die vom Architekten angestrebte Grenzenlosigkeit.

La maison dispose d'un bassin rectangulaire percé dans la surface de marbre du toit qui ne brise en rien la vue sur l'océan. L'absence de balustrade sur le toit souligne encore l'impression d'« infinité » recherchée par l'architecte.

The interiors have the same sense of openness and minimal purity that the rooftop evokes. Natural light is omnipresent, as is whiteness.

Genau wie die Dachterrasse vermittelt auch der Innenraum Offenheit und puren Minimalismus. Sonnenlicht und Helligkeit sind der alles beherrschende Eindruck.

On retrouve à l'intérieur le même sentiment d'ouverture et de pureté minimaliste que le toit évoque. La lumière naturelle est omniprésente, avec la blancheur.

DILLER SCOFIDIO + RENFRO
New York, New York [USA]
2007

Hypar Pavilion Lawn

Address: West 65th Street, between Amsterdam Avenue and Broadway, New York, NY 10023, USA, www.lincolncenter.org | Area: 1022 m² | Client: Lincoln Center for the Performing Arts | Cost: not disclosed | Collaboration: Lincoln Center project designed in collaboration with FXFowle, Mathews Nielsen Landscape Architects (Landscape Architect), Frank Ross (Horticulturist)

As part of their long-standing Lincoln Center for the Performing Arts redevelopment project, Diller Scofidio + Renfro designed "a twisting lawn that acts as an occupiable grass roof over a glass pavilion restaurant." The Hypar Lawn is located in Lincoln Center's North Plaza and is oriented away from the noise of the city "to create a bucolic urbanism." The geometry of the lawn occupies the ceiling surface of the restaurant framing views to the plaza and the street. Tall fescue grass was chosen for the lawn because of its durability. DS+R explains the environmental aspects of this project as follows: "The increased thermal mass of the grass roof dramatically reduces the mechanical loads of the restaurant below. Water is drained through the structural columns underneath the lawn surface."

Als Teil ihrer langwierigen Sanierung des Lincoln Center for the Performing Arts konzipierten Diller Scofidio + Renfro „eine in sich verdrehte Rasenfläche, die als begehbares Grasdach auf einem gläsernen Restaurant-Pavillon fungiert". Der Hypar Lawn auf der North Plaza des Lincoln Center ist mit dem „Rücken" zur lärmenden Stadt orientiert und schafft so „eine urbane Idylle". Die Rasengeometrie definiert die Dachoberfläche des Restaurants und rahmt Ausblicke auf die Plaza und die Straße. Beim Rasengras fiel die Wahl auf den besonders ausdauernden Rohrschwingel. DS+R erläutern die Umweltaspekte dieses Projekts folgendermaßen: „Dank der gesteigerten Wärmespeicherkapazität des Grasdachs lässt sich die mechanische Belastung des Restaurantgebäudes dramatisch reduzieren. Wasser wird durch die tragenden Säulen unter der Rasenfläche abgeführt."

Dans le cadre de leur projet à long terme de rénovation du Lincoln Center for the Performing Arts, Diller Scofidio + Renfro ont imaginé «une pelouse onduleuse qui donne un toit herbeux accessible au public à un restaurant dans un pavillon en verre». La pelouse du pavillon Hypar est située sur la North Plaza du Lincoln Center et orientée du côté opposé aux bruits de la ville «afin de créer un certain urbanisme bucolique». Sa forme correspond au plafond du restaurant, encadré par des vues sur la plaza et la rue. La fétuque élevée a été choisie pour la pelouse en raison de sa durée de vie. DS+R expliquent le caractère écologique du projet comme suit: «La masse thermique accrue du toit en pelouse réduit considérablement les charges mécaniques du restaurant en dessous. L'eau est drainée dans les colonnes structurales sous la surface de l'herbe.»

The sloping lawn brings a welcome green space to an otherwise largely mineral environment. The rooftop space is an added public amenity above the café.

Der schräg abfallende Rasen bringt willkommenes Grün in diese von Stein dominierte Umgebung. Die Dachfläche über dem Café ist ein Bonus für die Menschen.

La pelouse en pente enrichit d'un espace vert bienvenu un environnement sinon essentiellement minéral. L'espace ainsi aménagé sur le toit crée un lieu public supplémentaire au-dessus du café.

In the heart of Lincoln Center, the rooftop lawn angles down to the large rectangular basin containing Henry Moore's sculpture Reclining Figure.

Das Rasendach im Herzen des Lincoln Center neigt sich zu dem großen rechteckigen Wasserbecken herab, in dem Henry Moores Skulptur Reclining Figure ruht.

Au centre du Lincoln Center, la pelouse sur le toit descend vers le vaste bassin rectangulaire qui contient la sculpture Reclining Figure d'Henry Moore.

Le Loft Restaurant, Hotel Stephansdom

Address: Praterstr. 1, 1020 Vienna, Austria, +43 1 906 16,
www.sofitel-vienna-stephansdom.com | Area: 800 m² | Client: UNIQA Praterstraße
Projekterrichtungs GmbH | Cost: not disclosed | Collaboration: Pipilotti Rist

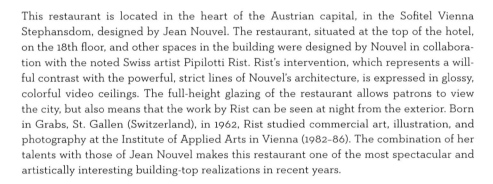

This restaurant is located in the heart of the Austrian capital, in the Sofitel Vienna Stephansdom, designed by Jean Nouvel. The restaurant, situated at the top of the hotel, on the 18th floor, and other spaces in the building were designed by Nouvel in collaboration with the noted Swiss artist Pipilotti Rist. Rist's intervention, which represents a willful contrast with the powerful, strict lines of Nouvel's architecture, is expressed in glossy, colorful video ceilings. The full-height glazing of the restaurant allows patrons to view the city, but also means that the work by Rist can be seen at night from the exterior. Born in Grabs, St. Gallen (Switzerland), in 1962, Rist studied commercial art, illustration, and photography at the Institute of Applied Arts in Vienna (1982–86). The combination of her talents with those of Jean Nouvel makes this restaurant one of the most spectacular and artistically interesting building-top realizations in recent years.

Dieses Restaurant liegt im Herzen der österreichischen Hauptstadt in dem von Jean Nouvel konzipierten Sofitel Vienna Stephansdom. Die Gastronomie im obersten, 18. Stockwerk sowie weitere Räumlichkeiten des Hotels gestaltete Nouvel in Zusammenarbeit mit der bedeutenden Schweizer Künstlerin Pipilotti Rist. Rists Intervention, die in mutwilligem Kontrast zu der beeindruckenden Strenge von Nouvels Architektur steht, hat die Gestalt einer vielfarbigen Lichtdecke. Die raumhohe Rundumverglasung gestattet den Restaurantgästen nicht nur einen ungehinderten Blick über die Stadt, sondern sie macht Rists Werk bei Nacht von außen sichtbar. Die 1962 in Grabs im Kanton St. Gallen geborene Künstlerin studierte Gebrauchs-, Illustrations- und Fotografik an der Hochschule für Angewandte Kunst in Wien (1982–86). Dieses Restaurant auf oberstem Niveau, für das Rist und Nouvel ihre Talente vereinten, verkörpert einen der spektakulärsten und interessantesten künstlerischen Entwürfe der letzten Jahre.

Le restaurant est situé au cœur de la capitale autrichienne, dans le Sofitel Vienna Stephansdom, réalisé par Jean Nouvel. Il occupe le sommet de l'hôtel, au 18e niveau, et a été conçu, avec d'autres espaces du complexe, par Nouvel en collaboration avec l'artiste suisse très remarquée Pipilotti Rist. Son travail, qui contraste volontairement avec les lignes puissantes et strictes de l'architecture de Nouvel, prend la forme de plafonds vidéo brillants et colorés. Le vitrage du restaurant sur toute sa hauteur donne vue sur la ville aux clients mais permet également à l'œuvre de Rist d'être admirée de l'extérieur la nuit. Née à Grabs (Saint-Gall, Suisse) en 1962, elle a étudié l'art publicitaire, l'illustration et la photographie à l'Institut des arts appliqués de Vienne (1982–86). L'association de son talent et de celui de Jean Nouvel font du restaurant l'une des toitures aménagées les plus spectaculaires et artistiquement intéressantes de ces dernières années.

As seen from the outside, the building seems to float between the colorful artworks by Pipilotti Rist.

Von außen scheint es, als werde das Gebäude von den farbenfrohen Werken der Künstlerin Pipilotti Rist getragen.

Vu de l'extérieur, le bâtiment semble flotter entre les œuvres colorées de Pipilotti Rist.

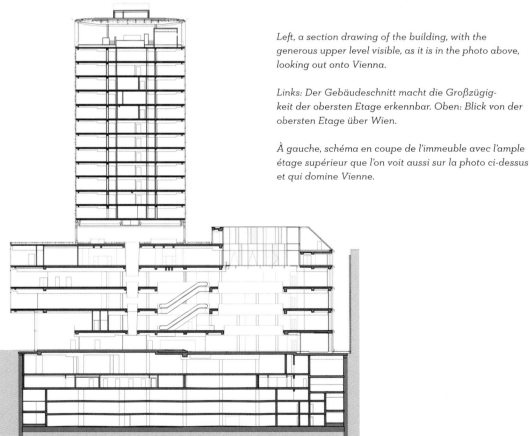

Left, a section drawing of the building, with the generous upper level visible, as it is in the photo above, looking out onto Vienna.

Links: Der Gebäudeschnitt macht die Großzügigkeit der obersten Etage erkennbar. Oben: Blick von der obersten Etage über Wien.

À gauche, schéma en coupe de l'immeuble avec l'ample étage supérieur que l'on voit aussi sur la photo ci-dessus et qui domine Vienne.

FRANK O. GEHRY
Paris [FRANCE]
2008–14

Louis Vuitton Foundation

Address: 8 Avenue du Mahatma Gandhi, Bois de Boulogne, 75116 Paris, France,
+33 1 40 69 96 00, www.fondationlouisvuitton.fr | Area: 11 000 m² | Client: Fondation
Louis Vuitton, Bernard Arnault, President | Cost: not disclosed

Commissioned by Bernard Arnault, head of LVMH, the Louis Vuitton Foundation can be called the masterpiece of Frank O. Gehry. In terms of inspiration and quality of construction, as well as its practicality for the exhibition of art, it goes beyond earlier works by the California architect. Located at the edge of the Jardin d'Acclimatation with views of the skyscrapers of La Défense, the building has visible elements made of wood and 13 500 square meters of glass, resembling "a glass cloud," but also a ship with billowing sails. The core of the building, dubbed the "Iceberg," is made of 19 000 separately molded sheets of fiber-reinforced Ductal concrete. Gehry sought inspiration from the glass roofs of the Grand Palais in Paris, but also from such structures as the nearby Palmarium (1893) in the Jardin des Serres d'Auteuil. Intended for the exhibition of contemporary art, the facility opened with works such as a mirror and mosaic colonnade by Olafur Eliasson. The building includes 11 art galleries and an auditorium with a capacity of 350, but a visit to the Foundation could not be complete without a tour of its numerous rooftop terraces, which look down on the architecture and out to the city.

Den von Bernard Arnault, Unternehmensleiter von LVMH, in Auftrag gegebenen Bau der Fondation Louis Vuitton darf man als Frank O. Gehrys Meisterwerk bezeichnen. Sowohl bezüglich der Grundidee und der Qualität der Bauausführung als auch hinsichtlich der Eignung des Baus zum Ausstellungsraum für Kunst geht das Projekt über frühere Werke des in Kalifornien ansässigen Architekten deutlich hinaus. Das am Rand des Jardin d'Acclimatation mit Blick auf die Wolkenkratzer von La Défense gelegene Bauwerk zeichnet sich durch sichtbare Holzelemente und 13 500 m² Glasfläche aus; es ähnelt einer „Glaswolke" oder auch einem Schiff unter vollen Segeln. Den Kern des Bauwerks mit dem Beinamen „Eisberg" bilden 19 000 einzeln geformte Platten aus Ductal-Faserbeton. Gehry fand seine Inspiration beim Glasdach des Pariser Grand Palais und bei Bauten wie dem Palmarium (1893) des nahegelegenen Jardin des Serres d'Auteuil. Die als Ausstellungsraum für zeitgenössische Kunst vorgesehene Einrichtung zeigte bei der Eröffnung so bedeutende Werke wie eine Spiegel- und Mosaikkolonnade von Olafur Eliasson. Das Gebäude beherbergt elf Ausstellungsräume und ein 350 Gäste fassendes Auditorium. Ohne einen Spaziergang über die zahlreichen Dachterrassen, die mit Ausblicken auf die Architektur und die Stadt aufwarten, bliebe ein Besuch der Fondation jedoch unvollständig.

Commandée par Bernard Arnault qui dirige LVMH, la Fondation Louis Vuitton peut être considérée comme le chef-d'œuvre de Frank O. Gehry. En termes d'inspiration et de qualité de construction autant que sur le plan pratique pour exposer l'art, la Fondation va bien au-delà des réalisations antérieures de l'architecte californien. Situé à la lisière du Jardin d'acclimatation avec vue sur les gratte-ciel de La Défense, le bâtiment est composé d'éléments en bois visibles, mais aussi de 13 500 m² de verre qui le font ressembler à un « nuage en verre » selon les journalistes, mais aussi à un navire aux voiles gonflées par le vent. Le cœur de l'édifice, l'« iceberg », est fait de 19 000 panneaux de béton fibré Ductal moulés individuellement. Gehry s'est inspiré des verrières du Grand Palais, à Paris, mais aussi du Palmarium voisin de 1893, dans le Jardin des serres d'Auteuil. Destinée à accueillir des expositions d'art contemporain, la Fondation a ouvert ses portes avec des œuvres comme le miroir et la colonnade de mosaïque d'Olafur Eliasson. Elle contient onze galeries d'art et un auditorium de 350 places, mais la visite ne saurait être complète sans un tour des nombreuses terrasses du toit pour admirer l'architecture d'en haut et la ville au-dehors.

The building has numerous covered or uncovered rooftop spaces that visitors can accede to freely. Below, a plan showing the upper-level terraces. Right page, visitors seen between the billowing sheets of glass.

Das Bauwerk besitzt zahlreiche teils überdachte, teils offene Dachflächen, die für Besucher frei zugänglich sind. Unten: Ein Plan der höher gelegenen Terrassen. Rechte Seite: Besucher zwischen den wogenden Glasflächen.

Le bâtiment possède sur son toit de nombreux espaces couverts ou non auxquels les visiteurs peuvent accéder librement. Ci-dessous, un plan des terrasses du niveau supérieur. Page de droite, des visiteurs entre les vitres gonflées.

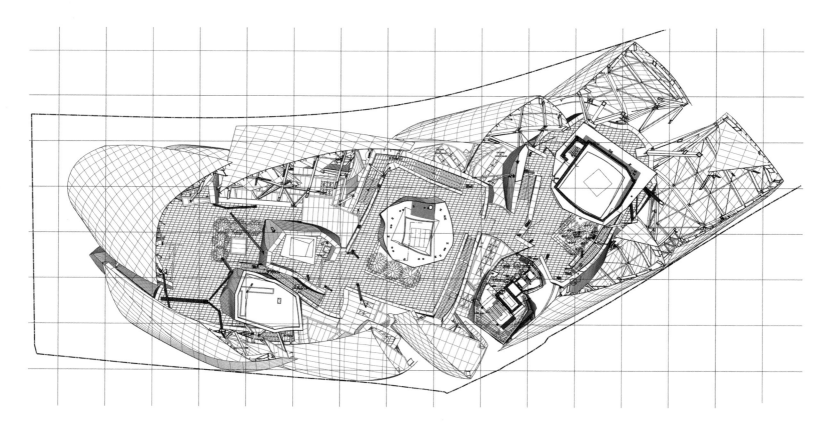

Frank O. Gehry combines wood, steel, and glass in a sculptural pattern that opens out onto terraces such as the ones seen on these two pages, with the Défense business district visible in the distance (above).

Frank O. Gehry verbindet Holz, Stahl und Glas zu einem skulpturalen Gebilde, das sich zu Terrassen wie die auf diesen beiden Seiten abgebildeten öffnen, im Hintergrund das Pariser Büroviertel La Défense (oben).

Frank O. Gehry associe le bois, l'acier et le verre dans un motif sculptural qui ouvre sur des terrasses comme celles que l'on voit sur ces deux pages, avec La Défense visible au loin (ci-dessus).

ANDREW FRANZ
New York, New York [USA]
2012–13

Lower Manhattan Loft

Address: not disclosed | Area: 279 m² (interiors), 74 m² (terraces) | Client: not disclosed
Cost: not disclosed | Collaboration: Jaime Donate (Associate)

This loft was created in the top floor and roof of an 1884 warehouse in the Tribeca North area of Manhattan. The original building served as a warehouse for a variety of tenants, including a soap company, a wrought-iron pipes and fittings manufacturer, a metal spinning company, and several grocers and purveyors. The top-floor loft space was once occupied by the Romanoff Caviar Company. The refurbished space is intended to be open for purposes of entertainment with a fluid link between the living area and the outdoor terrace, with views toward the Hudson River, a connection heightened by the use of a 14-square-meter retractable glass roof. The architect has intentionally combined new materials with recuperated elements from the original industrial-style building, typical of this part of New York, while energy-efficient mechanical systems heighten the ecological aspect of the project. The outdoor terrace uses Ipe wood for the deck, reclaimed bluestone pavers, powder-coated steel planters, and a mixture of native plants. The large skylight over the lower-level living space is made with galvanized steel and low-e glass. Andrew Franz was also responsible for interior design, including the custom kitchen.

Dieses Loft entstand auf der obersten Etage und dem Flachdach eines 1884 errichteten Lagerhauses im Norden von Manhattans Stadtteil Tribeca. Das Bestandsgebäude diente den unterschiedlichsten Mietern als Warenlager, darunter ein Seifenfabrikant, ein Hersteller gusseiserner Rohre und Fittings, eine Metalldrückerei sowie eine Reihe von Lebensmittelhändlern und -lieferanten. Das Loft auf der obersten Etage wurde einst von der Romanoff Caviar Company genutzt. Der sanierte Bereich soll nun der Bewirtung von Gästen dienen, mit einem fließenden Übergang vom Wohnbereich zu der Außenterrasse mit Blick zum Hudson River – eine Verbindung, die das 14 m² große einfahrbare Glasdach zusätzlich stärkt. Bewusst kombinierte der Architekt neue Materialien mit aufgearbeiteten Elementen des ursprünglichen, für diese New Yorker Gegend typischen Industriebaus; energieeffiziente Haustechnik betont den „grünen" Anspruch des Projekts. Auf der Außenterrasse kam für das Deck Ipe-Holz zum Einsatz, außerdem wiederverwertete Bluestone-Platten, Pflanzcontainer aus pulverbeschichtetem Stahl und verschiedene heimische Pflanzen. Die große Dachfensterfläche über dem Wohnbereich auf der unteren Ebene besteht aus Wärmedämmglas in einem galvanisierten Stahlrahmen. Auch die Innenraumgestaltung oblag Andrew Franz, einschließlich der maßgefertigten Küche.

Le loft a été aménagé au dernier étage et sur le toit d'un entrepôt de 1884 dans le quartier Tribeca du Nord de Manhattan. Le bâtiment d'origine a servi de hangar à de multiples locataires, parmi lesquels une savonnerie, un fabricant de tuyaux et accessoires de tuyauterie en fer forgé, une entreprise de métal repoussé, plusieurs épiciers et fournisseurs divers. Le dernier étage a aussi été occupé par les caviars Romanoff. L'espace a été remis à neuf à des fins de divertissement et bénéficie d'une communication fluide entre l'espace de vie et la terrasse, d'où la vue sur l'Hudson est rehaussée par le toit ouvrant en verre de 14 m². L'architecte a délibérément associé les matériaux neufs et des éléments récupérés sur le bâtiment d'origine au style industriel typique de cette partie de New York, tandis que des équipements techniques à faible consommation renforcent le caractère écologique du projet. La terrasse utilise du bois d'ipé et des pavés de pierre bleue récupérés pour la plate-forme, est agrémentée de jardinières en acier au revêtement poudré et d'un mélange de plantes locales. La grande lucarne au-dessus du niveau inférieur est en acier galvanisé et verre à faible émissivité. Andrew Franz a également été chargé de l'architecture intérieure, dont la cuisine personnalisée.

The warm, interior, double-height space has a stairway leading up to the rooftop, seen in the plan and section drawings on this page.

Aus dem einladenden Innenraum mit doppelter Deckenhöhe führt eine Treppe auf das Dach, dessen Anlage auf dem Grundriss und in dem Gebäudeschnitt auf dieser Seite zu sehen ist.

Le chaleureux espace intérieur double hauteur dispose d'un escalier pour monter sur le toit, représenté sur le plan et les schémas en coupe de cette page.

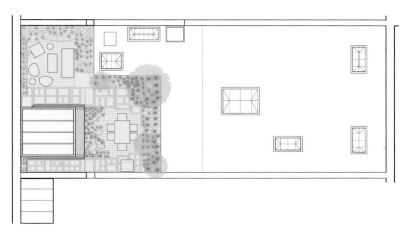

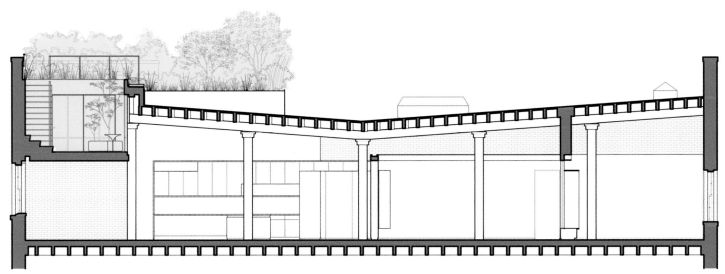

The relatively small terrace appears as a kind of green oasis looking out on the Hudson River in the distance.

Die relativ kleine Terrasse erscheint als eine angenehme grüne Oase mit Blick auf den Hudson River im Hintergrund.

La terrasse de dimensions modestes donne l'impression d'une oasis de verdure avec vue sur l'Hudson au loin.

MICHAEL VAN VALKENBURGH
Chicago, Illinois [USA]
2002–15

Maggie Daley Park

Address: 337 E. Randolph St., Chicago, IL 60601, USA, +1 312 552 3000, www.maggiedaley-park.com | Area: 10.7 hectares | Client: Guilford Transportation | Cost: $55 million

It was on the occasion of renovations to the 4000-car underground Lakeside parking garage adjacent to Millennium Park that Maggie Daley Park was created as a partial renovation of existing portions of Grant Park, thus unifying Daley Bicentennial Plaza, the Cancer Survivors Garden, and Peanut Park. The designers describe it as "curvilinear, topographically dramatic, and relentlessly heterogeneous." Organized on two diagonal axes, the park has an area for active recreation, including a 1.2-hectare play garden, a café, a rock-climbing park, and a seasonal ice-skating ribbon nestled in an evergreen grove. In the summer, the skating ribbon serves as a paved path, allowing for circulation and access to the climbing walls. In the other direction (northeast-to-southwest) a lawn valley and a network of paths provides opportunities for peaceful recreation engagement with open green space and views of Chicago and Lake Michigan. The way in which this park is realized above an underground garage makes it almost impossible to tell that it is, in fact, a very large rooftop.

Angelegentlich der Renovierung der 4000 Stellplätze fassenden Lakeside-Tiefgarage neben dem Millennium Park entstand als Teilrenovierung eines Abschnitts des Grant Park der Maggie Daley Park, der nun die Daley Bicentennial Plaza, den Cancer Survivors Garden und den Peanut Park zusammenfasst. Die Gestalter beschreiben ihn als „kurvenreich, mit dramatischer Topografie und kompromisslos heterogen". Dieser Park, der sich an zwei diagonalen Achsen orientiert, beinhaltet unter anderem ein Freizeitgelände mit einem 1,2 ha großen Spielplatz, ein Café, einen Boulderpark und im Winterhalbjahr eine von immergrünen Gehölzen gesäumte Eisbahn. Im Sommer wird die Bahn zum befestigten Spazierweg, über den auch die Kletterwände erreichbar sind. In der anderen Richtung (Nordost–Südwest) laden ein Rasental und verschlungene Pfade zu ruhiger Entspannung in weiten grünen Räumen ein mit Blick auf die Skyline von Chicago und den Lake Michigan. Aufgrund der riesigen Dimension der darunterliegendender Tiefgarage ist der Park auf den ersten Blick kaum als Dachkonstruktion zu erkennen.

Maggie Daley Park a été créé à l'occasion des rénovations du parking souterrain Lakeside de 4000 places, adjacent au Millennium Park, et renouvelle en partie certaines portions du Grant Park en regroupant la Daley Bicentennial Plaza, le Cancer Survivors Garden et Peanut Park. Les créateurs décrivent le parc comme «curviligne, à la topographie spectaculaire et absolument hétérogène». Articulé autour de deux axes en diagonale, il comporte une zone de loisirs actifs avec un terrain de jeux de 1,2 hectares, un café, un terrain d'escalade et une piste sinueuse de patin à glace à la saison, nichée dans un bosquet à feuilles persistantes. L'été, c'est un chemin pavé destiné à la promenade qui donne accès aux murs d'escalade. Dans l'autre direction (nord-est-sud-ouest), un vallon herbeux et un réseau de sentiers permettent des loisirs plus paisibles dans des espaces verts dégagés avec vue sur Chicago et le lac Michigan. La manière dont le parc a été réalisé au-dessus d'un parking souterrain ne permet presque pas de se rendre compte qu'il s'agit en fait d'un toit de très grandes dimensions.

In this aerial view of Chicago, Maggie Daley Park is visible in the middle of the image, with Frank O. Gehry's Jay Pritzker Pavilion on the left, in Millennium Park.

Der Maggie Daley Park liegt etwa in der Mitte dieser Luftaufnahme von Chicago, mit Frank O. Gehrys Jay Pritzker Pavilion links daneben im Millennium Park.

Le Maggie Daley Park apparaît au milieu de cette vue aérienne de Chicago avec le pavillon Jay Pritzker de Frank O. Gehry à gauche, dans Millennium Park.

Although the park appears to be at ground level, it is located on the roof of a large parking facility. In the image on the right page below, the playful atmosphere of the park is visible where the contrast with the neighboring city could not be more apparent.

Der Park erscheint zwar ebenerdig, doch er befindet sich auf dem Dach einer großen Tiefgarage. Das Foto gegenüber unten zeigt die spielerische Atmosphäre des Parks; der Kontrast zum benachbarten Hochhausbezirk könnte deutlicher nicht sein.

Bien que construit sur le toit d'un vaste parking, le parc semble véritablement au niveau du sol. L'ambiance ludique du parc ressort de la photo ci-contre en bas où le contraste avec la ville juste à côté ne saurait être plus visible.

A plan of the park assumes a curvilinear design, in contrast to the alignments of nearby Grant Park for example.

Grundriss des Parks, der – anders als beispielsweise der nahegelegene Grant Park – auf eine geschwungene Linienführung setzt.

Plan du parc où sa configuration curviligne contraste avec, par exemple, les alignements du Grant Park voisin.

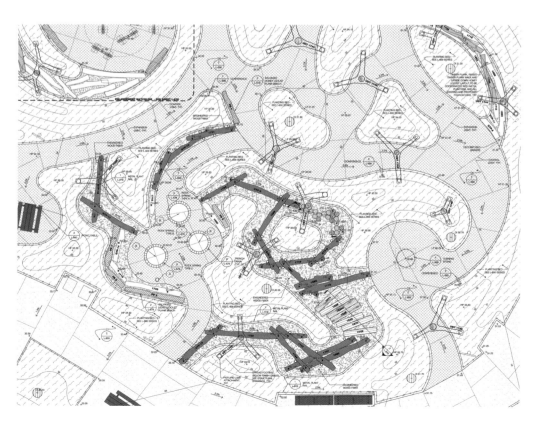

KEN SMITH
New York, New York [USA]
2004–05

Museum of Modern Art Roof Garden

Address: n/a | Area: 948 m² (north roof), 669 m² (south roof)
Client: Museum of Modern Art | Cost: not disclosed

Ken Smith's Museum of Modern Art Roof Garden can only be viewed from neighboring buildings. Set atop MoMA's expansion by Japanese architect Yoshio Taniguchi, it cannot be visited or even seen by museumgoers. Using 185 plastic rocks, 560 artificial boxwood trees, 136 kilos of clear crushed glass, four tons of recycled rubber mulch, and white stones (roof ballast) already purchased by the institution before it was decided to make a "garden," Ken Smith created a work he likens to camouflage. His intention, he says, was to take "the art of camouflage and the artifice of simulation a step further by using the simulation itself as a source for design speculation." Peter Reed, former Curator of the Department of Architecture and Design at MoMA, states that "by playing with notions of the artificial and natural, Smith points to the fact that much of landscape design recalls an ideal nature but is, in fact, a highly artificial construct intended to conceal what lies below or beyond. Given the highly artificial environment and limitations of the setting, it seems fitting to impose the imagery of imitated nature onto a built construction."[1]

Ken Smiths Dachgarten auf dem Museum of Modern Art kann nur von benachbarten Gebäuden aus gesehen werden. Er liegt auf dem MoMA-Erweiterungsbau des japanischen Architekten Yoshio Taniguchi und ist für die Museumsbesucher weder zugänglich noch einzusehen. Aus 185 Kunststofffelsen, 560 künstlichen Buchsbäumen, 136 kg weißem Glasschotter, 4 t Recycling-Gummischnitzeln sowie weißem Schotter, den das Museum bereits als Dachkies bestellt hatte, bevor die Entscheidung für den „Garten" fiel, schuf Ken Smith ein Werk, das er mit einem Tarnmuster vergleicht. Seine Absicht sei es gewesen, „die Kunst der Camouflage und die Künstlichkeit der Simulation weiter auf die Spitze zu treiben und die Simulation selbst als Quelle für Designideen zu nutzen." Peter Reed, ehemaliger Kurator für Architektur und Design am MoMA, konstatiert: „Smith spielt mit Vorstellungen von Künstlichkeit und Natürlichkeit und verweist so auf die Tatsache, dass sich Landschaftsgestaltung häufig auf eine Idealvorstellung der Natur bezieht, dabei aber ein überaus künstliches Konstrukt ist, um das darunter oder dahinter Gelegene zu verbergen. Angesichts der hochkünstlichen Umgebung und der vorgegebenen Beschränkungen scheint es angemessen, der Architektur die Bildsprache imitierter Natur zuzuordnen."[1]

Le jardin créé par Ken Smith sur le toit du Museum of Modern Art peut uniquement être vu depuis les immeubles voisins. Il occupe le sommet de l'extension du MoMA réalisée par l'architecte japonais Yoshio Taniguchi et ne peut être visité, ni même vu, par le public du musée. À l'aide de 185 rochers en plastique, 560 buis artificiels, 136 kg de verre pilé, 4 t de paillis de caoutchouc recyclé et des pierres blanches (lestage de toiture), Ken Smith a créé une œuvre qu'il compare à un camouflage. Son intention était de pousser «un peu plus loin l'art du camouflage et l'artifice de la simulation en utilisant cette dernière comme une source de spéculation créative». Peter Reed, ancien conservateur du département Architecture et design au MoMA, déclare qu'«en jouant avec les notions d'artificiel et de naturel, Smith attire l'attention sur le fait que si la plupart des créations paysagères rappellent une nature idéale, elles sont en fait des constructions totalement artificielles dont le but est de dissimuler ce qu'il y a en dessous ou au-delà. Étant donné le caractère extrêmement artificiel de l'environnement et les restrictions imposées par le cadre, il semble pertinent d'imposer l'imagerie de la nature imitée dans une structure construite[1]».

1   Peter Reed, *Groundswell*, Museum of Modern Art, New York, 2005

Ken Smith certainly innovated with this rooftop garden, meant only to improve the view of the museum from neighboring buildings. In the tradition of the Japanese dry garden, it contains no plants.

Der Dachgarten von Ken Smith ist etwas völlig Neues; sein einziger Zweck ist der schöne Blick auf das Museum von den benachbarten Gebäuden aus. Wie im japanischen Trockengarten finden sich auch hier keine Pflanzen.

Ken Smith a innové avec ce jardin en toiture dont la seule fonction est de fournir une plus belle vue sur le musée depuis les immeubles voisins. Dans la tradition des jardins secs japonais, il ne contient pas de plantes.

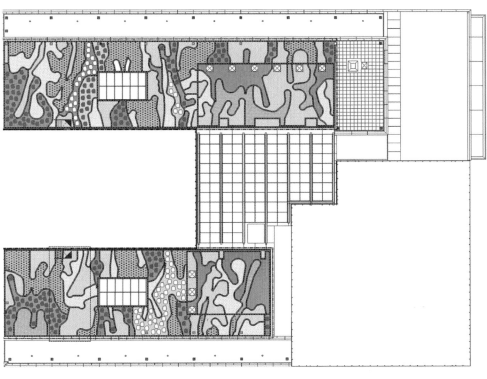

Especially when seen from above, the garden seems quite natural and "real"—when in fact it is made up of such elements as recycled glass and rubber mulch.

Besonders beim Blick von oben erscheint der Garten ganz natürlich und „echt" – tatsächlich aber besteht er aus Elementen wie Altglas und Gummischnitzeln.

C'est surtout vu d'en haut que le jardin semble naturel et «réel» – alors qu'il est en réalité composé de verre et de paillis de caoutchouc recyclé, parmi d'autres éléments.

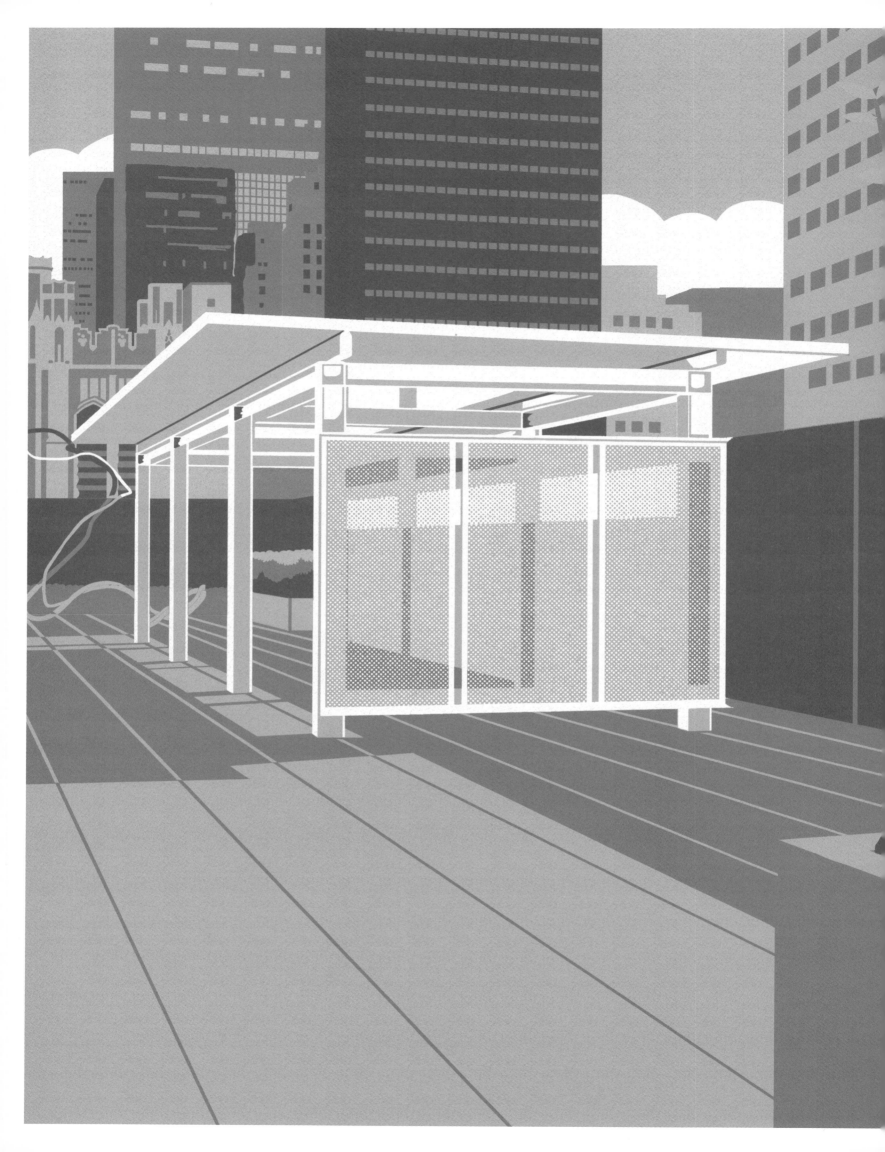

FRANÇOIS DE MENIL
New York, New York [USA]
2004–05

Museum Tower Roof Garden

Address: n/a | Area: 418 m² | Client: The Board of Managers of the Museum Tower C | Cost: not disclosed | Collaboration: Kohn Pederson Fox Associates (Architect of Record), Fisher Maran (Lighting Designer)

Accessible only to tenants of the Museum Tower at 15 West 53rd Street, this eighth-floor space looks down on the Abby Aldrich Rockefeller Sculpture Garden of the Museum of Modern Art. According to the architect, the small steel pavilion pays homage to both Mies van der Rohe and to Philip Johnson's Glass House. A stainless-steel and brass sculpture titled *Chinatown*, by the artist Forrest Myers, further emphasizes the dialogue with the Museum of Modern Art. The architect explains: "The roof terrace becomes an outdoor room that is discovered progressively. Entering the terrace, the copse of birch trees draws one to the north and the view over the MoMA garden below. From there the pavilion's perforated metal panels create an intriguing screen providing glimpses of something beyond. The pavilion then reveals the Myers sculpture, which anchors the terrace's east end."

Von diesem Außenraum auf der achten Etage, der nur den Bewohnern des Museum Tower an der Adresse 15 West 53rd Street zugänglich ist, fällt der Blick auf den Abby Aldrich Rockefeller Sculpture Garden des Museum of Modern Art. Der Architekt gestaltete den kleinen weißen Stahlpavillon als Huldigung an Mies van der Rohe sowie an Philip Johnsons Glass House. Zugleich unterstreicht die Skulptur *Chinatown*, die der Künstler Forrest Myers aus Edelstahl und Messing formte, den Dialog mit dem Museum of Modern Art. Der Architekt erklärt: „Die Dachterrasse wird zum schrittweise erschlossenen Freiraum. Beim Betreten der Terrasse lenkt die Birkengruppe den Besucher in Richtung Norden, hin zum Ausblick auf den darunter gelegenen MoMA-Garten. Die halbdurchsichtigen perforierten Metallpaneele des Pavillons locken mit Andeutungen; dann gibt der Pavillon den Blick auf Myers' Skulptur frei, die dem östlichen Teil der Terrasse Gewicht gibt."

Accessible seulement aux locataires de la Museum Tower, 15 West 53rd Street, l'espace aménagé au 8ᵉ niveau surplombe le jardin de sculptures Abby Aldrich Rockefeller du Museum of Modern Art. Selon l'architecte, le petit pavillon en acier rend hommage à la fois à Mies van der Rohe et à la Glass House de Philip Johnson. Une sculpture en acier inoxydable et bronze de l'artiste Forrest Myers, baptisée *Chinatown*, intensifie encore le dialogue avec le Museum of Modern Art. L'architecte explique : «La terrasse sur le toit devient une véritable pièce extérieure à découvrir progressivement. En entrant, le bosquet de bouleaux attire vers le nord et la vue sur le jardin du MoMA en contrebas. Puis les panneaux en métal perforé du pavillon créent comme un écran fascinant à travers lequel on aperçoit ce qu'il y a au-delà. Le pavillon dévoile alors la sculpture de Myers qui fixe l'extrémité est de la terrasse.»

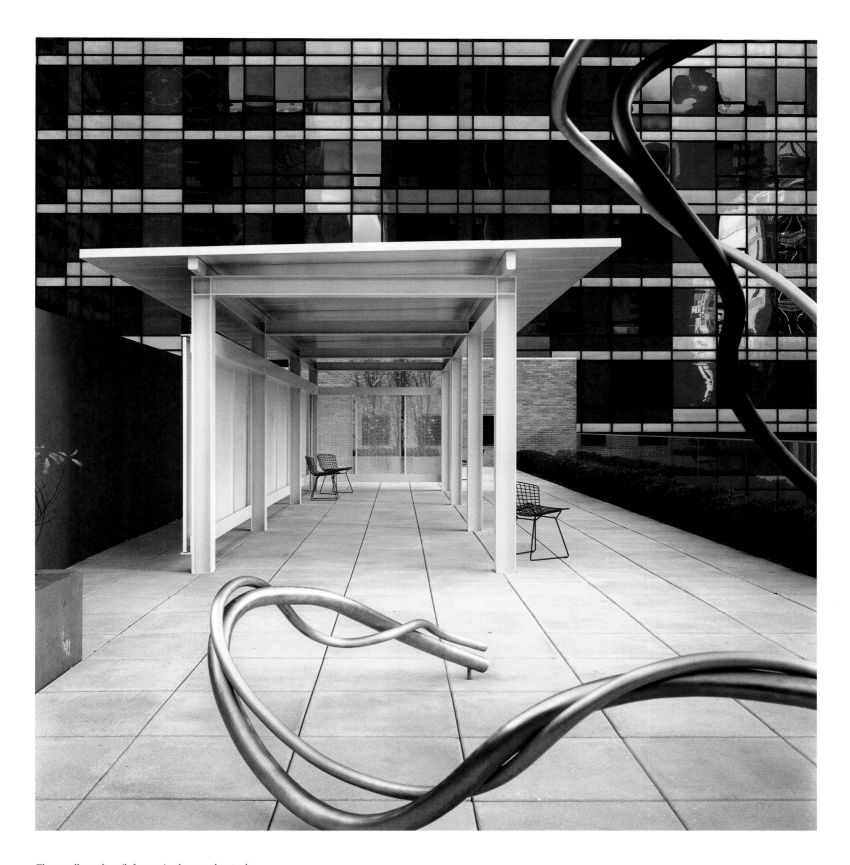

The small pavilion (left page) takes on classical
grandeur in this dense urban setting. Above, a
view of the installation with parts of the sculpture
Chinatown by Forrest Myers is visible.

Der Pavillon (links) zeigt sich in der dichten
Umgebung in klassisch vornehmem Design; im
Foto oben Blick auf die Installation, mit Teilen
der Forrest-Myers-Skulptur Chinatown.

Le petit pavillon (à gauche) acquiert une grandeur
véritablement classique du fait de la simplicité de
son design dans un contexte urbain aussi dense.
Ci-dessus, vue de l'installation avec la sculpture
Chinatown de Forrest Myers visible en partie.

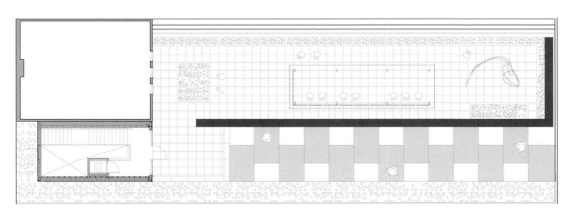

GUSTAFSON PORTER
London [UK]
2013–15

New Ludgate

Address: 1 & 2 New Ludgate, London EC4, UK, www.landsecurities.com
Area: 7000 m² | Client: Land Securities | Cost: not disclosed | Architects: Sauerbruch Hutton,
Fletcher Priest | Collaboration: Land Securities

This project involved the public realm landscape for 1 and 2 New Ludgate, designed by Sauerbruch Hutton and Fletcher Priest. A part of the development is a large south-facing roof terrace on the fifth floor of the Fletcher Priest-designed 1 New Ludgate. Here, a "curvilinear white Corian bench provides generous seating. Its form wraps around the edges of the terrace, growing in height and allowing ample soil depth for the intensive planting scheme." The designers explain their planting scheme: "The gently undulating landform is planted with colorful bands of perennial plants mixed with ornamental grasses in loose, natural arrangements. Plants are grouped together according to color and form. Bands of yellow flowering evergreen euphorbias contrast with the tall blue flowering spikes of eryngium, echinopsis and aster; low hummocks of flowering thyme are seen against the towering purple balls of alliums, all framed by the plumes of tall ornamental grasses. Using a mix of low and taller perennials and grasses provides a natural permeable boundary that allows spectacular views to St. Paul's and the City of London beyond."

Dieses Projekt ist Teil einer Landschaft im öffentlichen Raum an der Adresse 1 und 2 New Ludgate, gestaltet von den Büros Sauerbruch Hutton und Fletcher Priest. Zu der Bebauung gehört eine große, nach Süden offene Dachterrasse auf der 5. Etage des von Fletcher Priest entworfenen Gebäudes 1 New Ludgate. Eine „geschwungene Bank aus weißem Corian bietet viele Sitzgelegenheiten. Sie zeichnet die Form der Terrasse nach und umfasst mit ihrer bis auf die Höhe der Rückenlehne ansteigenden Sitzfläche die Beete mit genügend Bodentiefe für eine dichte Bepflanzung." Zu den Beeten sagen die Gestalter: „Die leicht welligen Flächen sind mit winterharten Stauden bepflanzt, zwischen denen in lockeren, natürlichen Arrangements Ziergräser stehen. Die Pflanzen sind nach Farbe und Form gruppiert. Bänder gelb blühender immergrüner Euphorbien kontrastieren mit den hohen blauen Blütenständen von Mannstreu, Kugeldisteln und Astern; niedrige blühende Thymiankissen setzen sich gegen hoch aufragende violette Blütenkugeln von Lauchpflanzen ab, das Ganze umrahmt von wogenden Ziergräsern. Die Kombination aus niedrigen und höheren Stauden und Gräsern schafft eine natürliche, durchlässige Grenze; dahinter schweift der Blick spektakulär zur St. Paul's Cathedral und über die Londoner Innenstadt."

Le projet comprend l'aménagement paysager de l'espace public du 1 et 2 New Ludgate, conçu par Sauerbruch Hutton et Fletcher Priest. La vaste terrasse sud sur le toit du 5e niveau du 1 New Ludgate, créée par Fletcher et Priest, est l'un des éléments de sa mise en valeur. Un «banc curviligne en Corian blanc fournit de multiples possibilités de s'asseoir. Sa forme s'enroule autour de la terrasse, tandis que sa hauteur croissante permet une plus grande profondeur de sol pour les plantations intensives prévues». Les créateurs expliquent leur projet de plantation : «Les douces ondulations du terrain sont plantées de vivaces en bandes colorées, mêlées à des herbes ornementales disposées de manière informelle et naturelle. Les végétaux sont groupés par couleur et forme. Des lignes d'euphorbes au feuillage persistant et aux fleurs jaunes contrastent avec les hautes bractées florales bleues des panicauts, echinopsis et asters, tandis que de bas monticules de thym en fleur se détachent sur les imposantes boules violettes des aulx d'ornement, le tout encadré par les aigrettes de hautes herbes ornementales. Le mélange de vivaces et d'herbes basses ou plus hautes crée une frontière naturelle ouverte avec des vues spectaculaires sur St. Paul et la City de Londres par derrière.»

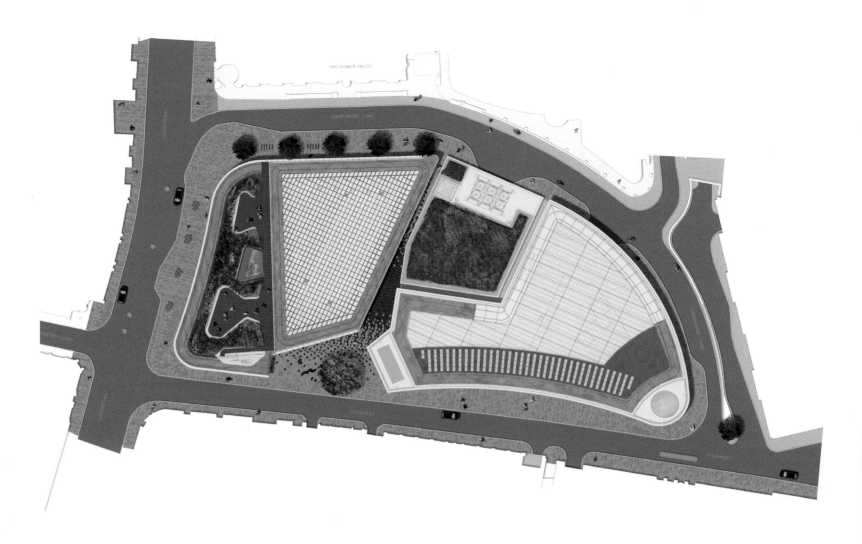

Above, a plan of the main rooftop and, on the right page, a view from the New Ludgate building toward St. Paul's Cathedral.

Oben: Plan der Hauptdachfläche. Rechts: Blick vom New-Ludgate-Gebäude auf die St. Paul's Cathedral.

Ci-dessus, plan du toit principal et page de droite, vue du New Ludgate vers la cathédrale St. Paul.

Right, a section drawing of the building showing planted areas, where colorful perennial plants, such as those seen on the right page, create an atmosphere that breaks with the dominant mineral aspect of the city.

Rechts: Der Gebäudeschnitt zeigt die bepflanzten Flächen. Mit bunten winterharten Gewächsen entsteht dort eine Atmosphäre, die mit dem von Stein geprägten Stadtbild bricht (rechte Seite).

À droite, schéma en coupe du bâtiment avec les zones plantées où des vivaces très colorées, comme celles que l'on voit sur la page de droite, créent une ambiance qui rompt avec le caractère minéral dominant de la City.

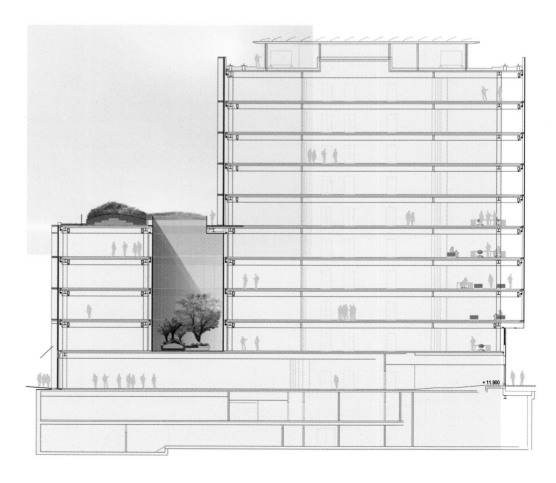

JOSÉ ANTONIO SOSA + MAGÜI GONZÁLEZ
Las Palmas de Gran Canaria [SPAIN]
2009

Old City Hall Renovation

*Address: Plaza de Santa Ana 1, 35001 Las Palmas de Gran Canaria,
Las Palmas, Spain | Area: 3500 m² | Client: Spanish Ministry of Housing | Cost:
€5 217 600 | Collaboration: Miguel Santiago, Reveriego y Asociados*

The old "Casas Consistoriales" (City Hall) building of Las Palmas had been void of functional contents. It is located outside of the present-day administrative center of the city, but at the heart of its historic center on the Plaza de Santa Ana. A new courtyard made with recycled timber was created like "a stack of open wooden cages." The architects explain that the design can be likened to a "series of boxes of intense golden old wood creating an interior forest." A wooden deck was created on the roof of the building with a view of surrounding historic buildings. The wooden "box" visible on the roof has a window pattern that recalls a barcode, an element that the architects also liken to the forms of a forest. The entire addition to the rooftop is not visible from the street, nor indeed from most neighboring buildings.

Das alte Rathaus, die „Casas Consistoriales", von Las Palmas war lange ohne Funktion. Zwar liegt es im Herzen des historischen Stadtkerns an der Plaza de Santa Ana, jedoch außerhalb des heutigen Verwaltungszentrums der Stadt. Aus Altholz schufen die Architekten einen neuen Hofraum, den sie mit einem „Stapel offener Holzkäfige" vergleichen. Die Architekten erklären ihre Gestaltung als eine „Reihe von Kästen aus kräftig goldfarbenem altem Holz, die im Innenraum einen Wald erwachsen lassen". Auf dem Dach des Gebäudes wurde ein Holzdeck mit Blick auf benachbarte historische Bauten verlegt. Dem „Kasten" aus Holz auf dem Dach verleihen seine Fenster ein Muster, das an einen Strichcode erinnert; auch hier ziehen die Architekten den Vergleich zum Wald. Von der Straße, ja sogar von den meisten Gebäuden in der Umgebung aus ist von dem Dachaufbau nichts zu sehen.

L'ancien «Casas Consistoriales» (hôtel de ville) de Las Palmas était vidé de tout contenu fonctionnel. Il est situé à l'écart du centre administratif actuel de la ville, mais au cœur du centre historique, sur la Plaza de Santa Ana. Une nouvelle cour en bois d'œuvre recyclé y a été créée qui rappelle «des cages en bois empilées». Les architectes expliquent que le design peut être comparé à une «série de cubes en bois ancien d'un ton doré intense qui créent une forêt intérieure». Une plate-forme en bois avec vue sur les bâtiments historiques voisins a été installée sur le toit. Les fenêtres du «cube» en bois bien visible sur le toit forment un motif qui rappelle un code-barres et que les architectes comparent aussi à une forêt. L'ajout sur le toit n'est pas visible depuis la rue, ni de la plupart des bâtiments environnants.

The rooftop installation visible above hardly emerges from the line of the original building, as can be seen in the section drawing below.

Oben: Die hier sichtbare Dachaufbau überragt die ursprüngliche Dachhöhe nur minimal, wie auch der Gebäudeschnitt unten zeigt.

La construction sur le toit visible ci-dessus dépasse à peine du bâtiment d'origine, comme en témoigne le schéma en coupe ci-dessous.

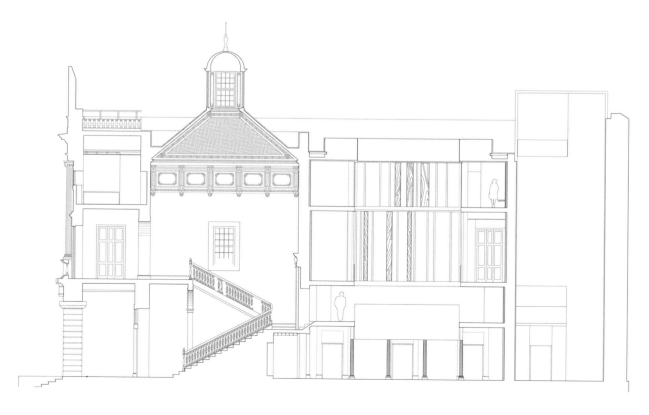

The wood and glass box created by the architects on the roof has openings that are meant to recall the sequences of a barcode.

Der „Kasten" aus Holz und Glas, den die Architekten auf das Dach setzten, soll mit seinen Öffnungen an die Streifenfolge eines Strichcodes erinnern.

Le cube de bois et de verre créé par les architectes sur le toit présente des ouvertures censées rappeler un code-barres.

JEAN NOUVEL
Sydney [AUSTRALIA]
2010–14

One Central Park

Address: 1 & 3 Carlton Street and 2 Chippendale Way, Sydney NSW 2008, Australia
Area: 67626 m² (gross tower floor area) | Client: Frasers Property Australia and Sekisui
House Australia | Cost: $230 million | Collaboration: PTW Architects, Patrick Blanc

The One Central Park project called for the construction of several buildings on the site of an old brewery located near the Central Business District of Sydney. Nouvel's contribution involves a 34-story residential apartment building and a smaller (12-story) apartment structure, sitting on a shared podium that includes recreational and retail spaces. The architect collaborated with Patrick Blanc, the noted French botanist and designer of "vertical gardens." These gardens cover no less than 50% of the buildings' façades. The architects explain: "Hydroponic walls, horizontal tubs, and support cables integrated into the tower's façades accommodate a wide variety of climbing plants and creepers. These act as a natural solar control mechanism, changing with the seasons, protecting the apartments from direct sunlight in summer while storing a maximum of sun in winter." A monumental cantilevered plateau juts from the larger building near its top. A common room and a panoramic terrace are located here, and a motorized heliostat (mirror for directing sunlight) is fixed to the cantilever framework and reflects light to a part of the park that is in the shadow of the tower. The heliostat has night lighting designed by the French artist Yann Kersalé.

Das Bauprojekt One Central Park in Sydney sah eine ganze Anzahl von Neubauten auf einem innenstadtnahen ehemaligen Brauereigelände vor. Nouvels Beitrag besteht aus einem 34-geschossigen Apartmenthaus und einem kleineren, zwölfgeschossigen Wohngebäude auf einem gemeinsamen Unterbau, in dem unter anderem Freizeiteinrichtungen und Geschäfte untergebracht sind. Der Architekt kooperierte mit Patrick Blanc, dem bekannten französischen Botaniker und Gestalter „vertikaler Gärten". Blancs Gärten bedecken ganze 50 % der Fassadenfläche der beiden Gebäude. Die Architekten erläutern: „Hydrokulturwände, waagerechte Wannen sowie in die Fassaden integrierte Tragseile bieten den unterschiedlichsten Kletter- und Kriechpflanzen Halt; sie fungieren als natürlicher, saisonaler Regulator, der die Wohneinheiten im Sommer vor direkter Sonneneinstrahlung schützt und im Winter ein Höchstmaß an Sonnenenergie speichert. Ein monumentales auskragendes Plateau entspringt dem größeren der beiden Gebäude auf Höhe einer der oberen Etagen. An dem freitragenden Rahmen, der eine gemeinschaftlich nutzbare Panoramaterrasse trägt, ist ein motorisierter Heliostat befestigt, der Sonnenlicht in den vom Hochhaus beschatteten Freiraum reflektiert. Die nächtliche Lichtinstallation am Heliostat entwarf der französische Lichtkünstler Yann Kersalé.

Le projet One Central Park prévoyait la construction de plusieurs immeubles à l'emplacement d'une ancienne brasserie, proche du Central Business District de Sydney. La contribution de Nouvel comprend un immeuble résidentiel de trente-quatre niveaux et un autre moins haut (douze niveaux) d'appartements sur un socle commun occupé par des espaces de loisirs et de vente au détail. L'architecte a travaillé avec Patrick Blanc, le célèbre botaniste français créateur des «jardins verticaux». Ces derniers ne couvrent pas moins de 50 % des façades. Les architectes expliquent: «Des murs hydroponiques, des bacs horizontaux et des câbles de soutien intégrés aux façades des tours accueillent une grande variété de plantes grimpantes et rampantes. Ces dernières agissent comme un mécanisme de contrôle solaire naturel au fil des saisons et de leurs transformations, protégeant les appartements de l'ensoleillement direct en été et emmagasinant un maximum de soleil en hiver.» Un immense plateau en porte-à-faux dépasse de la plus haute tour près du sommet. Il accueille une salle commune et une terrasse panoramique, tandis qu'un héliostat (miroir qui redirige la lumière du soleil) motorisé y est fixé et renvoie la lumière vers une partie du parc située à l'ombre de la tour. L'éclairage nocturne de l'héliostat a été conçu par l'artiste français Yann Kersalé.

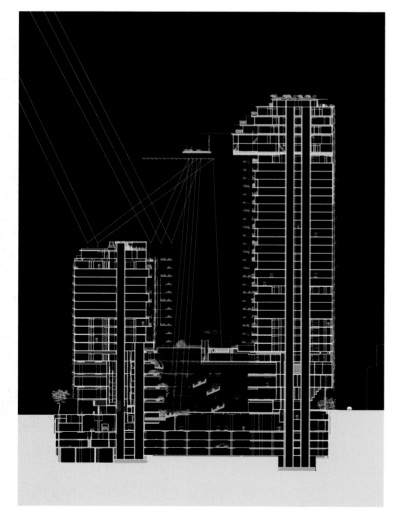

In this aerial view of the city, One Central Park is visible to the right of the center of the image with its protruding rooftop terraces.

Auf diesem Luftbild der Stadt sieht man rechts der Mitte One Central Park mit den auskragenden Dachterrassen.

Sur cette vue aérienne de la ville, One Central Park est bien visible à droite du centre avec les terrasses en saillie de son toit.

A section drawing shows the spectacular cantilevered outdoor terrace of the building, also seen on the right page.

Der Gebäudeschnitt zeigt die spektakuläre freitragende Außenterrasse des Bauwerks, die auch rechts zu sehen ist.

Le schéma en coupe montre l'extraordinaire terrasse en porte-à-faux vue sur la page de droite.

The open, extended terrace area is planted and offers a remarkable view over the city. Above, each floor has a green terrace.

Die mit Pflanzen gestaltete große Terrassenfläche bietet einen hervorragenden Blick über die Stadt. Oben: Auf allen Etagen finden sich grüne Terrassen.

La vaste terrasse ouverte est plantée et jouit d'une vue remarquable sur la ville. Ci-dessus, chaque étage possède aussi sa terrasse végétalisée.

Left page, red, one of the preferred colors of Jean Nouvel, dominates a passageway leading to the terrace. Right, a plan of level 29 of the building.

Links: Rot zählt zu Jean Nouvels Lieblingsfarben und dominiert einen Durchgang zur Terrasse. Rechts: Grundriss des 29. Stockwerks.

Page de gauche, le rouge, l'une des couleurs préférées de Jean Nouvel, domine dans ce passage qui mène à la terrasse. À droite, un plan du 29e niveau.

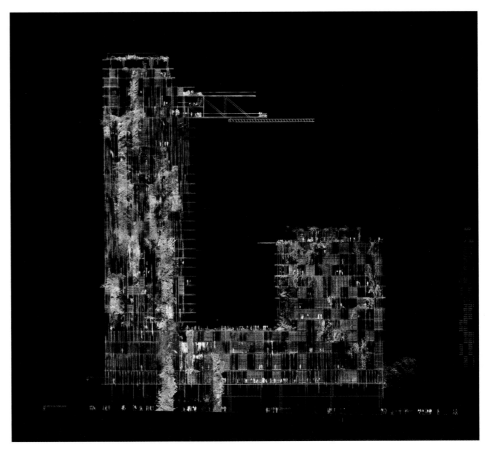

HMWHITE
New York, New York [USA]
2011–12

Penthouse Gardens

Address: not disclosed
Area: 604 m² (garden), 1172 m² (apartment) | Client: not disclosed | Cost: $1 million
Collaboration: Steve E. Blatz (Architect), Antonio Pio Saracino

This is a multilevel residential roof garden created for a contemporary penthouse. The intention of the garden designers is to "blur transitions between interior and exterior spaces." Architectural geometry is contrasted with "soft topographic forms and vegetation to create a harmonious and elegant residential landscape floating in the downtown Manhattan skyline." The garden designers have employed three different systems within the garden: "modulated flooring, topographic surface, and vertical vegetation." The project won the Interior Design Magazine Best of Year award in 2013, and the Chicago Athenaeum Museum of Architecture & Design American Architecture Award (2014). The Athenaeum commented: "Up on the roof, the architects transformed barren tar and unsightly mechanical equipment into a glorious haven with not only the lush grass specifically requested by the owner but also a wildflower meadow. Stretching along one side is an ipe deck folded into peaks and bleachers envisioned as lounging space for parties... At one end of the deck, it ramps up to surround a hot tub. The chaise longues nearby are ideal for admiring the Woolworth Building and 1 World Trade Center."

Dieser Privatgarten über mehrere Ebenen wurde für ein modernes Penthouse gebaut, mit dem erklärten Ziel der Gartengestalter, „die Grenzen zwischen Drinnen und Draußen [zu] verwischen". Der geradkantigen Architektur sind „weiche Geländeformen und Grün" gegenübergestellt; so wurde „direkt vor der Skyline von Downtown Manhattan eine harmonisch-elegante Wohnlandschaft" angesiedelt. Die Gartengestalter verbanden in dem Dachgarten drei verschiedene Gestaltungsansätze: „Bodenmodule, Flächen mit Topographie und vertikales Grün". Nachdem das Interior Design Magazine das Projekt 2013 als bestes Design des Jahres auszeichnete, gewann es 2014 den American Architecture Award des Architektur- und Design-Museums Chicago Athenaeum. Aus der Begründung des Museums: „Eine Dachfläche mit kahler Teerpappe und unansehnlicher Gebäudetechnik verwandelten die Architekten in eine herrliche Oase mit den vom Bauherrn geforderten hohen Gräsern und zusätzlich einer Blumenwiese, neben der sich ein zu Gipfeln und Bänken aufgefaltetes Deck aus Ipé-Holz als Lounge-Bereich für Partys erstreckt. [...] An einem Ende steigt das Deck zu einer erhöhten Fläche an, in die ein Hottub eingelassen ist. Liegen bieten dort einen perfekten Blick auf das Woolworth Building und das One World Trade Center."

Le jardin à plusieurs niveaux a été créé sur le toit d'un immeuble résidentiel pour un appartement de grand standing contemporain. Les créateurs ont voulu « effacer toute transition entre les espaces intérieurs et extérieurs. » Pour cela, la géométrie de l'architecture contraste avec des « formes topographiques douces et la végétation pour donner naissance à un paysage résidentiel harmonieux et élégant, qui semble flotter dans la ligne d'horizon du centre de Manhattan. » Trois techniques différentes ont été utilisées : « les sols modulaires, la surface topographique et la végétation verticale. » Le projet a remporté le prix Best of Year du magazine Interior Design Magazine en 2013 et l'American Architecture Award du Chicago Athenaeum Museum of Architecture & Design (2014) qui l'a décrit en ces termes : « au sommet du toit, les architectes ont transformé le goudron aride et les installations techniques disgracieuses en un merveilleux refuge doté, en plus de l'épaisse pelouse spécifiée par le propriétaire, d'une prairie de fleurs sauvages. Une plate-forme en bois d'ipé longe l'un des côtés, ses plis forment des sommets et des gradins conçus comme un espace-salon où donner des fêtes... À l'une de ses extrémités, la plate-forme monte pour entourer un jacuzzi. Les chaises-longues à côté sont parfaitement disposées pour admirer la vue sur le Woolworth Building et le 1 World Trade Center. »

This view (also see illustration on the cover of this book) shows the location of the Penthouse Gardens with the Freedom Tower in the World Trade Center area visible on the right side. Wood and varied planting typologies contrast with the powerfully urban environment.

Dieser Blick (siehe auch Buchumschlag) macht die Lage des Dachgartens deutlich – rechts der Mitte ragt der Freedom Tower auf dem Gelände des World Trade Center auf. Holz und wechselnde Pflanzentypologien stehen im Kontrast zu der gewaltigen Hochhauskulisse.

Cette vue (voir aussi l'illustration en couverture du livre) montre l'emplacement des jardins avec la Freedom Tower du World Trade Center visible sur le côté droit. Le bois et des plantes variables contrastent avec l'environnement fortement urbanisé.

With the Freedom Tower again dominating the skyline, the large terrace (604 square meters) seems to be a private park in the sky. The plan below shows the hot tub and paved areas in contrast with the green plantings.

Auch hier dominiert der Freedom Tower die Skyline. Die großzügige Dachterrasse (Gesamtfläche 604 m²) wirkt wie ein privater Park in luftiger Höhe. Auf der Planzeichnung ist der Whirlpool ebenso zu sehen wie die mit der Begrünung kontrastierenden Pflasterflächen.

Avec la Freedom Tower qui domine la ligne d'horizon, la vaste terrasse (604 m²) semble un parc privé en plein ciel. On voit sur le plan ci-dessous le jacuzzi et les surfaces pavées qui contrastent avec la verdure des zones plantées.

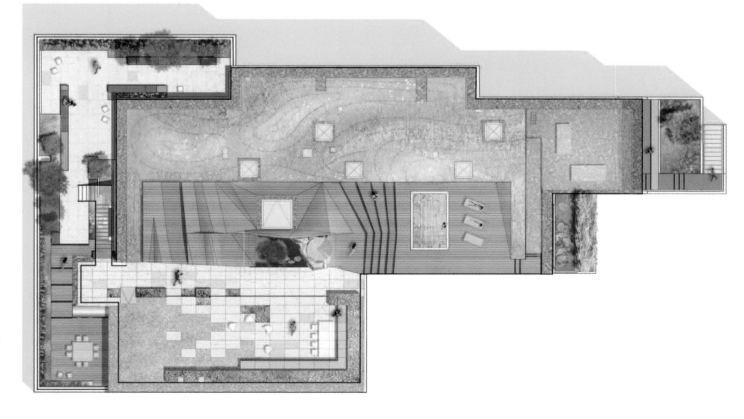

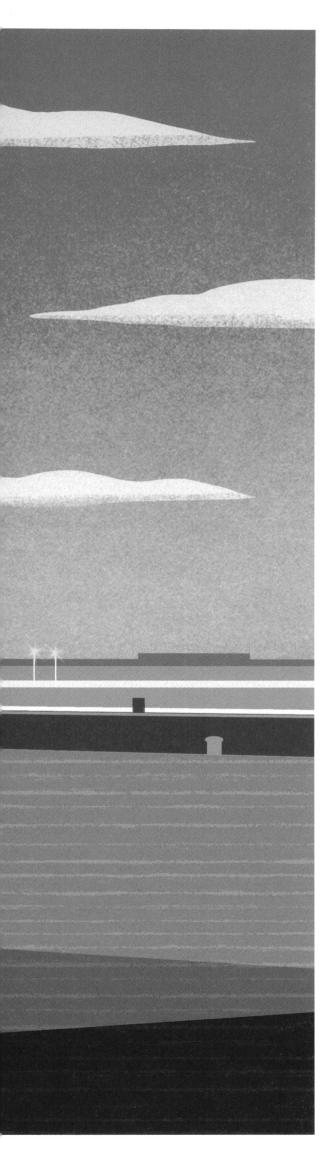

Port House

Address: not disclosed | Area: 12 800 m²
Client: Antwerp Port Authority | Cost: not disclosed

This new headquarters building for the Antwerp Port Authority is intended to house a staff of 500 people. A central atrium is used to direct visitors either to public counters, or to offices and meeting rooms. Two underground levels for car and bicycle parking are included in the scheme, which is made up of a former fire station topped by a crystalline, four-story addition on its roof. The unexpected rooftop design is asymmetrically placed over a central courtyard, thus allowing light into the older building. The erection of two large concrete pillars containing stairs and lifts, as well as a number of steel columns that touch ground in the courtyard, allowed the architects to leave the original building untouched. ZHA states: "The new volume is enclosed by articulated surfaces of triangular glass panels which are slightly rotated with respect to one another to achieve ever-changing reflections that enhance its diamond-shaped geometry."

Das neue Hauptgebäude der Antwerpener Hafenbehörde soll einmal 500 Beschäftigten Platz bieten. Aus dem zentralen Atrium werden die Besucher entweder zu Kundenschaltern oder zu Büro- und Besprechungsräumen dirigiert. Zwei Kellergeschosse mit Auto- und Fahrradstellplätzen sind Teil des Gesamtplans, in dessen Rahmen ein ehemaliges Feuerwehrhaus mit einem kristallförmigen vierstöckigen Erweiterungsbau überbaut wird. Damit weiterhin Licht in das Bestandsgebäude fällt, ist der außergewöhnliche Aufbau über dem zentralen Innenhof asymmetrisch aufgesetzt. Die Aufständerung auf zwei mächtigen Betonpfeilern, in denen sich Treppen und Aufzüge befinden, sowie auf mehreren im Innenhof verankerten Stahlpfeilern ermöglichte es den Architekten, das Bestandsgebäude unangetastet zu lassen. Die Architekten halten fest: „Das neue Raumvolumen ist von einer Hülle aus dreieckigen Glasflächen umschlossen, die leicht gegeneinander gekippt sind und so ständig wechselnde Reflexionen hervorrufen, die die kristallförmige Geometrie zur Geltung bringen."

Le nouveau siège des autorités portuaires d'Anvers doit accueillir cinq cents employés. Un atrium central donnera aux visiteurs accès aux comptoirs de services au public ou aux bureaux et salles de réunions. Deux niveaux souterrains destinés à un parking pour voitures et vélos sont inclus à l'ensemble — une ancienne caserne de pompiers surmontée d'un bâtiment cristallin de quatre niveaux posé sur son toit. La forme inattendue du toit est disposée de manière asymétrique au-dessus d'une cour centrale afin de laisser la lumière pénétrer dans le bâtiment ancien. La construction de deux immenses piliers de béton, qui contiennent les escaliers et les ascenseurs, et de nombreuses colonnes en acier ancrées dans le sol de la cour a permis aux architectes de conserver intact le bâtiment d'origine. ZHA avait déclaré : « Le nouveau volume est enclos dans des surfaces articulées dont les panneaux de verre triangulaires sont légèrement inclinés les uns vers les autres afin de produire des reflets toujours changeants qui rehaussent sa géométrie en forme de diamant. »

In this project, the late Zaha Hadid essentially proposed to turn a rooftop into the site of a new, connected building, totally transforming the older structure.

Für dieses Projekt machte die jüngst verstorbene Zaha Hadid im Grund ein Dach zum Bauplatz eines neuen Bauwerks, das mit dem bestehenden Bau verbunden ist, ihn aber völlig verwandelt.

Avec ce projet, feu Zaha Hadid se proposait surtout de transformer un toit en un nouveau bâtiment connexe, métamorphosant véritablement la structure plus ancienne.

The forward-leaning design of the new rooftop structure gives the esplanade around the building a contemporary feel. Below, the space beneath the main volume and above the old structure.

Das nach vorn orientierte Design des neuen Dachbaus gibt der Esplanade um den Altbau eine moderne Anmutung. Unten: Der Raum zwischen dem neuen und dem alten Bau.

La nouvelle construction penchée vers l'avant confère un caractère contemporain à l'esplanade qui entoure le bâtiment. Ci-dessous, l'espace sous le volume principal et sur la structure d'origine.

The added volume is anchored in the atrium of the old building, with dramatic, angled black supports. Below, a section drawing shows the relation of one element to the other.

Dramatische schwarze Schrägstützen verankern den hinzugefügten Baukörper im Atrium des alten Gebäudes. Unten: Der Schnitt zeigt, wie die Elemente zueinander in Beziehung stehen.

Le nouveau volume est ancré dans l'atrium du bâtiment ancien par d'énormes piliers noirs inclinés. Ci-dessous, schéma en coupe qui montre le rapport des différents éléments les uns aux autres.

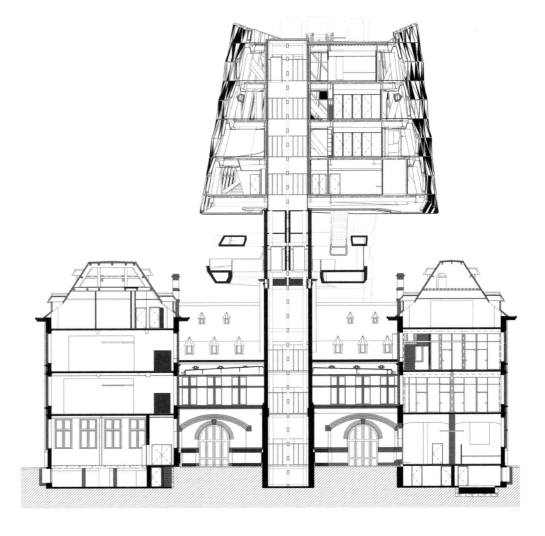

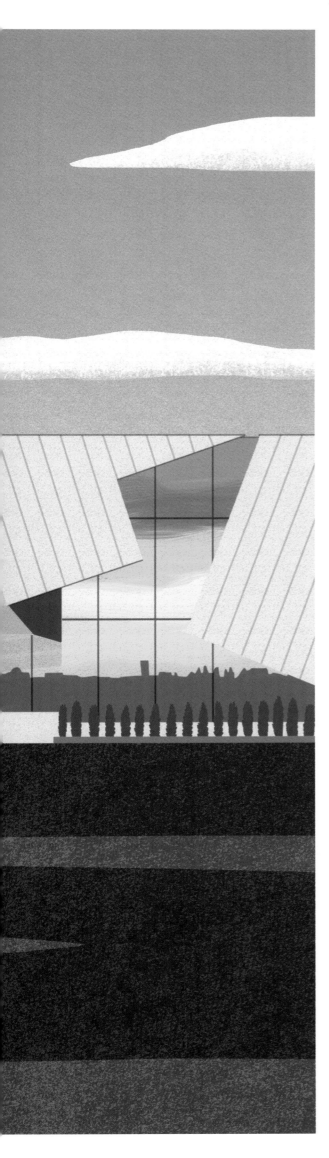

ERIC OWEN MOSS
Culver City, California [USA]
2013–14

Pterodactyl

Address: 3540 Hayden Boulevard, Culver City, CA 90232, USA | Area: 1548 m²
Client: Samitaur Constructs | Cost: not disclosed

Pterodactyl includes an office building and parking garage in a complex of new and remodeled buildings in Culver City. The four-level parking, 800-car structure built in 1998 is a straightforward and inexpensive construction—steel frame, metal decks, regular bays, and ingress/egress ramps at opposite ends of the public, west face of the project. The required fireproofing of the structural steel was treated as a finish material, and precisely applied to the steel frame but not to the metal deck spanning between the beams. The office building is formed by the intersection of nine rectangular boxes, lifted one level above the garage roof, stacked either on top of, or adjacent to, each other, along the west edge of the garage roof. Boxes are supported on the steel-column grid extended from the parking structure below. Essentially this project concerns the construction of a new building on top of the old parking garage.

Zum Bauprojekt Pterodactyl gehört auch ein Bürogebäude mit Parkhaus auf einem Areal mit neuen und renovierten Bauten in Culver City. Bei dem bereits 1998 errichteten vierstöckigen Parkhaus mit Platz für 800 Pkw handelt es sich um eine einfache, kostengünstige Stahlrahmen-Metalldeck-Konstruktion mit Parkbuchten; die Zu- und Abfahrtrampen sind an den Außenseiten der nach Westen ausgerichteten Hauptfassade angeordnet. Der für das Stahltragwerk vorgeschriebene Brandschutzanstrich wurde als Endanstrich auf den Stahlrahmen aufgetragen, nicht jedoch auf das metallene Parkdeck zwischen den Trägern. Neun neben- und übereinanderliegende „Kisten" bilden über dem Parkhausdach, auf der Westen weisenden Dachkante, das Bürogebäude. Diese kastenförmigen Gebilde ruhen auf einem Raster aus Stahlsäulen, das aus dem Parkhaus nach oben weitergeführt wurde. Streng genommen handelt es sich bei dem Projekt um einen dem alten Parkhaus aufgesetzten Neubau.

Le Ptérodactyle intègre un immeuble de bureaux et un parking couvert à un complexe de bâtiments nouveaux et remaniés, à Culver City. Le parking de huit cents places à quatre niveaux construit en 1998 est un bâtiment sans prétention et peu onéreux — charpente en acier, plates-formes métalliques, places de stationnement normales et rampes d'entrée et de sortie à l'opposé de la face ouest côté rue. L'ignifugation requise de l'acier structurel a pris la forme d'un matériau de finition appliqué précisément sur la charpente en acier mais pas sur le tablier métallique entre les poutres. L'immeuble de bureaux résulte de l'intersection de neuf parallélépipèdes surélevés à un niveau au-dessus du toit du parking et empilés ou juxtaposés le long de son bord ouest. Ils sont portés par le réseau de colonnes en acier qui s'étend depuis le parking en-dessous. Le projet consiste pour l'essentiel à construire un nouveau bâtiment en haut de l'ancien parking couvert.

Eric Owen Moss totally transforms the rooftop of this parking facility, giving it an apparently disordered aspect that announces its contemporary presence.

Eric Owen Moss transformiert die Dachebene dieses Parkhauses radikal; die scheinbare Unordnung steht für ihre Modernität.

Eric Owen Moss a entièrement transformé le toit du parking pour lui donner un caractère de désordre apparent qui annonce sa présence contemporaine.

The new building is close to four other projects by Moss—Stealth, Umbrella, Slash, and Backslash. Here, the Umbrella is visible in the foreground.

Der Neubau liegt nahe an vier weiteren Projekten des Architekten - Stealth, Umbrella, Slash, Backslash. Hier ist im Vordergrund Umbrella zu sehen.

Le nouveau bâtiment est voisin de quatre autres projets de Moss — Stealth, Umbrella, Slash et Backslash. On voit ici Umbrella au premier plan.

The apparently jumbled appearance of the structure corresponds to an ordered process visible in the drawings below, where six rectangular volumes are "dropped" onto the parking lot.

Die ungeordnet scheinende Konstruktion entstand tatsächlich in einem völlig geordneten Prozess, der sich den Zeichnungen unten entnehmen lässt – sechs lange Quader wurden dafür über dem Parkhaus „fallen gelassen".

L'aspect apparemment confus de l'ensemble résulte d'un processus très ordonné visible dans les schémas ci-dessous qui montrent comment six volumes rectangulaires sont « tombés » sur le parking.

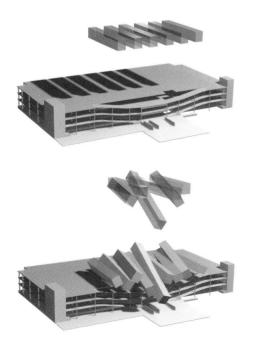

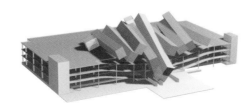

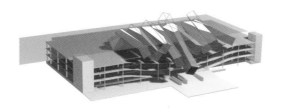

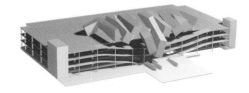

The stacking effect of the new office volumes is resolved in an orderly fashion as the image above and the plans on this page show.

Der Stapeleffekt der neuen Büroräume wurde auf einem sehr geordneten Weg erzielt, wie die Abbildung oben und die Pläne auf dieser Seite verdeutlichen.

L'impression d'empilement des nouveaux volumes de bureaux est obtenue très méthodiquement, comme le montrent la photo ci-dessus et les plans sur cette page.

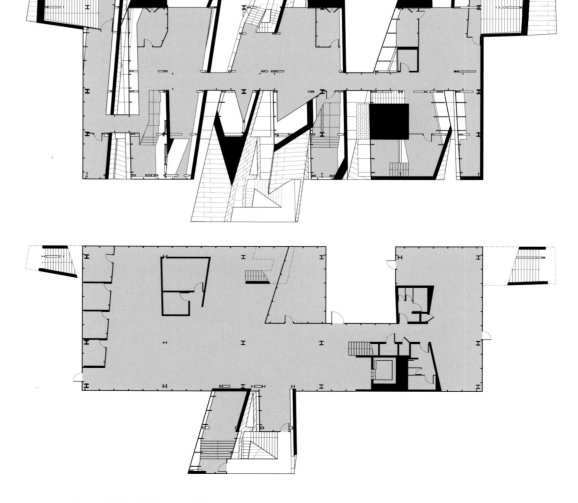

FOSTER + PARTNERS
London [UK]
2006–13

Radio Rooftop Bar, ME London

Address: 336-337 Strand, London WC2R 1HA,UK, www.radiorooftop.com | Area: 2150 m²
Client: Melia Hotels International | Cost: not disclosed

Located on the top (10th) floor of the ME London, a five-star hotel entirely designed inside and out by Foster + Partners, the name of the Radio Rooftop Bar is derived from the fact that the site of the hotel was the original home of the BBC on the Strand. It offers 180° panoramic views of London, from Renzo Piano's Shard tower to the Houses of Parliament and St. Paul's Cathedral. Accessed via an express lift, the bar has both interior and exterior seating areas. Entered through a steel and black corridor, the space has contoured white and black seating, and a triangular interior seating area. The architects explain: "The main challenge for the design of the bar was to maximize views and to create a space that would work at different times of the day, enabling the terrace to be used for lunch, dinner, and as a lounge bar late into the evening. The sense of drama and monochrome palette follow the striking formal language of the hotel, with minimal decoration."

In der obersten (10.) Etage des ME London, eines Fünf-Sterne-Hotels, das innen wie außen vollständig von Foster + Partners gestaltet wurde, befindet sich die Radio Rooftop Bar. Ihr Name leitet sich von der Tatsache her, dass dies der einstige Standort der BBC an der Straße Strand war. Die Bar bietet einen 180°-Panoramablick über London, von Renzo Pianos Hochhaus Shard bis zum Parlament und zur St. Paul's Cathedral. Ein Expressaufzug transportiert die Gäste in die Bar, die über Innen- und Außengastronomie verfügt. Über einen in Stahl und Schwarz ausgeführten Korridor gelangt man in das Lokal mit konturierten Sitzlandschaften in Schwarz-Weiß und einem dreieckigen Innenbereich. Der Kommentar der Architekten: „Die größte Herausforderung bei der Gestaltung dieser Bar bestand darin, den Ausblick maximal zu inszenieren und zugleich eine Räumlichkeit zu schaffen, die zu unterschiedlichen Tageszeiten in gleichem Maße nutzbar ist – als Terrassengastronomie für Mittags- und Dinnergäste ebenso wie als Lounge bis in den späten Abend hinein. Die dramatische Inszenierung und die monochrome Palette folgen bei minimaler Dekoration der markanten Formensprache des Hotelgebäudes."

Au dernier (10ᵉ) niveau du ME London, un hôtel cinq étoiles entièrement conçu à l'intérieur et à l'extérieur par Foster + Partners, le Radio Rooftop Bar doit son nom au fait que l'hôtel occupe l'emplacement du siège d'origine de la BBC, sur le Strand. Il offre des vues panoramique à 180° sur Londres, de la Shard tower de Renzo Piano aux Houses of Parliament et à la cathédrale St. Paul. Accessible par un ascenseur express, le bar possède des tables à l'intérieur et à l'extérieur. Après l'entrée par un couloir noir et acier, on découvre un espace aux sièges noirs et blancs galbés, triangulaire à l'intérieur. Les architectes expliquent : « Le principal défi de ce bar était d'optimiser les vues et de créer un espace qui fonctionne à différents moments de la journée, en permettant à la terrasse d'être occupée à midi, pour le diner et sous forme de "lounge bar" pour prolonger la soirée. Le caractère théâtral et la gamme monochrome font écho au langage formel très expressif de l'hôtel au décor minimaliste. »

Right, a floor plan of the rooftop level. The lounge area (left) is at the tip of the triangular building.

Rechts: Grundriss der Dachetage. Der Loungebereich (links) ist an der Spitze des dreieckigen Gebäudes angesiedelt.

À droite, plan du sommet du toit. La partie lounge (à gauche) occupe la pointe du bâtiment triangulaire.

The Radio Rooftop Bar was thus named because its site was the original home of the BBC (above). Right page, outdoor and indoor view of the rooftop terraces.

Oben: Mit ihrem Namen verweist die Radio Rooftop Bar darauf, dass dies der Originalstandort der BBC war. Rechts: Die Dachterrassen von außen und von innen betrachtet.

Le Radio Rooftop Bar a été nommé ainsi car il occupe l'emplacement du siège d'origine de la BBC (ci-dessus). Page de droite, vue extérieure et intérieure de la terrasse sur le toit.

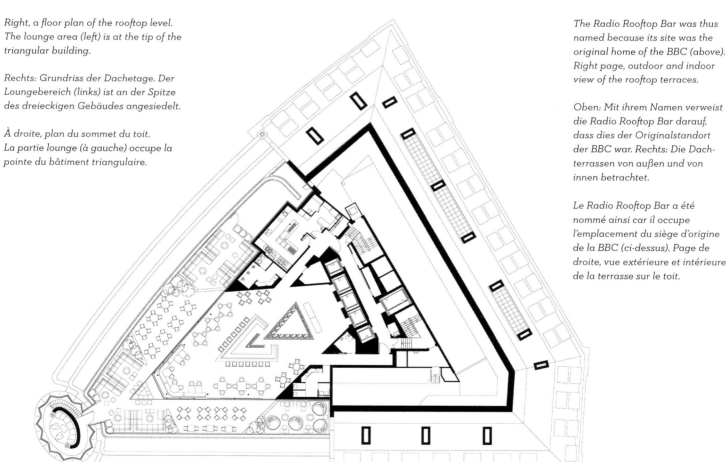

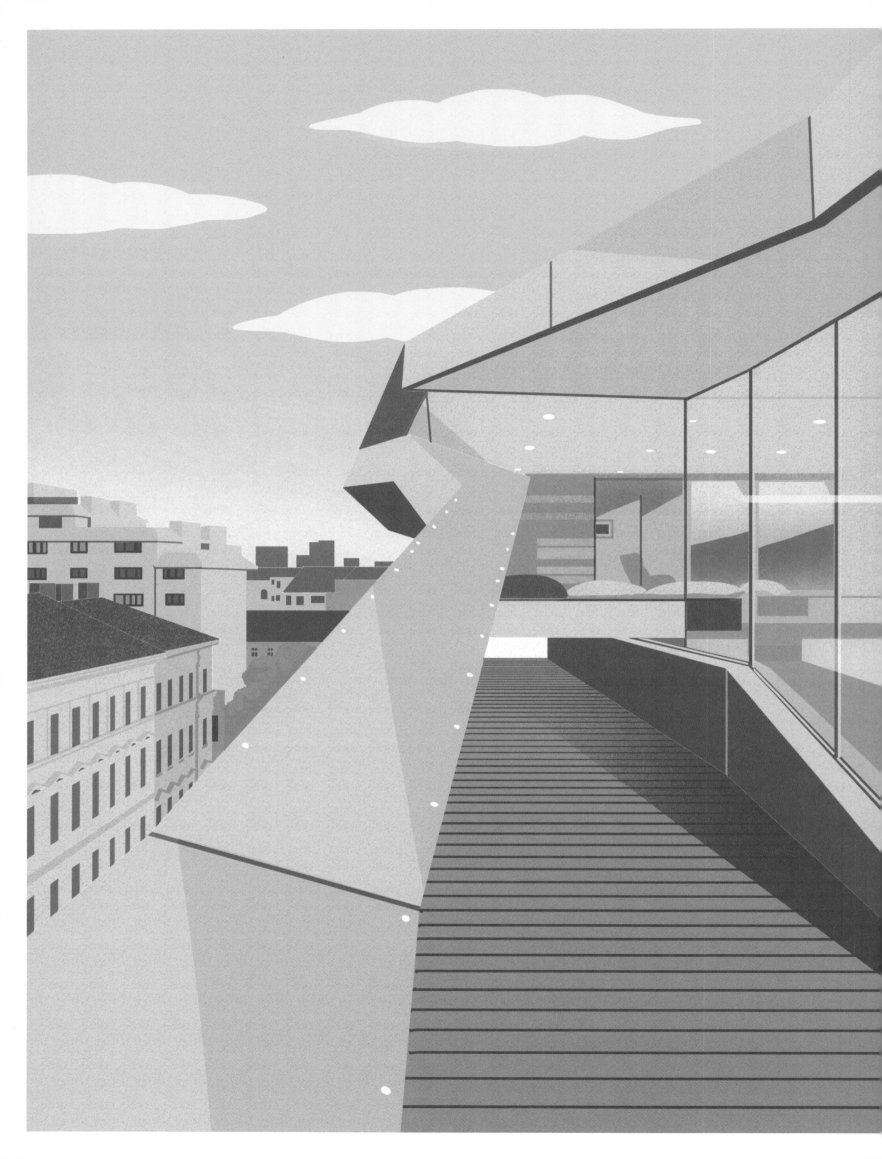

DELUGAN MEISSL
Vienna [AUSTRIA]
2003

Ray 1 House

Address: not disclosed | Area: 230 m² | Client: not disclosed
Cost: not disclosed

The architects sought to willfully contrast the "dynamic form" of this rooftop penthouse with the more "static" shape of the flat-topped 1960s office building on which it was added. Referring to the existing alignments formed by buildings on either side, Ray 1 was imagined as a "permeable border zone" between the earth and the sky. The architects state: "Recesses and folds create transparent zones and sheltered terraced landscapes on both sides of the building, providing opportunities for experiencing the structure's open layout, from the entrance all the way up to the accessible roof area." The outer surface or shell of the new structure is covered in Alucobond, an aluminum sandwich panel. The functional aspects of the residence are signified by different floor levels inside.

Die Architekten kontrastierten bewusst die „dynamische Gestalt" dieses Dachaufbaus mit der eher „statischen" Form des Flachdach-Bürogebäudes aus den 1960er-Jahren, auf das er aufgesetzt wurde. Ray 1 nimmt Bezug zur Anordnung der benachbarten Gebäude, und das Design selbst beruht auf der Vorstellung eines „durchlässigen Grenzbereichs" zwischen Himmel und Erde. Die Architekten sagen dazu: „Rücksprünge und Faltungen schaffen transparente Zonen und geschützte terrassierte Landschaften auf beiden Gebäudeseiten, wodurch sich die Möglichkeit ergibt, den weitgehend offenen Grundriss zu erleben, vom Eingang bis hin zur begehbaren Dachfläche." Die äußere Haut des Neubaus ist mit Alucobond belegt, einem Aluminiumverbundstoff. Innen sind die unterschiedlichen Bereiche ihrer Funktion nach auf unterschiedlichen Niveaus angeordnet.

Les architectes ont ici délibérément cherché le contraste entre la « forme dynamique » de l'appartement de standing installé sur le toit et la masse plus « statique » de l'immeuble de bureaux à toit plat des années 1960 auquel il a été ajouté. En référence aux alignements d'immeubles qui le bordent des deux côtés, Ray 1 a été imaginé comme une « zone frontière perméable » entre la Terre et le ciel. Les architectes déclarent : « Les plis et les replis de la construction créent des zones transparentes et des terrasses abritées des deux côtés qui sont autant d'opportunités de tester la disposition ouverte de l'ensemble, depuis l'entrée et jusqu'à la zone du toit accessible. » La surface extérieure, ou coque, de la nouvelle structure est couverte d'Alucobond, un panneau sandwich d'aluminium. Différents niveaux à l'intérieur marquent les aspects fonctionnels du logement.

The futuristic design of the penthouse (above) creates interior spaces that are equally unexpected, with full-height glazing and the outdoor terrace seen on the right page.

Das futuristisch gestaltete Penthouse (oben) schafft nicht weniger überraschende Innenräume mit deckenhoher Verglasung und der vorgelagerten Terrasse rechts.

Le design futuriste de l'appartement de standing (ci-dessus) crée des espaces intérieurs tout aussi inattendus, page de droite, le vitrage sur toute la hauteur et la terrasse.

A real sense of continuity between the outdoor terrace and the interior is established with full-height glazing.

Die deckenhohe Verglasung sorgt für ein echtes Gefühl der Kontinuität zwischen Terrasse und Innenraum.

Le vitrage pleine hauteur crée une continuité réelle entre la terrasse et l'intérieur.

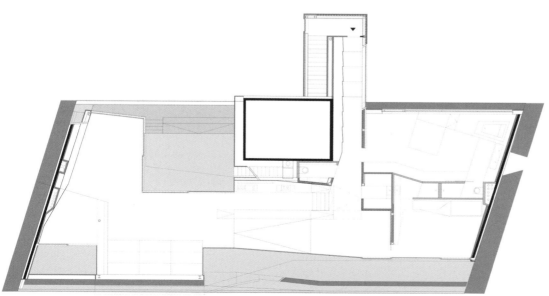

Opaque surfaces are contrasted with the numerous large windows. Left, a floor plan shows the exterior spaces in darker grey.

Undurchsichtige Flächen stehen im Kontrast zu den zahlreichen großen Fenstern. Auf dem Grundriss links sind die Außenflächen grau schattiert.

Les surfaces opaques contrastent avec les nombreuses grandes fenêtres. À gauche, un plan montre les espaces extérieurs en gris plus sombre.

SPONGE / IOU
Amsterdam [THE NETHERLANDS]
2006–07

Ronald McDonald VU-Kinderstad

*Address: De Boelelaan 1117, 1081 HV Amsterdam, The Netherlands, +31 20 444 44 44,
www.vumc.nl | Area: 1000 m² | Client: Ronald McDonald VU Huis /Kinderstad
Cost: €3.5 million | Collaboration: Rupali-Gupta*

The "Kinderstad" (Dutch for "children's city") project was a product of the Young Architects Competition of the Dutch National Board of Architects (BNA) together with the Ronald McDonald Children's Foundation (Kinderfonds). In 2003, Björn van Rheenen, Rupali Gupta, and Roland Pouw won the first prize and received the appointment to realize the winning design for both the exterior and interior, as well as project management. Björn van Rheenen and Roland Pouw were the project architect and manager. "Kinderstad" is located adjacent to the children's ward on the ninth floor of the eastern wing of the Medical Center of Amsterdam Free University (VU Amsterdam). It is located on the roof and was built with glass and 20 000 titanium tiles. According to the architects: "The basic idea of the concept of 'Kinderstad' is to put children in contact with the outside, with nature. This idea was realized by the use of natural materials (wood, stone, and photo prints), a completely open façade, and big roof windows that allow natural light to come in while giving the impression that 35 meters above you the sky and the weather are within your grasp."

Das Projekt „Kinderstad" (Kinderstadt) ging aus einem Nachwuchswettbewerb hervor, den der Bund Niederländischer Architekten (BNA) gemeinsam mit der McDonald's Kinderhilfe ausschrieb. 2003 gewannen Björn van Rheenen, Rupali Gupta und Roland Pouw den ersten Preis, womit sie den Auftrag für Projektmanagement und Bauausführung ihres Konzepts einschließlich der Innengestaltung erhielten. Björn van Rheenen und Roland Pouw fungierten als leitender Architekt bzw. Projektmanager. Die „Kinderstad" liegt direkt neben der Kinderstation auf der neunten Etage des Ostflügels der Klinik der Freien Universität Amsterdam (VU Amsterdam). Glas sowie 20 000 Titanplättchen dominieren die Konstruktion auf dem Dach. Die Architekten erläutern: „Grundidee des Entwurfs für die ‚Kinderstad' war es, Kinder in Kontakt mit der Außenwelt, der Natur zu bringen. Diese Idee mithilfe natürlicher Materialien realisiert (Holz, Stein, Fotodrucke), einer völlig offenen Fassade sowie großflächiger Oberlichter, die Tageslicht hereinlassen und zugleich den Eindruck vermitteln, als seien Himmel und Wetter 35 m darüber mit Händen greifbar."

Le projet «Kinderstad» («ville des enfants» en néerlandais) est le résultat du concours de jeunes architectes organisé par l'Association professionnelle des architectes néerlandais (BNA) avec la fondation Ronald McDonald Kinderfonds. En 2003, Björn van Rheenen, Rupali Gupta et Roland Pouw ont remporté le premier prix et ont reçu commande de réaliser l'intérieur et l'extérieur du projet gagnant, gestion de projet comprise. Björn van Rheenen et Roland Pouw étaient l'architecte et le chef de projet. «Kinderstad» est adjacent au quartier pédiatrique, situé au 9ᵉ niveau de l'aile est du Centre médical de l'Université libre d'Amsterdam (VU Amsterdam). Installé sur le toit, il est construit en verre et 20 000 carreaux de titane. Pour les architectes : «L'idée de base du concept "Kinderstad" est de permettre aux enfants le contact avec l'extérieur, avec la nature. Pour cela, des matériaux naturels (bois, pierre et tirages photos) ont été utilisés, la façade est entièrement ouverte et les grandes fenêtres du toit font entrer la lumière du jour en donnant l'impression que le ciel et le temps qu'il fait, 35 m plus haut, sont à portée de la main.»

The added volume stands out from the original building, seeming to float above the brick structure, with a cantilever hanging over one end.

Der aufgesetzte Raumkörper setzt sich deutlich vom ursprünglichen Gebäude ab. Er scheint über dem Ziegelbau, über den er auf einer Seite auskragt, zu schweben.

Le volume ajouté se détache du bâtiment d'origine et semble flotter au-dessus des murs de brique, avec un porte-à-faux dépassant à une extrémité.

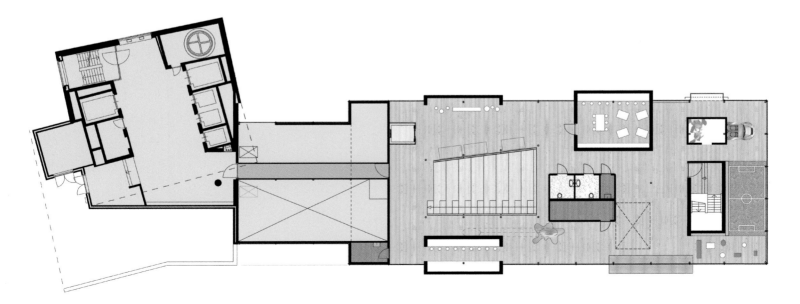

The interior spaces are bright and warm, somewhat in contrast with the rather dark exterior appearance of the rooftop addition.

Die Innenräume wirken anders als die etwas düstere äußere Anmutung des Dachaufbaus hell und anheimelnd.

Les espaces intérieurs sont gais et chaleureux, quelque peu en contraste avec l'aspect extérieur plutôt sombre.

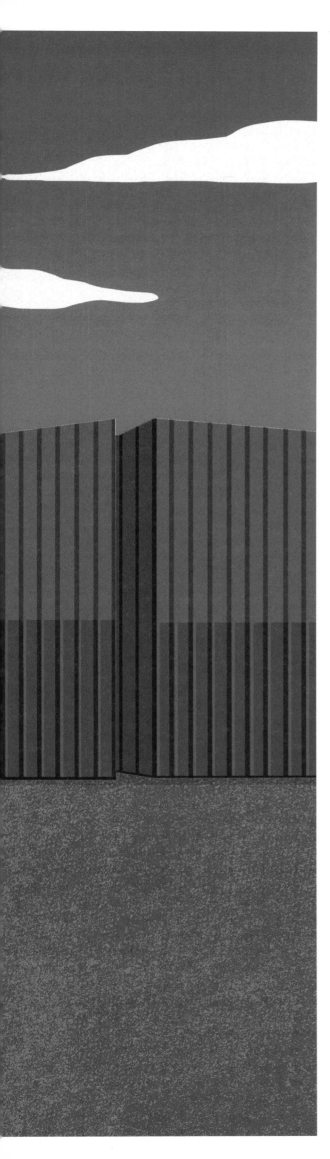

JAG
Lisbon [PORTUGAL]
2013–15

Roofbuildinghouse

Address: Rua Joaquim António de Aguiar, Lisbon, Portugal | Area: 220 m² + 45 m²
Client: Lucy and Mathieu Gerardin | Cost: €200 000 | Collaboration: Inês Forte, Maria
João Costa, Gonçalo Castro, Rita Fernandes, Rita Andrade da Costa

This project involved the rehabilitation of a building in Lisbon originally built in the 1930s. The Franco-British couple who acquired the space had exclusive access to the terraces and rooftop of the building, which offers views over the city including the St. Jorge Castle and the historic center of Lisbon. The architects thus conceived a kind of "tree house" that willfully contrasts with the existing structure. Wood was selected as the main building material because of its ecological aspects, and because of its "technical and aesthetic characteristics." The architect explains: "This wood structure emerges from the rooftop, establishing its own space and defining its own spatial hierarchy, allowing a unique view, from the north to the south of the city. The result is what we call the Roofbuildinghouse, a hybrid and balanced structure that uses the forms of a rectangle based on the golden ratio rectangle and an isosceles triangle."

Dieses Projekt entstand im Rahmen der Sanierung eines in den 1930er-Jahren errichteten Lissaboner Gebäudes. Das französisch-britische Paar, das das Haus erwarb, hatte alleinigen Zugang zu den Terrassen und dem Flachdach, von dem der Blick weit über Lissabon bis hin zum Castelo de São Jorge und dem historischen Stadtzentrum reicht. Die Architekten konzipierten eine Art Baumhaus, das bewusst in Kontrast zum ursprünglichen Gebäude tritt. Aufgrund seiner ökologischen Vorzüge und seiner „technischen und ästhetischen Eigenschaften" wurde als Material überwiegend Holz verwendet. Die Architekten erläutern: „Die Holzkonstruktion erwächst aus dem Dach, sie definiert einen eigenen Raum und eine eigene Raumhierarchie mit einem einzigartigen Blick über die Stadt, von Nord bis Süd. Das Ergebnis bezeichnen wir als Roofbuildinghouse, ein hybrides, ausgewogenes Gefüge auf Basis eines Rechtecks nach dem Goldenen Schnitt und eines gleichseitigen Dreiecks."

Le projet comprend la rénovation d'un immeuble, construit dans les années 1930 à Lisbonne. Le couple franco-britannique qui a acquis cet espace dispose d'un accès exclusif aux terrasses et au toit avec vue sur la ville, notamment le château St. Jorge et le centre historique. Les architectes ont imaginé une sorte de «maison dans les arbres» qui contraste délibérément avec la structure existante. Le bois a été choisi comme principal matériau de construction pour des raisons écologiques et pour ses «caractéristiques techniques et esthétiques». L'architecte explique que «la structure en bois émerge au sommet du toit, créant son propre espace et définissant sa propre échelle spatiale en offrant une vue unique du Nord au Sud de la ville. Le résultat est ce que nous appelons la "Roofbuildinghouse", une structure hybride bien équilibrée qui combine la forme d'un rectangle calculé selon le nombre d'or et d'un triangle isocèle.»

The added rooftop volume is visible in plan and elevation below. Spiral stairways, both inside and out, lead up to the added wooden structure on the roof.

Unten: Grund- und Aufriss zeigen den auf das Dach aufgesetzten Bau. Drinnen wie draußen erschließen Wendeltreppen die neue Holzkonstruktion.

On voit le volume ajouté sur le plan et l'élévation ci-dessous. Des escaliers en colimaçon, à l'intérieur et à l'extérieur, mènent à la nouvelle construction en bois au sommet du toit.

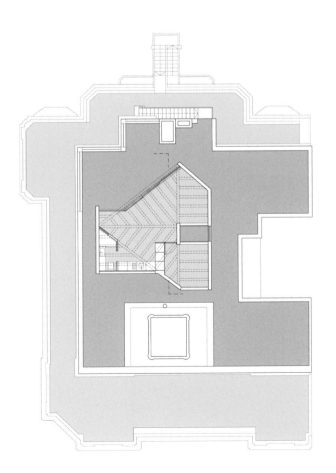

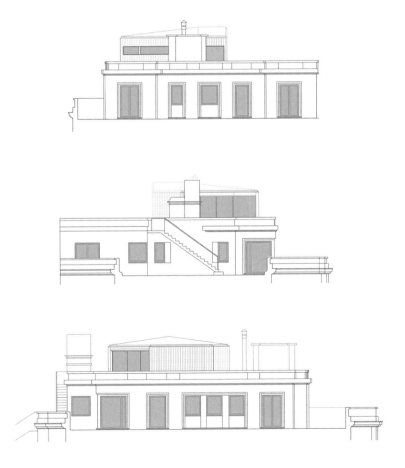

The added area on the roof presents a willful contrast with the white, colder elements of the original building. The architects compare the rooftop addition to a "treehouse."

Der neue Bereich auf dem Dach steht in bewusstem Kontrast zu den weißen, kälteren Elementen des ursprünglichen Gebäudes. Die Architekten vergleichen den Dachaufbau mit einem Baumhaus.

L'espace supplémentaire contraste délibérément avec les éléments blancs plus froids du bâtiment d'origine. Les architectes le comparent à une «maison dans les arbres».

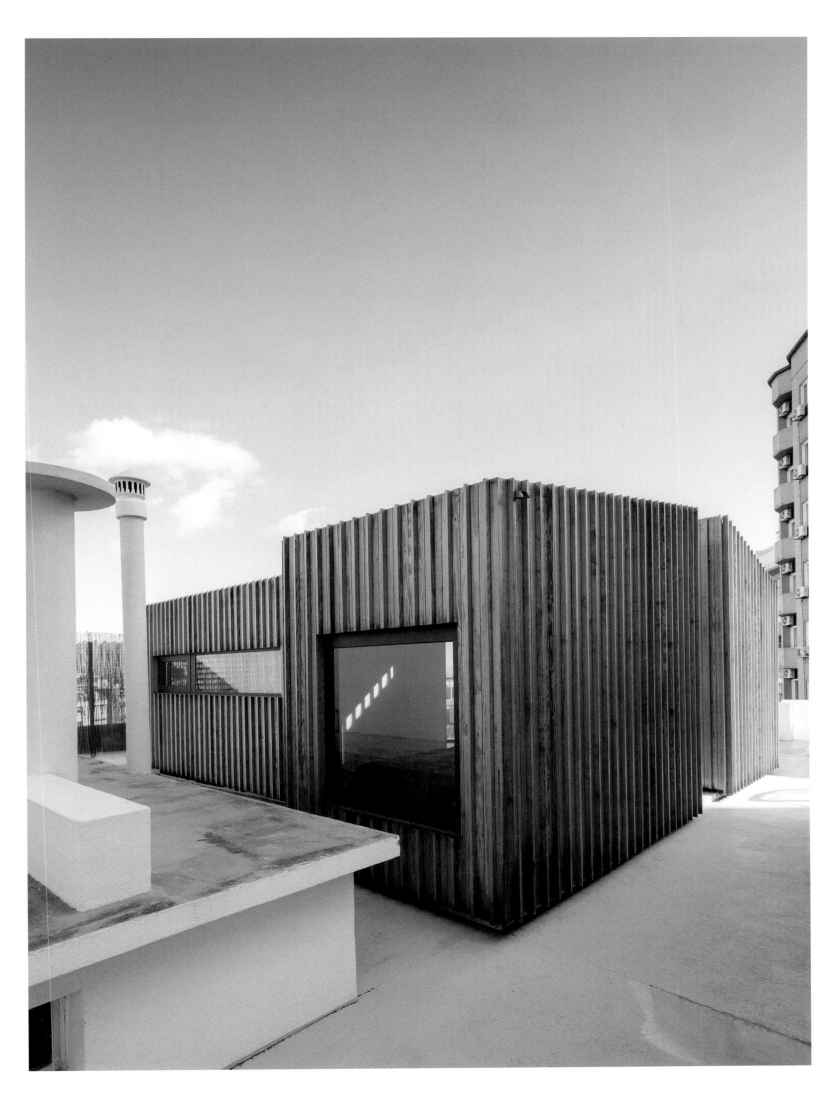

FOSTER + PARTNERS
London [UK]
2009-15

Rooftop Garden, Crossrail Place

Address: Crossrail Place, Canary Wharf, London E14, UK
Area: 34 837 m² (total), 3000 m² (roof garden) | Client: Canary Wharf Group PLC
Cost: not disclosed | Collaboration: Adamson Associates Architects

The project consists of the design of a mixed-use facility built above the new Canary Wharf Crossrail Station. Crossrail connects London from east to west. There are four levels of retail, a roof garden, pavilions, and station entrances unified by a grid-shell timber roof that wraps around the building. This 310-meter-long roof arches 30 meters over the park and stretches around the shops and entrances below. An opening in the center of the roof brings in light and water for irrigation purposes. According to the architects: "Its distinctive, latticed enclosure is planned to unify and enhance the station, as well as to further the central aim of the Crossrail project to open up London from east to west." Spruce glulam beams, only four of which out of 1418 are curved, support ETFE cushions that allow the garden areas below to support plant varieties first brought into England through the original West India Dock. The roof garden is accessible from ground level via two bridges. The concrete superstructure with glazed façades, and the wood and EFTE roof are the main elements employed.

Kern dieses Projekts war ein Bau über dem Bahnhof Canary Wharf der neuen Crossrail-Linie, die London auf der Ost-West-Achse erschließt. Dieser Geschäfte, einen Dachgarten, Pavillons sowie Bahnhofszugänge auf vier Ebenen umfassende Komplex wird vollständig von einer Holzgitterschale überspannt, einem 310 m langen Dach, das sich 30 m über die Gartenanlage wölbt und die Läden und Eingänge darunter umschließt. Eine Öffnung in der Dachmitte lässt Licht und Regenwasser für die Bewässerung hinein. Die Architekten kommentieren: „Die einzigartige Gitterhülle verleiht der Bahnstation Kohärenz und wertet sie auf; zugleich treibt sie das Hauptziel des Crossrail-Projekts, die Erschließung Londons in Richtung Osten und Westen, voran." Das Dach aus 1418 Fichten-Leimbindern, von denen nur vier gebogen sind, trägt ETFE-Folienkissen; so können auf den Gartenflächen darunter Pflanzenarten wachsen, die über das alte West India Dock erstmals nach England gelangten. Zwei Brücken erschließen den Dachgarten vom Straßenniveau aus. Die Betonüberbauung mit Glasfassaden sowie das Holz-ETFE-Dach sind die beherrschenden Elemente.

Le projet consiste à aménager un espace à usage mixte, au-dessus de la nouvelle gare Crossrail de Canary Wharf. Le Crossrail relie Londres d'Est en Ouest. L'ensemble comprend quatre niveaux de commerces, un jardin sur le toit, des pavillons et les entrées de la gare, tous réunis sous un toit en grid shell de bois qui s'enroule autour de la construction. Les arches du toit long de 310 m enjambent le parc à 30 m de hauteur et s'étendent jusqu'aux boutiques et aux entrées de la gare en dessous. Une ouverture au centre fait entrer la lumière et la pluie à des fins d'irrigation. Selon les architectes : « L'enceinte treillagée caractéristique vise à unifier et mettre en valeur la gare, ainsi qu'à promouvoir l'objectif central du projet Crossrail, à savoir ouvrir Londres d'est en ouest. » Des poutres en lamellé-collé d'épicéa, dont quatre seulement sont recourbées sur 1418, portent des coussins en ETFE grâce auxquels le jardin en dessous a pu être planté d'espèces végétales qui ont été introduites pour la première fois en Grande-Bretagne par les premiers docks des Indes occidentales. Le jardin est accessible depuis le rez-de-chaussée par deux passerelles. La superstructure de béton, les façades vitrées, le bois et le toit en EFTE sont les principaux éléments utilisés.

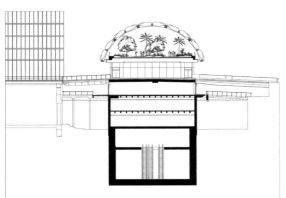
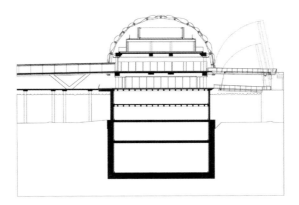

Section drawings show the lattice structure on top of the roof of the Crossrail station, with its enclosed garden seen on the following spread.

Die Querschnitte zeigen die Gitterstruktur des Dachs des Crossrail-Bahnhofs; auf der folgenden Doppelseite ein Blick in den überdachten Garten.

Les schémas en coupe montrent la structure treillissée du toit de la gare Crossrail avec le jardin clos que l'on voit sur la double page suivante.

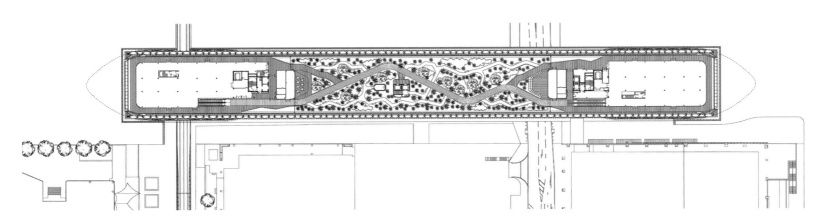

Searcy's, 30 St. Mary Axe

Address: 30 St. Mary Axe, London EC3A 8EP, UK, +44 20 70 71 50 25, www.searcys.co.uk
Area: 1400 m² | Client: Swiss Re | Cost: not disclosed

Searcy's occupies the top three floors of Norman Foster's 180-meter-tall Swiss Re building at 30 St. Mary Axe. Sold since its opening by Swiss Re, the building is commonly known in London as the Gherkin. It includes London's highest private members' club and a 70-seat restaurant, along with five private dining rooms and a bar offering a 360° view of London. Although access to Searcy's is normally reserved to club members or those working in the building, occasional public openings of the restaurant attract strong demand. The glass dome at the top of the building is available for private rental and is often used for weddings and product launches. The decor of Searcy's has been described as "glossy and minimalist" and there is near unanimity about the spectacular views from the uppermost level, which is reached by a spiral staircase. The architects state: "As an office tower, 30 St. Mary Axe embodies diverse values—about conserving energy, and making the workplace more enjoyable by bringing light, views, and fresh air deep into the heart of the interior. The materials in the restaurant are restrained but luxurious—polished black granite floor and dark silk gray walls, with tinted glazing on the façade reducing glare and solar gain."

Searcy's, Londons höchstgelegener Privatklub, nimmt die drei obersten Etagen in Norman Fosters 180 m hohen Swiss-Re-Gebäude an der 30 St. Mary Axe ein. Das inzwischen weiterverkaufte Haus heißt in London „Gurke". Hier befinden sich ein Restaurant mit 70 Plätzen, fünf separaten Speiseräumen und einer Bar mit Rundumblick über London. Eigentlich haben nur Klubmitglieder und Angestellte der Firmen im Gebäude Zutritt zum Searcy's. Ist das Restaurant aber ausnahmsweise für die Allgemeinheit geöffnet, ist die Nachfrage immer hoch. Der Raum unter der Glaskuppel wird gern für Hochzeiten und Produkteinführungen gebucht. Das Dekor von Searcy's gilt als „glanzvoll-minimalistisch". Einstimmigkeit herrscht über den spektakulären Blick aus der obersten Etage, die man über eine Wendeltreppe erreicht. Die Architekten kommentieren: „Als Bürohochhaus verkörpert 30 St. Mary Axe verschiedene Werte – Energieeffizienz ebenso wie ein angenehmeres Arbeitsklima dank Licht, Ausblicken und frischer Luft bis weit ins Gebäude. Die im Restaurant verwendeten Materialien sind zurückhaltend und dabei luxuriös – polierter schwarzer Granit für den Boden und dunkelseidengraue Wände, dazu eine getönte Verglasung, die zu starkes Sonnenlicht und aufgeheizte Räume verhindert."

Le Searcy's occupe les trois derniers étages de la tour Swiss Re construite par Norman Foster au 30 St. Mary Axe, haute de 180 m. Vendue par Swiss Re depuis son ouverture, l'édifice est connu sous le nom de «Cornichon» à Londres. Il comprend le plus haut club privé de Londres et un restaurant de 70 places avec cinq salles à manger privées et un bar avec une vue sur Londres à 360°. L'accès est normalement réservé aux membres du club ou aux personnes qui travaillent dans l'immeuble, mais le restaurant est parfois ouvert au public et fait alors l'objet d'une forte demande. La coupole de verre au sommet peut être louée et accueille souvent des mariages ou des lancements de produits. Le décor du Searcy's a été décrit comme «brillant et minimaliste» et les vues fantastiques depuis le dernier étage, accessible par un escalier en colimaçon, recueillent la quasi-totalité des suffrages. Les architectes expliquent: «En tant qu'immeuble de bureaux, le 30 St. Mary Axe incarne plusieurs valeurs – économies d'énergie, lieu de travail plus agréable par l'apport de lumière, de la vue et de l'air frais jusqu'au cœur même de l'édifice. Les matériaux utilisés pour le restaurant sont sobres, mais luxueux – sol de granite noir poli et murs gris tendus de soie sombre ou verre teinté en façade pour réduire l'éblouissement et l'apport solaire.»

Searcy's takes advantage of the spectacular view
on London offered by the rooftop location and the full
glazing. Right, the circular plan of the 39th floor.

Das Searcy's profitiert von dem spektakulären Blick
über London, der sich hier dank Dachlage und
Rundumverglasung bietet. Rechts: Der kreisrunde
Grundriss der 39. Etage.

Le Searcy's exploite la vue extraordinaire sur Londres
que l'on a au sommet du toit avec son vitrage pleine
hauteur. À droite, le plan circulaire du 39e niveau.

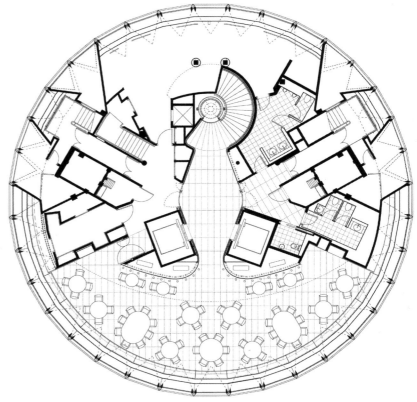

Because the mechanical plants have not been placed on the roof, as often occurs in skyscrapers, the very top of the building is completely glazed. The glass dome space is available for rental and special events.

Da auf dem Dach dieses Wolkenkratzers – anders als sonst häufig der Fall – keine Gebäudetechnik untergebracht ist, konnte die Spitze des Bauwerks komplett verglast werden. Die Glaskuppel kann für besondere Events gemietet werden.

Les équipements techniques n'ont pas été placés sur le toit comme c'est souvent le cas des gratte-ciel, ce qui a permis de vitrer entièrement le sommet de l'immeuble. L'espace sous la coupole de verre peut être loué pour des évènements exceptionnels.

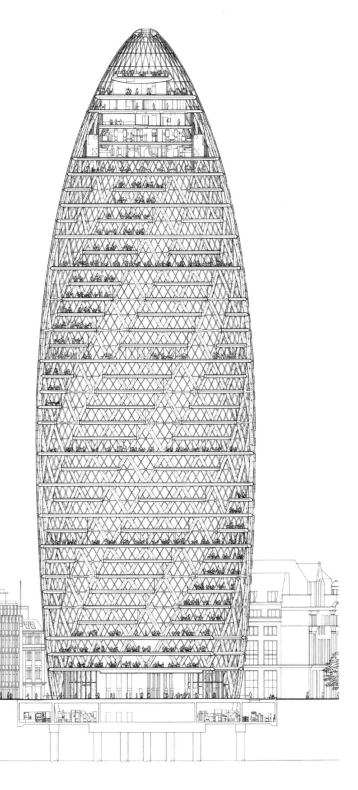

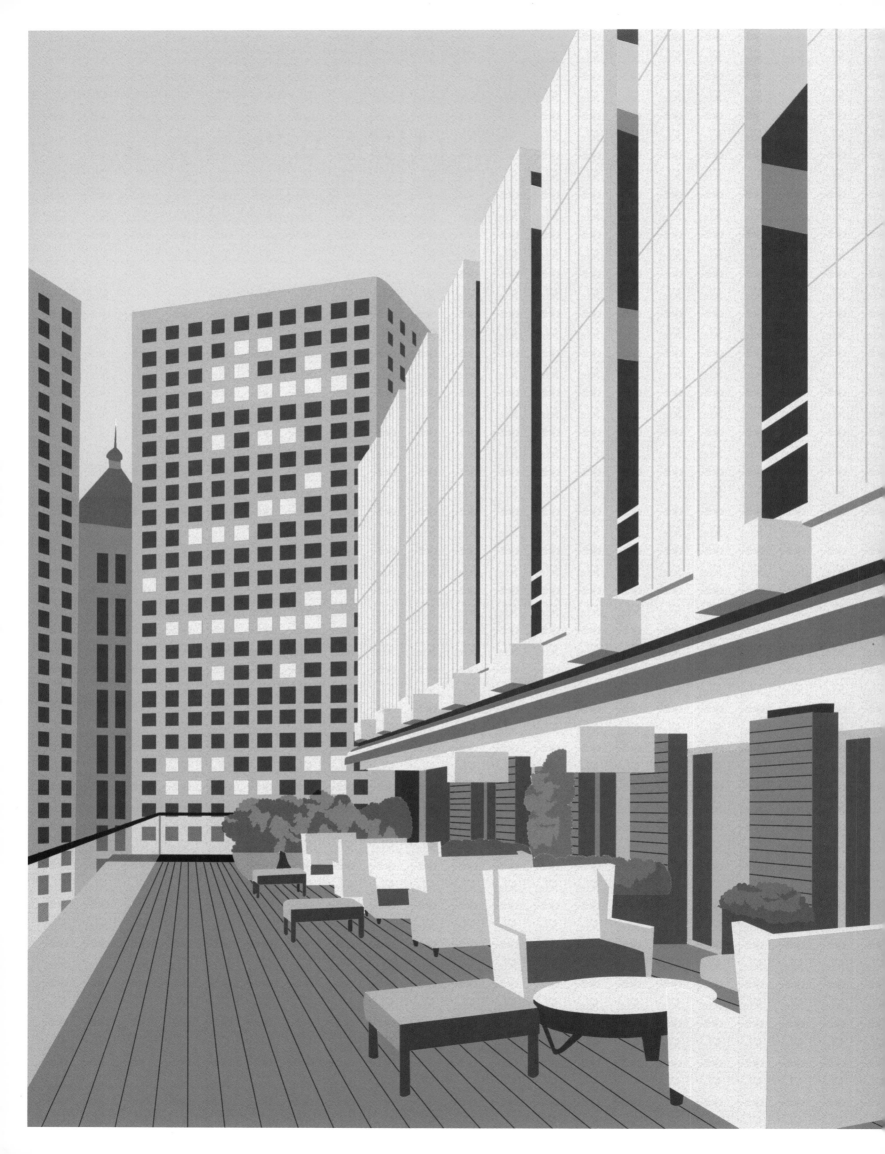

TSAO & MCKOWN
Hong Kong [CHINA]
2008

SEVVA Restaurant

*Address: Prince's Building, 10 Chater Road, Central, Hong Kong, China, +852 2537 1388,
www.sevva.hk | Area: 2044 m² | Client: Bonnie Gokson | Cost: not disclosed*

SEVVA, pronounced "savor," serves a mixture of Chinese and Western cuisines and is located on top of a designer shopping mall in the Prince's Building in Hong Kong's Central district. The restaurant features a 360° view of the heart of this very dynamic area. Designed by Calvin Tsao in close collaboration with the client, a well-known local personality Bonnie Gokson, SEVVA is made up of five enclaves, each with a different ambiance, with the whole intended to be a reflection of the client's cosmopolitan tastes. A vertical garden marks the main entrance walkway. The Bank Side area offers stunning views of Norman Foster's HSCB headquarters tower. Works of modern art, such as photos by Candida Hofer, mark the space. The Harbor Side space has a domed ceiling designed by the Australian lighting artist Ruth McDermott. The Taste Bar is a cocktail lounge, while a final space, the terrace, overlooks the panorama of Hong Kong's skyline.

Das Restaurant SEVVA wartet mit einem Mix chinesischer und westlicher Küchentraditionen auf. Es liegt im obersten Geschoss eines Designer-Shoppingcenters im Prince's Building im Hongkonger Stadtteil Central. Beeindruckend ist der Rundumblick im Herzen dieses äußerst dynamischen Viertels. In enger Zusammenarbeit mit der Bauherrin, der Stilikone Bonnie Gokson, gestaltete Calvin Tsao im SEVVA fünf separate Bereiche, jeden mit einem anderen Ambiente, um so den weltläufigen Geschmack der Auftraggeberin widerzuspiegeln. Ein Wandgarten markiert den Hauptzugang. Das Restaurant Bankside bietet einen überwältigenden Blick auf Norman Fosters Hochhaus für die HSBC-Zentrale. Fotos von Candida Hofer und andere moderne Kunst prägen diesen Bereich. Das Harbourside liegt unter einer hoch gewölbten Decke, einem Werk der australischen Lichtkünstlerin Ruth McDermott. Die Taste Bar bietet das Ambiente einer Cocktail-Lounge, während die Terrasse den Blick auf das Panorama von Hongkongs Skyline eröffnet.

Le SEVVA, prononcé « savor », situé au sommet d'une galerie marchande design dans le Prince's Building du quartier Central de Hong-Kong, sert une cuisine chinoise et occidentale. Le restaurant offre une vue à 360° sur le cœur de ce quartier extrêmement dynamique. Créé par Calvin Tsao en collaboration étroite avec le client Bonnie Gokson, une personnalité locale connue, le SEVVA est composé de cinq enclaves aux ambiances toutes différentes, le tout se voulant un reflet des goûts cosmopolites de ses clients. Le principal accès piétons est marqué par un jardin vertical. Du côté Bankside, les vues sur la tour de Norman Foster qui abrite le siège de HSCB sont saisissantes. L'espace est ponctué d'œuvres d'art moderne, notamment des photos de Candida Hofer. Le Harbourside présente un plafond à coupole créé par l'artiste lumière australienne Ruth McDermott. Le Taste Bar est un salon à cocktails et la Terrace tout au bout domine le panorama de Hong Kong.

An outdoor bar area looks out at the spectacular forms of Norman Foster's HSBC Headquarters (1986).

Beeindruckend ist der Blick von der Außenbar auf die spektakuläre Fassade von Fosters Zentrale der HSBC (1986).

L'espace bar extérieur a vue sur les sièges spectaculaires de la HSBC par Norman Foster (1986).

Above, a view across Kowloon Bay and, below, an overall plan of the rooftop restaurant and bar. Right page, from the bar looking out toward I. M. Pei's Bank of China Headquarters (1989).

Oben: Blick über die Kowloon Bay. Unten: Grundriss des Dachrestaurants mit Bar. Rechts: Blick von der Bar auf I.M. Peis Zentrale der Bank of China (1989).

Ci-dessus, vue de la baie de Kowloon et ci-dessous, plan d'ensemble du restaurant et du bar. Page de droite, vue depuis le bar sur le siège de la Bank of China par I. M. Pei (1989).

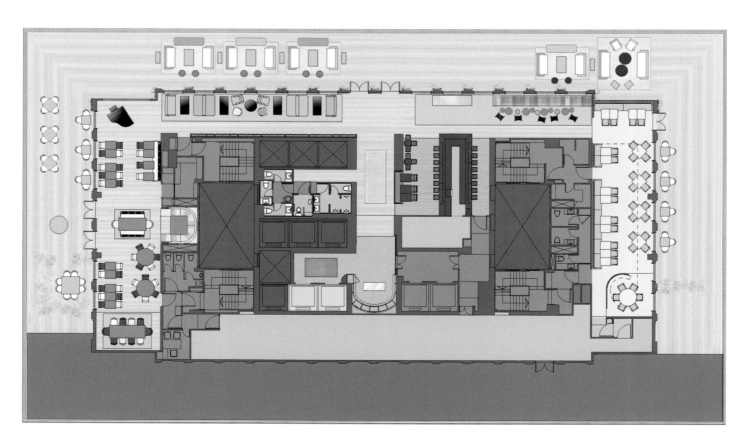

DWP
Bangkok [THAILAND]
2004

Sirocco Restaurant & Skybar

Address: 1055 State Tower, Silom Road, Bangkok 10500,
Thailand, +66 2624 9555, www.lebua.com/sirocco | Area: 500 m²
Client: The Dome at Lebua | Cost: not disclosed

The Sirocco Restaurant & Skybar is located in the Dome of the State Tower, a 247-meter-high skyscraper on Silom Road in the Bang Rak business district of the Thai capital. Built in 2001, it is the largest building in Southeast Asia. The golden dome at the top of the building is at the back of the restaurant space. Set above the Lebua Hotel on the 63rd floor of the building, the 150-seat restaurant Sirocco and its Skybar offer 360° views of the city. Finishes used include sandstone, timber veneers, gold leaf, and Thai silks. Air-conditioning is used for the outdoor dining area. Sirroco has been continually listed among the best restaurants in Thailand since its opening.

Das Sirocco Restaurant & Skybar befindet sich auf dem State Tower, einem 247 m hohen Wolkenkratzer an der Silom Road im Geschäftsviertel Bang Rak der thailändischen Hauptstadt. Das 2001 errichtete Gebäude ist das größte Südostasiens. Der Gastronomiebereich liegt direkt unterhalb der goldenen Kuppel auf dem Gebäudedach. Hier, in der 63. Etage, gleich über dem Lebua Hotel, bietet das Restaurant mit Skybar 150 Gästen einen Rundumblick über die City. Die Oberflächen wurden in Sandstein, Holzfurnier, Blattgold und thailändischen Seidenstoffen ausgeführt. Die Klimaanlage macht den Aufenthalt im Außenbereich angenehm. Das Sirocco gilt seit seiner Eröffnung durchgehend als eines der besten Restaurants Thailands.

Le Sirocco Restaurant & Skybar occupe le dôme de la State Tower, un gratte-ciel de 247 m à Silom Road, dans le quartier d'affaires Bang Rak de la capitale thaïlandaise. Construit en 2001, c'est le plus grand d'Asie du Sud-Est. La coupole dorée au sommet est située à l'arrière du restaurant. Au 63e niveau, le restaurant Sirocco de 150 places et son Skybar, au-dessus de l'hôtel Lebua, offrent des vues à 360° sur la ville. Les finitions comprennent du grès, des placages de bois, des feuilles d'or et des soies thaï. Les espaces de restauration extérieurs bénéficient de l'air conditionné. Depuis son ouverture, le Sirocco a toujours figuré sur la liste des meilleurs restaurants du pays.

Below, a city view shows the State Tower, on top of which the Sirocco Restaurant & Skybar is located. Right, the golden dome of the building, which is visible from a great distance.

Die Stadtansicht unten zeigt den State Tower, auf dessen Dach sich das Sirocco Restaurant & Skybar befindet. Rechts: Die bereits von Weitem sichtbare goldene Kuppel.

Ci-dessous, vue de la ville avec la State Tower qui abrite le Sirocco Restaurant & Skybar. À droite, la coupole dorée visible de loin.

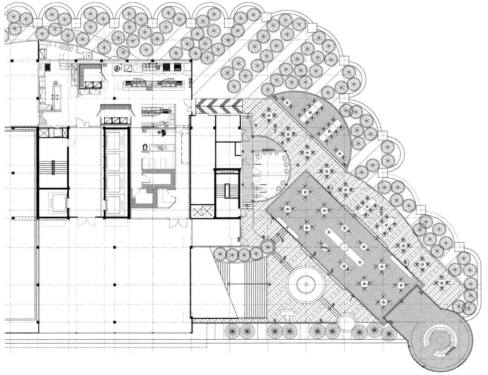

Left, a plan of the rooftop and its terraces.
As can be seen in the image above, Sirocco
offers a remarkable view of the city.

*Links: Grundriss der Dachfläche und der
Terrassen. Das Foto oben zeigt auch den
herrlichen Ausblick über die Stadt.*

*À gauche, plan du toit et de ses terrasses.
On le voit sur la photo ci-dessus, le Sirocco
dispose d'une vue exceptionnelle sur la ville.*

MOSHE SAFDIE
Bishan [SINGAPORE]
2012–15

SkyHabitat

Address: 7 Bishan Street 15, Singapore 579827, Singapore, www.skyhabitat.com.sg
Area: 5200 m² (L14 bridge), 5200 m² (L26 bridge), 4655 m² (L38 bridge)
Client: CapitaLand Residential Singapore | Cost: not disclosed
Collaboration: DCA Architects Pte Ltd (Executive Architects), Shane Coen
and Partners (Landscape Design)

Located in the neighborhood of Bishan, a residential area in the suburban area of Singapore, this 38-story residential complex develops a matrix of homes with private terraces, balconies, and common gardens, "bringing landscape into the air and maintaining porosity on the skyline." The strong stepping form of the complex "recalls the community texture of ancient hillside developments and provides for lush vertical greenery, multiple orientations relative to the sun, naturally ventilated units, and generous views, all without compromising planning or structural efficiency." The two stepping towers are linked by three bridging sky gardens, creating a series of interconnected streets, gardens, and terraces far above ground level that provide a variety of areas for recreation and congregation.

Mit dieser 38-stöckigen Wohnanlage in Bishan, einem Außenbezirk Singapurs, wurde eine Matrix von Wohneinheiten mit privaten Terrassen und Balkonen sowie Gemeinschaftsgärten umgesetzt, die „Landschaft in die Luft erhebt und dabei die Durchlässigkei der Skylines zu erhält". Die prägnant abgetreppte Silhouette des Komplexes „nimmt Bezug auf die Gemeinwesen alter Hangsiedlungen und ermöglicht eine üppige Vertikalbegrünung, unterschiedliche Ausrichtungen zur Sonne, natürlich durchlüftete Wohneinheiten großzügige Ausblicke, ohne die planerische und konstruktive Effizienz zu einzuschränken". Zwischen den beiden abgetreppten Türmen erstrecken sich drei Brücken mit Himmelsgärten, die unterschiedliche Wegeverbindungen, Gärten und Terrassen hoch über der Erde schaffen, die sich als Erholungs- und Gemeinschaftsraum anbieten.

Situé dans le quartier de Bishan, une zone résidentielle suburbaine de Singapour, le complexe résidentiel de 38 niveaux déploie une matrice de logements aux terrasses privées, balcons et jardins communs, pour «transporter le paysage dans les airs tout en conservant la porosité de la ligne d'horizon». La forme en escalier strict du complexe «rappelle le tissu communautaire d'anciens lotissements à flanc de coteau et permet une végétation verticale luxuriante, des orientations multiples par rapport au soleil, des unités naturellement ventilées et des vues généreuses, le tout sans aucun compromis en termes de planification ou d'efficacité structurelle». Les deux tours en escaliers sont reliées par trois jardins en plein ciel sur des passerelles qui créent des rues interconnectées, des jardins et des terrasses haut au-dessus du sol – autant de lieux de loisirs et de réunion.

Right page, the sky bridges that link the two main elements of the building are planted, as are many of the terraces and courtyard spaces of the building.

Rechts: Die Himmelsbrücken, die die beiden Gebäudehälften verbinden, sind ebenso bepflanzt wie viele der Terrassen und Höfe der Gebäude.

Page de droite, les passerelles qui relient les deux principaux éléments du complexe sont végétalisées, ainsi que bon nombre des terrasses et des cours.

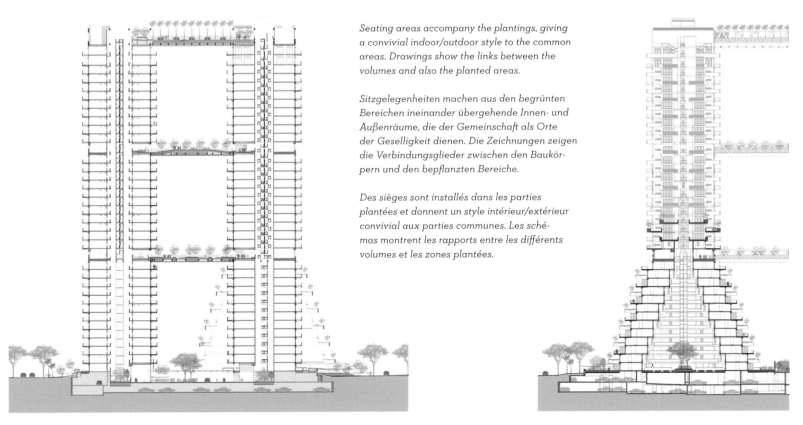

Seating areas accompany the plantings, giving a convivial indoor/outdoor style to the common areas. Drawings show the links between the volumes and also the planted areas.

Sitzgelegenheiten machen aus den begrünten Bereichen ineinander übergehende Innen- und Außenräume, die der Gemeinschaft als Orte der Geselligkeit dienen. Die Zeichnungen zeigen die Verbindungsglieder zwischen den Baukörpern und den bepflanzten Bereiche.

Des sièges sont installés dans les parties plantées et donnent un style intérieur/extérieur convivial aux parties communes. Les schémas montrent les rapports entre les différents volumes et les zones plantées.

1.2m

MOSHE SAFDIE
Marina Bay Sands [SINGAPORE]
2010

Skypark

*Address: 10 Bayfront Avenue, Singapore 018956, Singapore, +65 6688 8888, www.marinabay-sands.com/sands-skypark.html | Area: 929 000 m² (building), 10 000 m² (Skypark)
Client: Las Vegas Sands Corp. | Cost: $5 billion (including land cost) | Collaboration:
Aedas (Associate Architect), PWP Landscape Architecture, ARUP*

Marina Bay Sands is a high-density, mixed-use, urban complex. The project is based on guidelines developed by the Urban Redevelopment Authority of Singapore for expansion of its downtown through reclamation of the bay front. The program of 580 000 square meters dispersed over a 15.4-hectare site is organized around town-planning principles. Three 55-story hotel towers anchor the district. A 1.01-hectare Skypark connects the towers at a height of 190 meters, with a 65-meter cantilever at one end, the longest cantilever in a public building in the world. The Skypark superstructure was fabricated offsite and then the pieces of the structure were lifted 200 meters by 14 heavy lifts and put together at the top. The Skypark can accommodate 3900 people at any one time. The public observation deck, located on the cantilever and looking north over the Singapore Flyer, can host 900 people at a time. Its gardens include 250 trees and 650 plants, some up to eight meters tall. One of the signature amenities of the Skypark is the swimming area, which includes three linked 50-meter swimming pools and a 146-meter-long infinity edge overlooking the city.

Marina Bay Sands in Singapur ist ein dicht bebautes Areal mit Mischnutzung. Das Projekt beruht auf neuen Richtlinien zur Vergrößerung des Bezirks Downtown durch die Nutzung der Uferzone, die das Amt für Stadterneuerung erließ. Das 580 000 m² große Raumprogramm auf einem Areal von 15,4 ha orientiert sich an stadtplanerischen Grundsätzen; seinen Mittelpunkt bilden drei 55-stöckige Hoteltürme. Diese Türme sind auf einer Höhe von 190 m durch einen 1,01 ha großen Skypark verbunden, der auf einer Seite um 65 m auskragt – die weltweit weiteste Auskragung an einem öffentlichen Gebäude. Der Überbau wurde vorgefertigt angeliefert, mithilfe von 14 Schwerlastkränen stückweise auf 200 m Höhe gebracht und oben zusammengefügt. Auf dem Skypark können sich 3900 Besucher zugleich aufhalten. Allein auf der öffentlich zugänglichen Aussichtsplattform auf der Auskragung mit Blick auf das Riesenrad Singapore Flyer im Norden finden 900 Besucher Platz. Auf den Gartenflächen des Skypark wachsen 250 Bäume und 650 weitere Pflanzen, einige davon bis 8 m hoch. Berühmt ist der Poolbereich mit drei verbundenen 50-m-Becken und einer 146 m langen Infinity-Kante mit Blick über die Stadt.

Marina Bay Sands est un complexe urbain extrêmement dense à usage mixte. Le projet est basé sur des directives élaborées par les services de rénovation urbaine de Singapour pour agrandir le centre-ville en mettant en valeur le front de mer. L'ensemble de 580 000 m² répartis sur un site de 15,4 hectares est articulé autour de plusieurs principes urbanistiques. Les trois tours de l'hôtel de 55 niveaux ancrent le tout. Un Skypark de 1,01 hectare les relie à 190 m de hauteur, l'avancée de 65 mètres qui prolonge l'une de ses extrémités est le plus long porte-à-faux construit sur un bâtiment public au monde. La superstructure en a été préfabriquée hors site, puis les éléments de la structure ont été montés à 200 m par quatorze ascenseurs pour transports lourds et assemblés en haut. Le Skypark peut accueillir 3900 personnes en même temps. La plate-forme d'observation publique, sur le porte-à-faux, a vue au nord sur la grande roue Singapore Flyer et peut contenir 900 personnes. Les jardins comptent 250 arbres et 650 plantes, certains hauts de 8 m. Parmi les aménagements les plus marquants du Skypark, l'espace de baignade comprend trois bassins de 50 mètres en enfilade et une piscine à débordement de 146 mètres de long qui domine la ville.

*The Skypark looks almost like a curved
ocean liner perched on top of three skyscrapers
in this aerial view.*

*In dieser Luftaufnahme wirkt der Skypark
fast wie ein gekrümmter Ozeandampfer, der
auf drei Wolkenkratzern balanciert.*

*Sur cette vue aérienne, le Skypark fait
penser à un paquebot courbe perché au
sommet de trois gratte-ciel.*

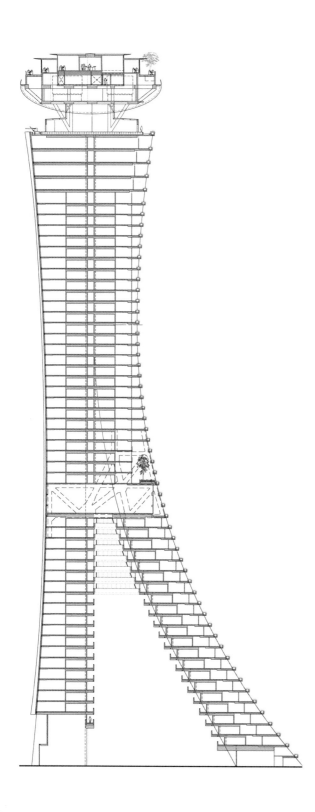

Drawings give an idea of the size of the trees planted on the roof and the relation to the 146-meter-long curved pool. Below, a general plan of the rooftop.

Die Zeichnungen vermitteln einen Eindruck von der Größe der Bäume auf dem Dach und von ihrem Größenverhältnis zu dem 146 Meter langen gebogenen Pool. Unten: Grundriss der Dachfläche.

Les schémas donnent une idée de la taille des arbres plantés sur le toit et de leur rapport à la piscine incurvée de 146 m de long. Ci-dessous, un plan général des aménagements du toit.

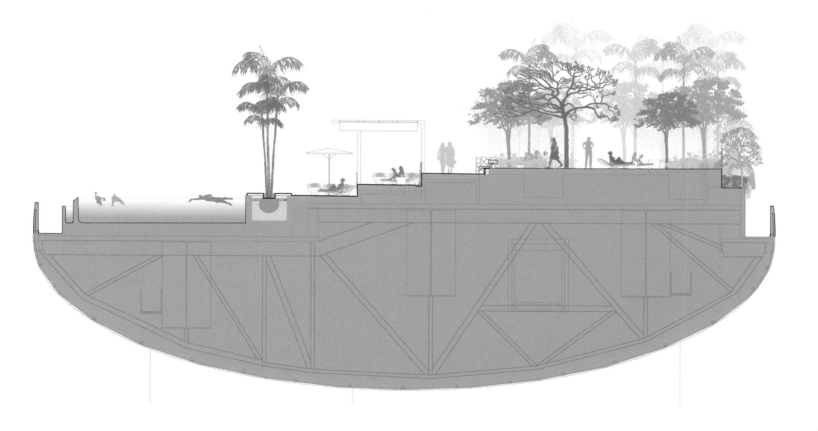

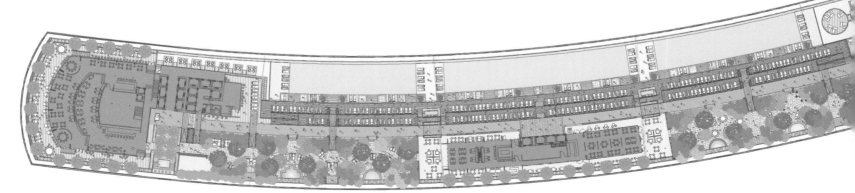

The Skypark and its observation platform
are cantilevered out 65 meters over the Marina
Bay Sands complex.

Der Skypark und sein Aussichtsdeck ragen
65 Meter über den Gebäudekomplex Marina
Bay Sands hinaus.

Le Skypark et sa plate-forme d'observation
dépassent de 65 m au-dessus du complexe
Marina Bay Sands.

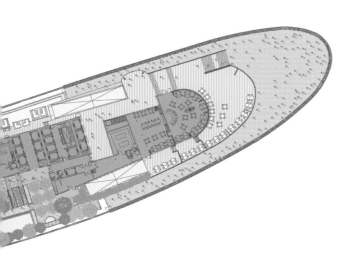

GUNN LANDSCAPE ARCHITECTURE
New York, New York [USA]
2014

SoHo Roof Terrace

Address: not disclosed | Area: 76 m² | Client: not disclosed | Cost: not disclosed
Collaboration: Shaler Ladd (Interior Designers), Vert Gardens, Inc. (Installation)

SoHo is, of course, the area south of Houston Street in Lower Manhattan, formerly a gallery district but now given over more to residences, fashion stores, and restaurants. For this penthouse garden, Gunn Landscape Architecture used custom-designed teak planters and created a heated plunge pool for the clients. A kitchen and dining space with an adjoining seating area and an outdoor fireplace are also part of the outdoor design. The dining table faces uptown with a distant view of the Empire State Building. As the architects describe the plantings: "Our palette incorporates the green leaves and puffy plumes of the Grace Smokebush, a finely curated selection of perennial grasses and meadow plantings, and maple branches, which add a sculptural display when covered with a blanket of winter's snow."

SoHo, das Gebiet südlich der Houston Street in Lower Manhattan, war früher ein Galerienviertel, heute jedoch finden sich hier vor allem Privatwohnungen, Modegeschäfte und Restaurants. Für diesen Penthouse-Garten benutzte das Büro Gunn Landscape Architecture maßgefertigte Pflanzkübel aus Teak und baute den Eigentümern ein beheiztes Tauchbecken. Eine Küche und ein Essplatz mit angrenzender Sitzgruppe sowie ein Kamin gehören ebenfalls zu der Außeneinrichtung. Vom Esstisch blickt man Richtung Uptown und sieht in der Ferne das Empire State Building. Zur Bepflanzung erläutern die Architekten: „Zu unserer Pflanzpalette gehören der sommergrüne, weiche Blütenwolken tragende Perückenstrauch ‚Grace', eine sorgfältige Auswahl mehrjähriger Gräser und Wiesenpflanzen sowie Ahornzweige, die dem Garten, wenn sie im Winter mit Schnee bedeckt sind, eine skulpturale Anmutung hinzufügen."

SoHo, le quartier au Sud de Houston Street, dans Lower Manhattan, était autrefois surtout connu pour ses galeries mais est aujourd'hui plus occupé par des résidences, boutiques de mode et restaurants. Pour le jardin de cet appartement de luxe, Gunn Landscape Architecture a choisi des jardinières faites sur mesure en bois de teck et a créé un bassin chauffé. L'aménagement extérieur comprend aussi une cuisine et un espace repas, attenant à des sièges devant une cheminée extérieure. La table domine le haut de la ville avec au loin l'Empire State Building. Les architectes décrivent les plantations en ces termes : « La palette comprend les feuilles vertes et les aigrettes cotonneuses de l'arbre à perruque, des herbes vivaces et plantes de prairies sélectionnées avec soin, ainsi que des branches d'érable qui font une impression très sculpturale lorsqu'elles sont couvertes de neige en hiver. »

The relatively small area of the terrace (76 m²) has led the designers to confine the greenery to planters aligned along the edges of the space, which is made convivial with an outdoor fireplace.

Da die Terrasse mit 76 m² über relativ wenig Grundfläche verfügt, beschränkten die Gestalter alles Grün auf Pflanzkübel entlang der Terrassenränder; ein Außenkamin sorgt für Wohlbehagen.

La surface relativement modeste de la terrasse (76 m²) a incité les créateurs à limiter la verdure à des jardinières alignées sur les côtés de l'espace qui doit sa convivialité à une cheminée extérieure.

Below, a plan of the rooftop terrace showing the planted areas and the furnishings.

Unten: Der Grundriss der Dachterrasse zeigt die Pflanzflächen und die Möblierung.

Ci-dessous un plan de la terrasse montre les parties plantées et l'ameublement.

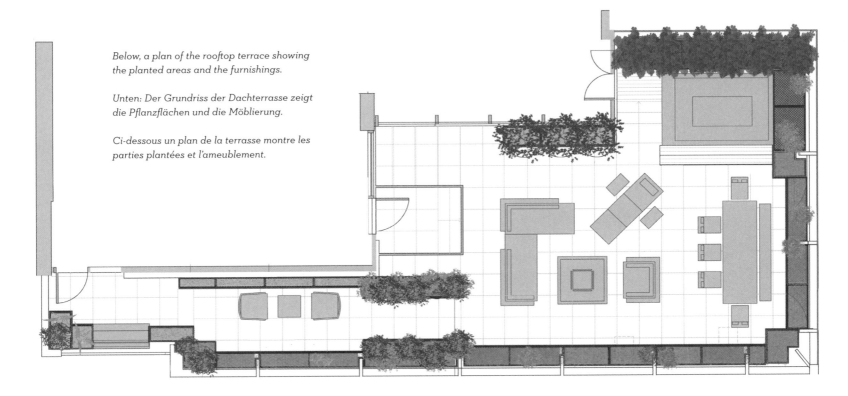

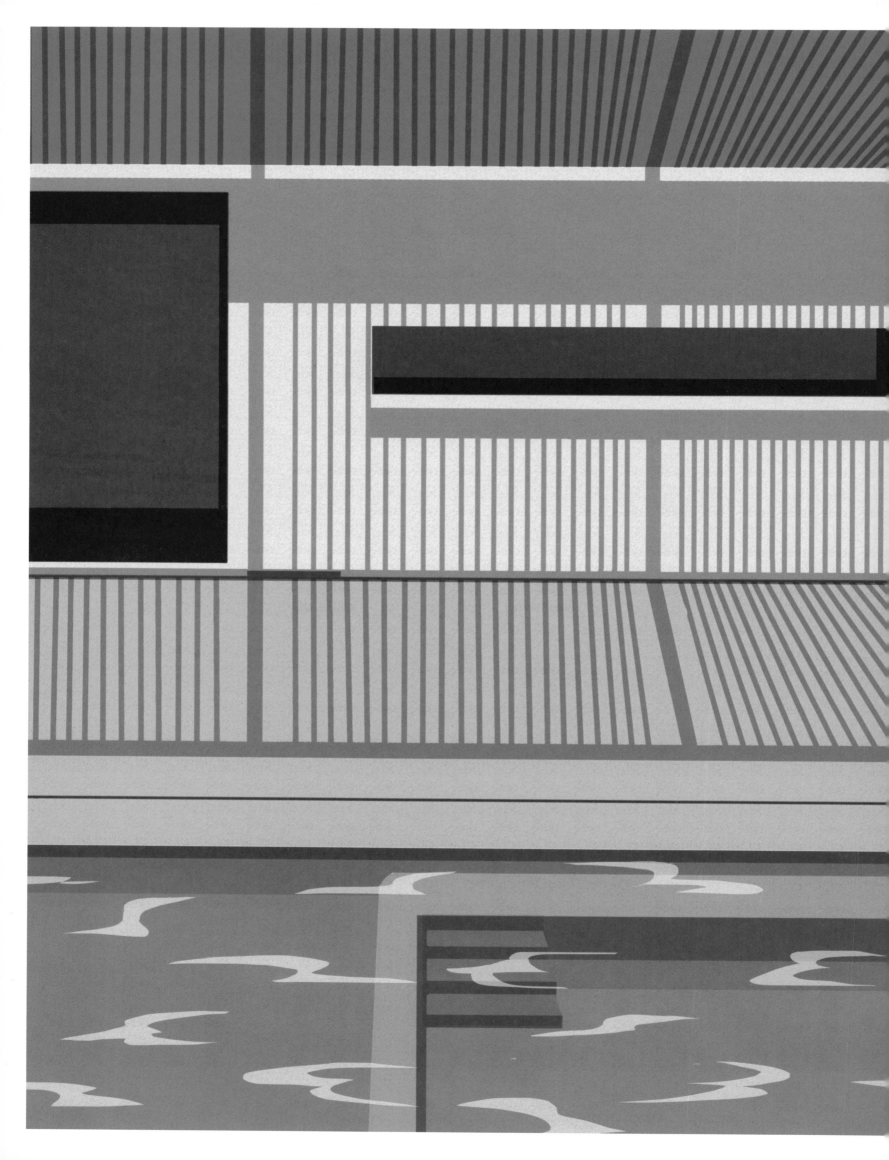

VLADIMIR DJUROVIC
Beirut [LEBANON]
2008-13

SST Building Private Rooftop

Address: not disclosed | Area: 400 m² | Client: not disclosed
Cost: not disclosed | Collaboration: Aquarius (Water Features),
Pépinières Peter Holman (Plants), Parissis (Steel Works)

Vladimir Djurovic's mastery of space and volumes has brought him a large number of private and public commissions, often for powerful and wealthy clients ranging from the Aga Khan to Lakshmi Mittal. In this instance, he conceived what he calls "a place of refuge." The rooftop garden, he says, "is a space seemingly floating in open skies and an endless horizon." The space includes a panoramic bar, and a discreet kitchen and barbecue area. A cantilevered shade structure provides shelter. Chinese medium gray granite and wood are used for most surfaces. Located not far from the Ramlet al-Baida beach at the southern end of the Corniche, the rooftop offers uninterrupted views of the coastline and sea. A long, rectangular reflecting pool gives the impression that the rooftop itself extends directly into the sea and the horizon.

Vladimir Djurovics meisterhafter Umgang mit Raum und Volumen hat ihm bereits zahlreiche private und öffentliche Aufträge eingebracht, darunter von so vermögenden, einflussreichen Bauherren wie dem Aga Khan und Lakshmi Mittal. In diesem Fall entwarf er einen „Zufluchtsort", wie er selbst sagt. Der Dachgarten sei „ein Raum, der zwischen dem weiten Himmel und einem unendlichen Horizont zu schweben scheint". Zu dem Programm zählen eine Panoramabar und ein separater Koch- und Grillbereich. Ein freitragendes Schattendach bietet Schutz. Die Oberflächen sind überwiegend in mittelgrauem chinesischem Granit und Holz ausgeführt. Die nahe des Strands Ramlet al-Baida am Südende der Seepromenade von Beirut gelegene Dachterrasse bietet einen unverstellten Blick auf den Küstenverlauf und das Meer. Ein langes, rechteckiges Spiegelbecken vermittelt den Eindruck, als erstreckte sich diese Dachfläche selbst bis ins Meer und zum Horizont.

La maîtrise de l'espace et des volumes de Vladimir Djurovic lui a valu de nombreuses commandes publiques et privées, souvent pour des clients riches et puissants, de l'Aga Khan à Lakshmi Mittal. Ici, il a créé ce qu'il appelle «un refuge». Le jardin sur le toit est, selon ses mots, «un espace qui semble flotter en plein ciel et dans un horizon infini». Il comprend un bar panoramique, une cuisine discrète et un espace barbecue. Le tout est abrité sous une structure en porte-à-faux qui l'ombrage. La plupart des surfaces sont en granit de Chine gris moyen et en bois. Situé non loin de la plage de Ramlet al-Baïda, à l'extrémité sud de la Corniche, le toit offre une vue parfaitement dégagée sur la ville et le littoral. Une longue piscine rectangulaire réfléchissante donne l'impression qu'il se prolonge jusque dans la mer et l'horizon.

Although he is known mainly as a garden designer, Vladimir Djurovic is also a talented architect who makes use of different materials with subtlety and sensibility.

Zwar ist Vladimir Djurovic vor allem als Gartengestalter bekannt, doch er ist auch ein begabter Architekt, der seine Materialien mit Geschick und Einfühlungsvermögen kombiniert.

Même s'il est surtout connu pour ses jardins, Vladimir Djurovic est aussi un architecte de talent qui sait tirer parti de différents matériaux avec subtilité et sensibilité.

Right, a plan of the rooftop terrace. Above, a view toward the Corniche Beirut, not far from the Central District, overlooking the sea.

Rechts: Grundriss der Dachterrasse. Oben: Blick zur Corniche Beirut nahe des Central District am Meer.

À droite, plan de la terrasse. Ci-dessus, vue vers la Corniche de Beyrouth, non loin du centre, qui domine la mer.

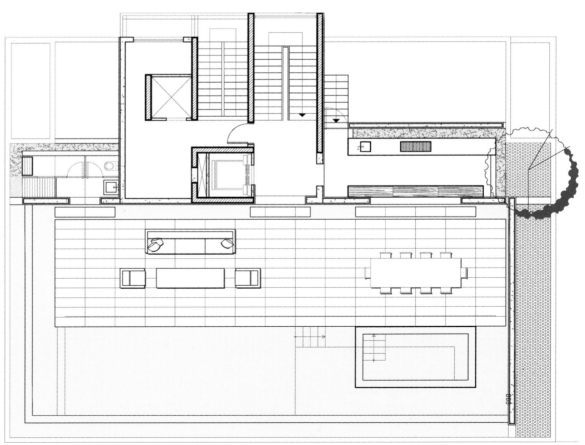

CETRARUDDY
London [UK]
2013

SushiSamba

Address: Heron Tower, 110 Bishopsgate, London EC2N 4AY, UK, +44 20 36 40 73 30,
www.sushisamba.com | Area: 1721 m² | Client: Samba Brands Management
Cost: not disclosed

SushiSamba, along with Duck & Waffle (also designed by CetraRuddy), is located high in the Heron Tower, the highest building in the City of London (third tallest in Greater London). Located on the 38th, 39th, and 40th floors of the building, the facility includes two restaurants and terraces, four bars, and a lounge. The architects explain: "The design imperative was to create distinct dining aesthetics that reflect the merging of Japanese, Peruvian, Brazilian, and English cuisines and cultures through fluid spatial relationships and the innovative composition of materials." SushiSamba has a 7.3-meter-high arched latticed bamboo ceiling and panoramic views leading to a bar that extends out onto the west terrace. Duck & Waffle is on the top level and is open 24 hours a day, seven days a week. Again, according to the architects: "The main dining room features a dynamic geometric ceiling of undulating yellow panels that pay homage to the great Brazilian architect, Oscar Niemeyer. Crafted warm materials include antique crackle wall tiles, darkened bronze and textured glass walls, weathered wood, and end-grain wood floors."

SushiSamba liegt wie das ebenfalls von CetraRuddy gestaltete Duck & Waffle hoch oben im Heron Tower, dem höchsten Bauwerk in der City of London und dritthöchsten von Greater London. Die Räumlichkeiten erstrecken sich von der 38. bis zur 40. Etage des Gebäudes; zu ihr gehören zwei Restaurants mit Terrasse, vier Bars und eine Lounge. Die Architekten erklären: „Die Designaufgabe bestand darin, eine bestimmte Ästhetik für die Verschmelzung japanischer, peruanischer, brasilianischer und englischer Kultur und Küchentradition zu schaffen, und zwar mithilfe der innovativen Zusammenstellung von Materialien und fließend ineinander übergehenden Räumen." Das SushiSamba, über dem sich ein 7,30 m hohes Bambusgitter wölbt, beeindruckt mit seinem Panoramablick, der auch die Bar auf der westlichen Terrasse umfasst. Das Duck & Waffle liegt auf der obersten Etage und ist an sämtlichen Wochentagen rund um die Uhr geöffnet. Auch hier äußern sich die Architekten: „Den Hauptraum prägt seine dynamische geometrische Decke aus gewellten gelben Tafeln, die eine Hommage an den großen brasilianischen Architekten Oscar Niemeyer sind. Verbaut wurden warme handwerkliche Materialien wie antike Wandkacheln mit Krakeleeglasur, patinierte Bronze und Zwischenwände aus Ornamentglas, verwittertes Holz sowie ein Bodenbelag aus Hirnholz."

Avec Duck & Waffle (également conçu par CetraRuddy), SushiSamba est situé très haut dans la Heron Tower, la plus haute tour de la City londonienne (et la troisième plus haute du Grand Londres). L'établissement en occupe les 38ᵉ, 39ᵉ et 40ᵉ niveaux et compte deux restaurants avec des terrasses, quatre bars et un «lounge». Les architectes expliquent: «L'impératif en termes de design était de créer des esthétiques distinctes qui reflètent le mélange de cuisines et de cultures japonaise, péruvienne, brésilienne et anglaise au travers de connexions spatiales fluides et de la composition innovante des matériaux.» SushiSamba, sous un plafond de 7,3 m de haut fait d'un treillis de bambou arqué, bénéficie d'une vue panoramique qui comprend le bar qui prolonge la terrasse ouest. Duck & Waffle, au dernier étage, est ouvert 24 h sur 24, sept jours par semaine. Là encore, selon les architectes: «La salle de restauration principale affiche un plafond géométrique de panneaux jaunes ondulés très dynamique, qui rend hommage au grand architecte brésilien Oscar Niemeyer. Les matériaux portant la marque chaleureuse de l'artisanat comprennent des dalles murales antiques craquelées, du bronze noirci et des parois en verre texturé, du bois patiné et des planchers en bois de bout.»

Above, the outdoor terrace with Norman Foster's "Gherkin" on the left and Renzo Piano's Shard in the distance.

Oben: Die Außenterrasse mit Norman Fosters „Gurke" (links) und im Hintergrund Renzo Pianos Shard.

Ci-dessus, la terrasse avec le Cornichon de Norman Foster à gauche et le Shard de Renzo Piano au loin.

The decor of the interior spaces (left page) is lively, but guests surely keep much of their attention focused on the generous view of the city. Right, a plan of the rooftop.

So interessant die Innenräume (linke Seite) auch gestaltet sein mögen – die Hauptaufmerksamkeit der Gäste gilt sicher dem weiten Blick über die Stadt. Rechts: Ein Grundriss der Dachgestaltung.

Le décor des espaces intérieurs (page ci-contre) est plein de vie mais l'attention des clients est certainement centrée avant tout sur la vue de la ville. À droite, plan du toit.

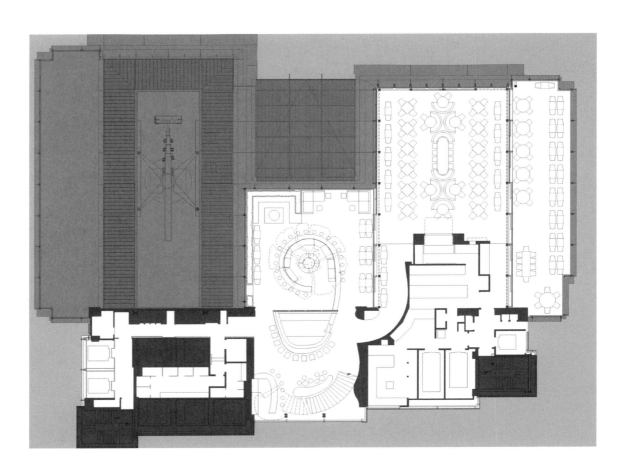

JAKOB + MACFARLANE
Paris [FRANCE]
2012

The Docks Rooftop Terrace

Address: Cité de la Mode et du Design, 34 Quai d'Austerlitz, 75013 Paris, France, www.citemodedesign.fr | Area: 4200 m² (accessible to the public) | Client: Caisse des Dépôts Cost: €25 million | Collaboration: Michel Desvigne (Landscape), Yann Kersalé (Lighting)

Located on the Quai d'Austerlitz in the 13th arrondissement of Paris, opposite the Ministry of Finance at Bercy, this project involved the renovation of a 1907 industrial warehouse made of concrete into a showplace for fashion and design. Using a new lightweight glass construction system called "plug-over," the architects sought to modernize the building with forms inspired by the flow of the River Seine. The program is a mix centered on the themes of design and fashion, including exhibition spaces, the IFM Fashion School, cafés, and an auditorium. A panoramic rooftop terrace and a purpose-designed exterior lighting system assure that the new facility attracts attention at night as well as during the day. On the landscaped roof level, a vast terrace is made accessible to the public onto which the functions sheltered by the plug-over are extended. The architects state: "The concept of plug-over at the roof level not only allows for maximum use of the building's envelope, but also creates a fluid and continuous public space. In this way the project extends the public promenades overlooking the Seine up to the enormous panoramic terrace, facilitating the descent to the river level in a great loop that greatly enhances its continuity."

Am Quai d'Austerlitz im 13. Arrondissement von Paris, gleich gegenüber dem Ministerium für Wirtschaft und Finanzen in Bercy, steht diese im Jahr 1907 errichtete Betonlagerhalle, die zu einem Ausstellungsort für Mode und Design umgebaut wurde. Die Architekten nutzten eine neue Glasleichtbaumethode, das Plug-over-System, um das Bauwerk mit Formen zu aktualisieren, die vom Dahinströmen der Seine inspiriert sind. Im Mittelpunkt des gemischten Raumprogramms stehen die Themen Mode und Design mit Ausstellungsräumen, dem Institut Français de la Mode, Cafés und einem Auditorium. Eine Panoramaterrasse auf dem Flachdach und eine für den Raum konzipierte Außenbeleuchtung garantieren, dass diese neue Stätte nachts ebenso viel Beachtung findet wie tagsüber. Die Dachlandschaft ist als riesige Terrasse öffentlich zugänglich, die von der Plug-over-Konstruktion umhüllten Funktionen wurden bis hier hinauf geführt. Die Architekten kommentieren: „Auf der Dachetage maximiert das Konzept des Plug-over nicht nur die Nutzung der Gebäudehülle, sondern lässt zugleich einen fließenden, kontinuierlichen öffentlichen Raum entstehen. So stellt sich diese Gestaltung als Fortführung der Uferpromenaden hinauf auf die gewaltige Panoramaterrasse dar, von der sie in einem weiten, die Kontinuität des Entwurfs betonenden Bogen erneut zum Uferniveau herabsteigen."

Situé quai d'Austerlitz, dans le 13e arrondissement de Paris, face au ministère des Finances de Bercy, le projet comprend la rénovation d'un entrepôt industriel en béton de 1907 pour en faire un centre de la mode et du design. À l'aide d'un nouveau système de construction légère en verre appelée «plug-over», les architectes ont voulu moderniser le bâtiment avec des formes inspirées par la Seine et ses méandres. L'ensemble mixte est centré sur la mode et le design et abrite des espaces d'exposition, l'école de mode IFM, des cafés et un auditorium. Une terrasse panoramique sur le toit paysager et l'éclairage extérieur spécialement conçu attirent l'attention sur le nouveau bâtiment de nuit comme de jour. La vaste terrasse est accessible au public et prolonge les espaces abrités par le plug-over. Les architectes déclarent : «Le concept de plug-over au niveau du toit permet l'exploitation maximale de l'enveloppe du bâtiment, tout en créant un espace public fluide et continu. En ce sens, le projet prolonge les promenades qui dominent la Seine jusqu'à l'immense terrasse panoramique, tandis qu'une vaste boucle redescend en douceur vers le fleuve et contribue pour beaucoup à la continuité de l'ensemble.»

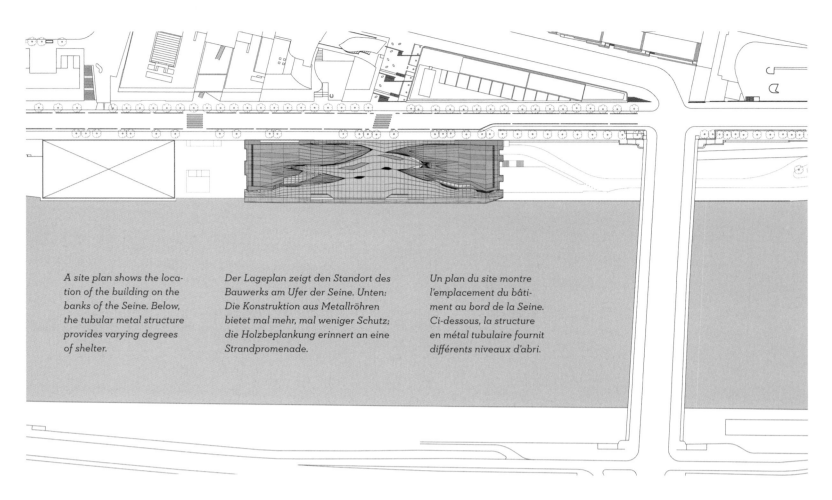

A site plan shows the location of the building on the banks of the Seine. Below, the tubular metal structure provides varying degrees of shelter.

Der Lageplan zeigt den Standort des Bauwerks am Ufer der Seine. Unten: Die Konstruktion aus Metallröhren bietet mal mehr, mal weniger Schutz; die Holzbeplankung erinnert an eine Strandpromenade.

Un plan du site montre l'emplacement du bâtiment au bord de la Seine. Ci-dessous, la structure en métal tubulaire fournit différents niveaux d'abri.

Metal and wood form the topography that
is inhabited by grasses and flowers. A wooden
surface brings to mind a seaside boardwalk.

Aus Metall und Holz entstand die Topografie,
auf der Blumen und Gräser wachsen. Die Holzbeplankung erinnert an eine Strandpromenade.

Bois et métal forment une topographie peuplée
de fleurs et d'herbes. Une surface en bois rappelle
une promenade en bord de mer.

The Hills at Vallco

Address: 10123 N Wolfe Rd, Cupertino, CA 95014, USA, www.thehillsatvallco.com
Area: 1 012 514 m², green roof integrated with a 12-hectare community park
and nature preserve | Client: Sand Hill Property Company | Cost: not disclosed
Collaboration: OLIN Landscape Architects

This project aims to create a vast, open, rooftop space "inspired by the natural ecology of the Cupertino foothills," and located above the existing 20-hectare Vallco Shopping Mall. The outdated, 40-year-old indoor shopping mall, which was 95% empty in June 2016, will be replaced by "a vibrant mixed-use town center and a community park and nature preserve." The complex, which aims for a LEED Platinum rating, will include 800 apartment units, office space for startups, as well as entertainment, retail, sports, and recreation spaces. Twelve hectares of publically accessible rooftop open space will comprise the largest green roof in the world and will include more than six kilometers of "walking/jogging trails, vineyards, orchards, organic gardens, an amphitheater, children's play areas, single-level amenities pavilions, and a refuge for native fauna." The complex is located very close to the large new headquarters of Apple Inc. that is currently under construction (Apple Campus 2, Norman Foster + Partners).

Oben auf der 20 ha großen Vallco Shopping Mall ist diese ausgedehnte, zum Himmel offene Dachlandschaft projektiert, „inspiriert durch die Bergausläufer bei Cupertino". Das vor 40 Jahren errichtete überalterte Einkaufszentrum mit 95 % Leerstand (Juni 2016) soll als „lebendiger Ortskern mit Mischnutzung sowie mit einem Nachbarschaftspark mit Naturflächen" neu erfunden werden. Für den Komplex wird das „LEED Platinum"-Siegel, das höchste Zertifikat für Grünes Bauen in den USA, angestrebt; er soll 800 Wohneinheiten, Büroflächen für Startup-Unternehmen sowie Einzelhandelsflächen, Sportplätze und Möglichkeiten für die aktive und passive Freizeitgestaltung umfassen. Die 12 ha große öffentlich zugängliche Dachfläche wird die weltweit umfangreichste Dachbegrünung umfassen, mit über 6 km „Spazier- und Joggingwegen, Reb- und Obstgärten, Biogemüsegärten, einem Amphitheater, Spielplätzen, eingeschossigen Bauten für diverse Zwecke sowie für die heimische Tierwelt reservierten Flächen". Der Komplex befindet sich in unmittelbarer Nähe der neuen, derzeit im Bau befindlichen Apple-Zentrale (Apple Campus 2, Norman Foster + Partners).

L'objectif du projet est de créer un vaste espace ouvert, « inspiré par l'environnement naturel des montagnes autour de Cupertino » sur le toit du centre commercial Vallco, qui occupe 20 hectares. Le centre commercial intérieur, vieux de 40 ans et désormais un peu dépassé, vide à 95 % en juin 2016, sera remplacé par « un centre de ville vibrant à usage mixte, un parc de quartier et une réserve naturelle. » Le complexe, qui vise la certification LEED Platine, comprendra 800 unités d'appartements, des espaces de bureaux pour startups et des espaces dédiés aux loisirs, au commerce, au sport et à la détente. Douze hectares du toit accessibles au public formeront le plus grand toit végétalisé du monde, avec plus de 6 km de « pistes de marche nordique ou jogging, des vignobles, des vergers, des jardins biologiques, un amphithéâtre, des terrains de jeux pour les enfants, des pavillons de services et un refuge pour la faune locale. » L'ensemble est situé à proximité immédiate du nouveau siège d'Apple Inc., actuellement en construction (Apple Campus 2, Norman Foster + Partners).

Above, a computer-generated image evokes the integration of the architecture of the complex into the rooftop gardens. Below, a sketch by Rafael Viñoly shows The Hills at Vallco in the foreground and the enormous ring of Norman Foster's Apple Campus 2 in the background.

Oben: Die computergerenderte Abbildung zeigt, wie sich die Architektur des Gebäudekomplexes mit den Dachgärten verzahnt. Unten: Auf der Zeichnung von Rafael Viñoly sieht man The Hills at Vallco im Vordergrund und dahinter die gewaltige Ringstruktur von Norman Fosters Apple Campus 2.

Ci-dessus, une image générée par ordinateur montre l'intégration de l'architecture dans les jardins sur le toit. Ci-dessous, un schéma de Rafael Viñoly montre au premier plan les collines de Vallco et l'immense anneau du Campus 2 d'Apple par Norman Foster à l'arrière-plan.

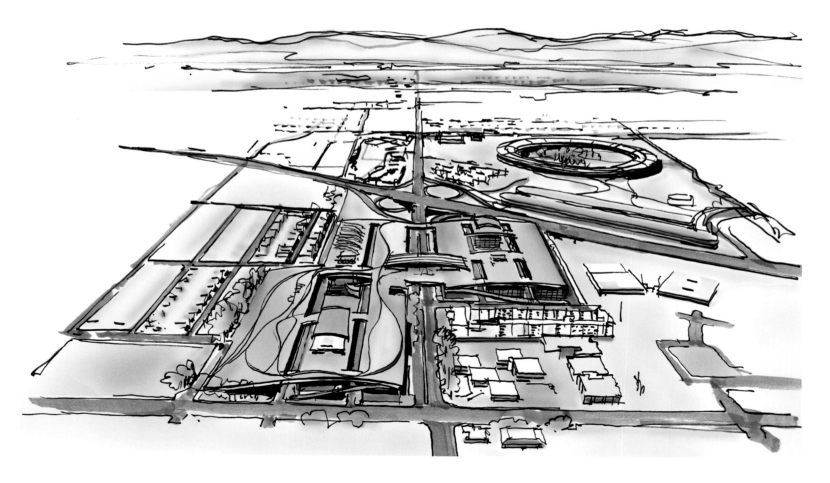

The rooftop gardens include nearly 6.5 kilometers of trails, vineyards, orchards, organic gardens, an amphitheater, children's play areas, amenities pavilions, and a refuge for native wildlife.

Die Dachgärten verfügen über nicht ganz 6,5 km Spazierwege, dazu Reb- und Obstgärten, Biogemüse-gärten, ein Amphitheater, Spielplätze, niedrige Bauten für diverse Zwecke sowie Flächen, die der heimischen Tierwelt vorbehalten sind.

Les jardins sur le toit comprennent 6,5 km de pistes, des vignobles, des vergers, des jardins biologiques, un amphithéâtre, des terrains de jeux pour les enfants, des pavillons de services et un refuge pour la faune locale.

Given its large scale, the rooftop garden should "reduce the urban heat island effect, improve public health, minimize water run-off, improve water and air quality, improve energy efficiency of the buildings, and promote bio-diversity."

Dank seiner gewaltigen Ausmaße soll der Dachgarten „den städtischen Wärmeinseleffekt reduzieren, die Gesundheit der Bevölkerung fördern, den Regenwasserabfluss minimieren, die Wasser- und Luftqualität verbessern, die Energieeffizienz der Gebäude verbessern und die Biodiversität fördern."

La grande taille du jardin sur le toit doit lui permettre de « réduire l'effet d'îlot thermique urbain, contribuer à une meilleure santé publique, contenir les écoulements d'eau, améliorer la qualité de l'eau et de l'air, accroître l'efficacité énergétique des bâtiments et promouvoir la biodiversité. »

BIG / JDS
Copenhagen [DENMARK]
2006–08

The Mountain

Address: Ørestads Boulevard 55, 2300 Copenhagen S, Denmark
Area: 33 000 m² | Client: Høpfner A/S, Danish Oil Company A/S
Cost: €34.873 million | Collaboration: Moe & Brødsgaard

The Mountain is an unusual project in that two thirds of its space is reserved to parking and only one third to housing. The idea of BIG and JDS was to create a kind of concrete hillside "covered by a thin layer of housing, cascading from the 1st to the 11th floor. Rather than doing two separate buildings next to each other—a parking block and a housing block—we decided to merge the two functions into a symbiotic relationship," say the architects. All of the apartments in this complex have "roof gardens facing the sun, amazing views, and street parking on the 10th floor." Conceived like a series of garden homes on top of a 10-story building, the concept provides for "suburban living with urban density." This idea is all the more surprising because Copenhagen is essentially flat, built largely on reclaimed land. Rainwater is recycled and used for drip irrigation of the extensive rooftop planters.

The Mountain ist insofern ein ungewöhnliches Projekt, als zwei Drittel davon als Parkhaus genutzt werden und lediglich ein Drittel als Wohnraum. BIG und JDS wollten eine Art Betonhügel schaffen, der „von einer dünnen Häuserschicht bedeckt ist, die von der 1. zur 11. Etage ansteigt. Anstatt zwei separate Bauten – ein Parkhaus und ein Wohnhaus – nebeneinanderzusetzen, beschlossen wir, beide Funktionen symbiotisch miteinander zu vereinen", erläutern die Architekten. Sämtliche Wohneinheiten in diesem Komplex verfügen über „zur Sonne ausgerichtete Dachgärten, einen überwältigenden Ausblick und einen wohnungsnahen Pkw-Stellplatz auf der 10. Etage." Das als Einfamilienhäuser mit Garten auf einem zehnstöckigen Gebäude konzipierte Projekt bietet „Vorstadtleben in urbaner Dichte". Das Konzept ist umso ungewöhnlicher, als Kopenhagen eigentlich flach ist, denn diese Stadt entstand auf größtenteils dem Meer abgetrotzten Flächen. Regenwasser wird gesammelt und über eine Tröpfchenbewässerungsanlage den großen Pflanztöpfen auf den Dächern zugeführt.

The Mountain est un projet inhabituel qui réserve les deux tiers de son espace aux parkings et un tiers seulement aux logements. L'idée de BIG et JDS était de créer un flanc de coteau en béton «couvert d'une fine couche de logements cascadant du 1er au 11e niveau. Plutôt que deux bâtiments distincts l'un à côté de l'autre – un pour le parking et un pour les appartements –, nous avons décidé de faire fusionner les deux fonctions en une relation symbiotique», expliquent les architectes. Les appartements ont tous des «jardins sur le toit face au soleil, des vues fantastiques et une place de stationnement sur rue au 10e niveau». Conçu comme une série de maisons avec jardin en haut d'un immeuble de 10 niveaux, l'ensemble permet de concilier la «vie suburbaine et la densité urbaine». L'idée est d'autant plus surprenante que Copenhague est une ville extrêmement plate, construite en grande partie sur des terrains gagnés sur la mer. L'eau de pluie est récupérée pour l'irrigation goutte-à-goutte des vastes jardinières du toit.

A section drawing shows how the residences are placed on top of the parking facility. Every rooftop is planted or offers terrace space to the apartments above.

Im Querschnitt erkennt man, wie die Wohneinheiten über den Parkflächen angeordnet sind. Alle Dachflächen sind entweder begrünt oder werden als Terrassenfläche für die Wohnungen darüber genutzt.

Un schéma en coupe montre comment les logements sont agencés au-dessus du parking. Les toits sont plantés ou forment la terrasse des appartements situés au-dessus.

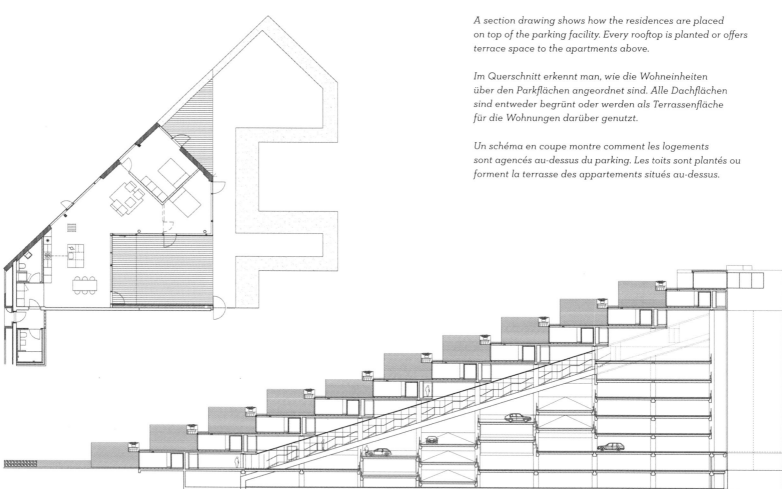

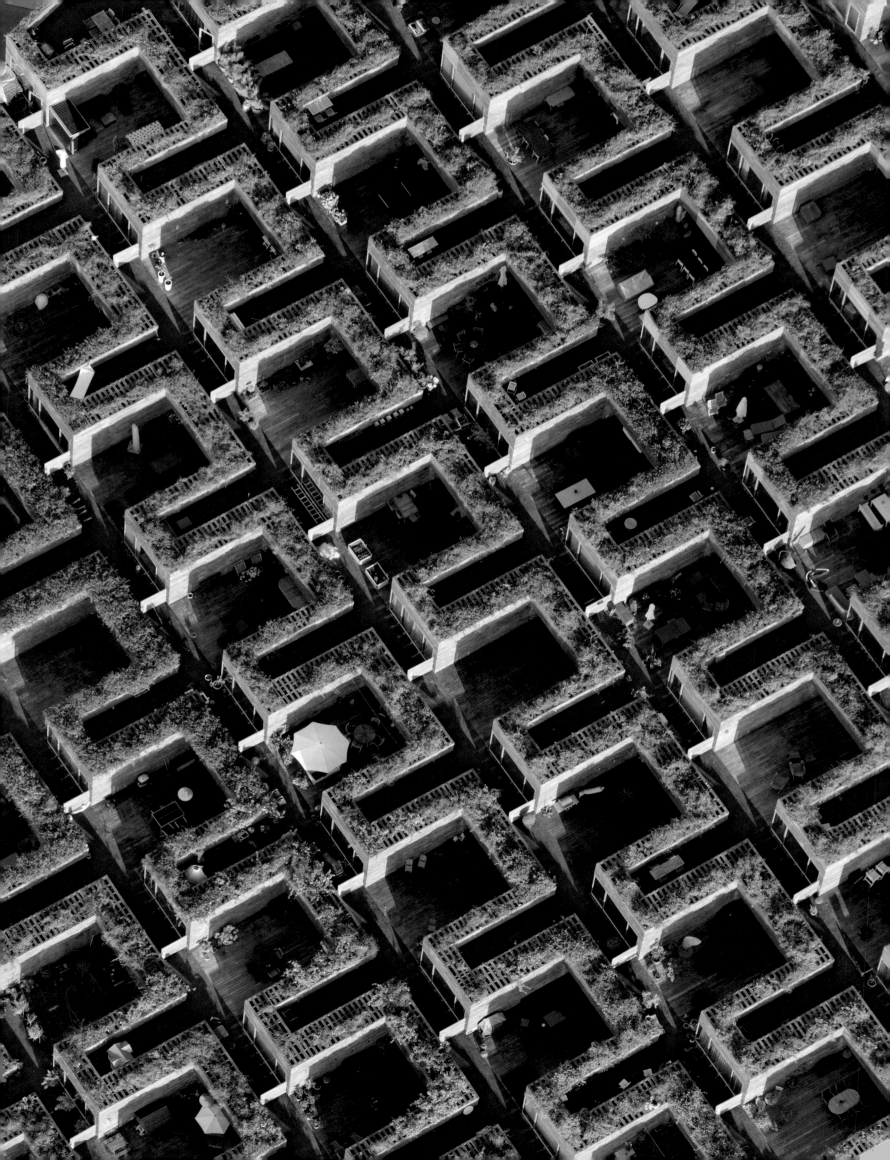

The density of the planting and the arrangement of the apartments give private space to every residence, as well as views of the city.

Durch die dichte Begrünung und die Anordnung der Wohnungen hat jede Einheit ihre Privatsphäre und einen Ausblick auf die Stadt.

La densité de la végétation et la disposition des appartements permettent à chacun de disposer de son espace personnel et de vues sur la ville.

In this side view, the disguised volume of the large parking lot appears as the angled surface on which the apartment units sit. The parking lot is what gives the mountain-like appearance to the building.

In dieser Seitenansicht stellt sich der versteckte Baukörper des großen Parkhauses als geneigte Fläche dar, auf der die Wohnungen stehen. Dem Parkhaus verdankt das Gebäude seine bergartige Anmutung.

Dans cette vue latérale, le volume dissimulé de l'immense parking prend la forme anguleuse qui sert de base aux appartements. C'est le parking qui donne au complexe sa forme de montagne.

GUNN LANDSCAPE ARCHITECTURE
New York, New York [USA]
2013

Tribeca Roof Terrace

*Address: not disclosed | Area: 186 m² | Client: not disclosed
Cost: not disclosed | Collaboration: Pembrooke & Ives (Architect),
Vert Gardens, Inc. (Installation and Maintenance)*

In this area surrounded by historic buildings, the architects created an enclave encircled by perimeter planting, used by the owner to entertain family and friends. Garden elements in containers are used to "soften the straight-lined geometry" of the existing space, while "a green roof brings a dose of zen answering the owner's adoration for more natural materials along with a sense of a forested setting fit for the urban context." A custom-designed step-up spa "takes advantage of a long linear space lined with a dense canopy of bamboo, becoming a connector for the areas off the master bedroom and living room." Tribeca, or the "Triangle below Canal" Street, is not far north from the site of the World Trade Center, as the presence of the Freedom Tower in an image here attests.

An diesem von historischen Gebäuden umgebenen Standort schufen die Architekten eine Enklave, die von Pflanzen eingefasst ist und in der die Eigentümer gern Familie und Freunde empfangen. Pflanzen in großen Töpfen lassen „die harte Geometrie" des Raums sanfter erscheinen, das „grüne Dach entspricht mit einer Dosis Zen der Liebe der Eigentümer zu natürlicheren Materialien und bringt gleichzeitig ein bisschen stadtgerechte Waldstimmung mit sich". Ein maßgefertigter Whirlpool „nutzt einen langen, schmalen, von dichtem Bambus gesäumten Weg, der die Bereiche vor dem Schlafraum und dem Wohnzimmer verbindet". Tribeca, das „Triangle below Canal Street", liegt nur wenig weiter nördlich als der einstige Standort des World Trade Center – gut zu erkennen an dem Freedom Tower, der auf einem der Fotos zu sehen ist.

Dans cette zone entourée de bâtiments historiques, les architectes ont créé une enclave encerclée par les plantations dans laquelle le propriétaire reçoit sa famille et ses amis. Des éléments de jardin dans des grandes jardinières «adoucissent la géométrie en lignes droites» de l'espace, tandis qu'«un toit végétalisé apporte une touche zen en réponse à l'amour du propriétaire pour les matériaux naturels, et insuffle une impression de décor forestier adapté au contexte urbain». Un spa surélevé sur mesure «tire profit d'un long espace linéaire doublé d'une épaisse voûte de bambou et fait le lien entre la chambre principale et le salon». La Tribeca ou «Triangle below Canal» Street, n'est pas très éloignée vers le sud du World Trade Center, comme en témoigne la présence de la Freedom Tower sur l'une des photos.

Right, a plan of the terrace areas and, on the left page, a view looking in the direction of the Freedom Tower at the former World Trade Center site.

Rechts: Grundriss der Terrassenbereiche. Links: Blick in Richtung des Freedom Tower am früheren Standort des World Trade Center.

À droite, plan des terrasses et page de gauche, vue dans la direction de la Freedom Tower, sur le site de l'ancien World Trade Center.

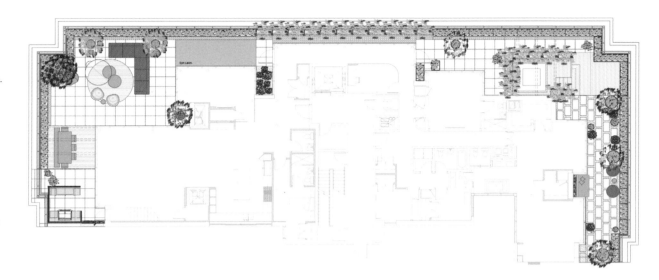

Below, gravel, stepping stones, and plants animate the narrow passages on the sides of the terrace (visible in the drawing above as well).

Unten: Kiesel, Trittsteine und Pflanzen beleben die schmalen Durchgänge entlang der Terrasse, wie auch auf der Zeichnung oben zu sehen ist.

Ci-dessous les graviers, pierres de gué et plantes animent les étroits passages sur les côtés de la terrasse (représentés aussi sur le schéma ci-dessus).

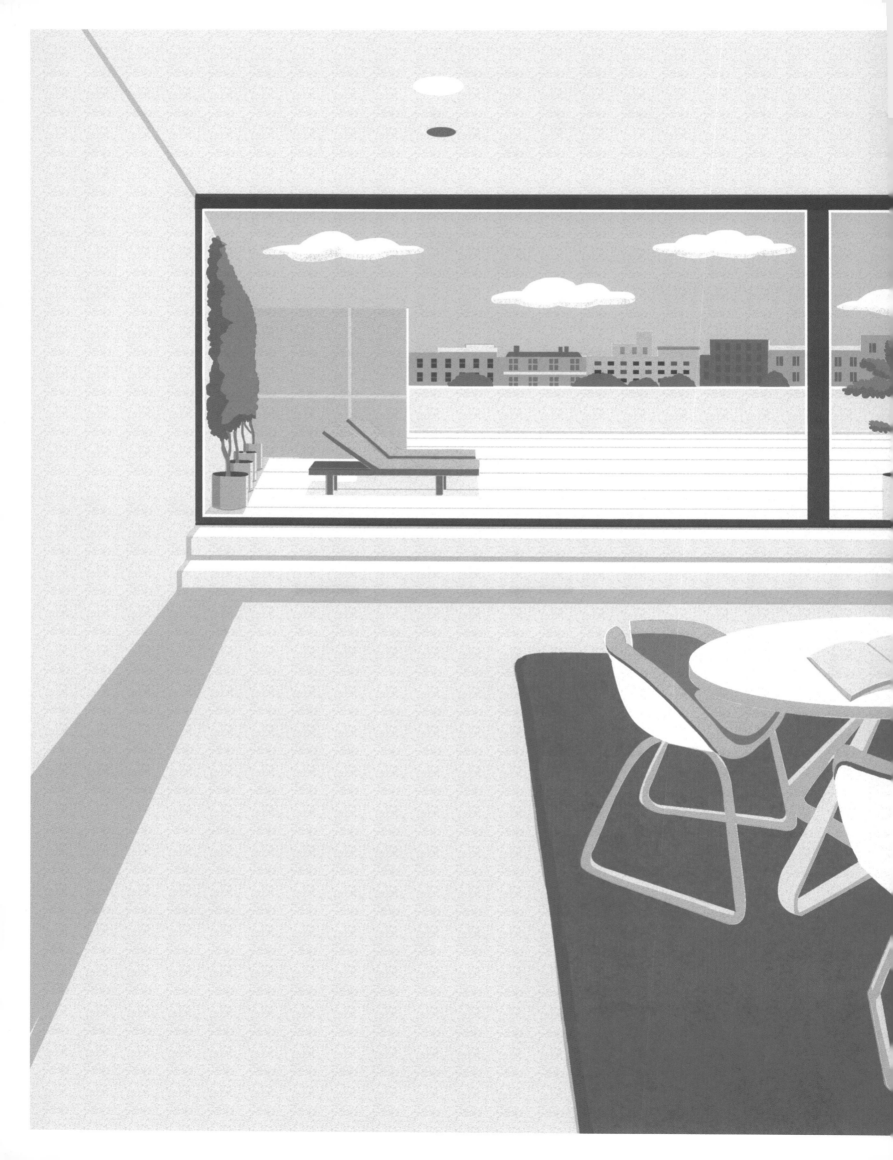

DELUGAN MEISSL
Vienna [AUSTRIA]
2013

TS 11

Address: not disclosed | Area: 200 m² | Client: not disclosed
Cost: not disclosed

This generously glazed penthouse seeks to dissolve the borders between interior and exterior. The architects state: "The occupant becomes a part of the urban fabric, the urban fabric a part of the interior." Inside, the living spaces form a continuum with slightly different floor levels for the seating area or dining space. White surfaces and black elements dominate the interior, with a use of Corian. A monolithic kitchen element made of black stone echoes an equally dark wall with individually configured shelves. The white bedroom space includes an integrated bathroom, conveying "a feeling of calmness and relaxation" according to the architects. A south-facing terrace is also finished and includes such elements as a cantilevered water basin and green spaces.

Dieses mit großzügigen Glasflächen versehene Penthouse will die Grenze zwischen drinnen und draußen auflösen. Die Architekten kommentieren: „Der Bewohner wird eins mit dem Stadtgefüge, das Stadtgefüge zum Teil des Innenraums." Die Wohnräume bilden ein Kontinuum mit leicht variierter Bodenhöhe für den Sitz- und den Essbereich. Weiße Oberflächen mit schwarzen Akzenten unter Verwendung von Corian dominieren die Innengestaltung. Ein monolithischer Küchenblock aus schwarzem Stein findet sein Echo in einer ebenso dunklen Wand mit einzeln angeordneten Ablagen. Der weiße Schlafraum mit dem integrierten Bad vermittelt ein Gefühl der „Ruhe und Entspannung", so die Architekten. Auch die nach Süden gewandte Terrasse ist vollständig gepflastert und verfügt über ein freitragendes Wasserbecken und Pflanzen.

L'appartement de standing aux vitrages généreux cherche à résorber les frontières entre intérieur et extérieur. Pour les architectes : « L'occupant devient une partie du tissu urbain, le tissu urbain une partie de l'intérieur. » Les espaces à vivre forment un tout continu avec de légères différences de niveau entre le coin salon et le coin repas. Les surfaces blanches et le mobilier noir dominent, ainsi que le Corian. Un élément de cuisine monolithique en pierre noire répond à un mur tout aussi noir garni d'étagères à la disposition personnalisée. La chambre toute blanche comprend une salle de bains intégrée qui, selon les architectes, transmet « un sentiment de calme et de relaxation ». Une terrasse au sud est, elle aussi, parfaitement décorée avec divers aménagements tels un bassin en porte-à-faux et des espaces verts.

Below and right, the added apartment seen in section and plan.

Unten und rechts: Querschnitt und Grundriss des Apartments auf dem Dach.

Ci-dessous et à droite, l'appartement en coupe et plan.

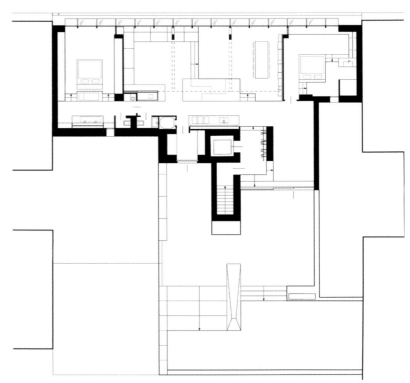

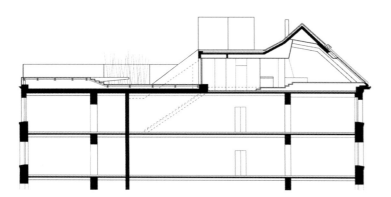

In the photo below, the white spaces of a bathroom blend seamlessly with the low bed and the large, angled windows. Right, the kitchen and living space.

Unten: Der weiße Badbereich und das niedrige Bett mit den großen, abgewinkelten Fensterwänden gehen nahtlos ineinander über. Rechts: Küche und Wohnbereich.

Sur la photo ci-dessous, les espaces blancs de la salle de bains se fondent en douceur avec le lit bas et la vaste fenêtre inclinée. À droite, la cuisine et le salon.

STEFANO BOERI
Milan [ITALY]
2008–14

Vertical Forest

Address: Via Gaetano de Castillia 9–11/Via Confalonieri 6, 20124 Milan, Italy,
www.residenzeportanuova.com | Area: 16 011 m² (tower E), 8045 m² (tower D)
Client: Hines Italia | Cost: not disclosed

Part of a broader urban renovation project carried out by Hines in Milan, the Vertical Forest (Il Bosco Verticale) by Boeri Studio includes two towers respectively 80 and 112 meters in height and was inaugurated in 2014. The towers were designed for a total of 460 inhabitants, but also include 780 trees, 5000 shrubs, 11 000 perennial plants, and, it seems, 1600 birds and butterflies. The reference to birds and butterflies is a pointer to the architect's ideas that such projects increase biodiversity. Boeri writes: "The biological architect relies on a screen of vegetation, needing to create a suitable microclimate and filter sunlight, and rejecting the narrow technological and mechanical approach to environmental sustainability." The vegetation was studied by the architects together with botanists and the plants were cultivated in a nursery in conditions similar to those that exist on the towers. The changing colors of the foliage also permit the towers to change in appearance with the passing seasons. These towers clearly change the urban roofscape with their gardens at every level.

Der Mailänder Bosco Verticale (der vertikale Wald) von Boeri Studio ist Teil eines umfassenden Stadterneuerungsprojekts durch das Büro Hines und wurde 2014 eingeweiht. Die beiden Wohntürme von 80 m bzw. 112 m Höhe sind für 460 Bewohner ausgelegt, es gibt darüber hinaus aber noch 780 Bäume, 5000 Sträucher, 11 000 Stauden sowie offenbar 1600 Vögel und Schmetterlinge. Indem er auch Vögel und Schmetterlinge erwähnt, will der Architekt darauf hinweisen, dass ein Projekt dieser Art zu größerer Biodiversität beitragen kann. Boeri schreibt: „Anstatt sich auf einen engen technologischen Nachhaltigkeitsansatz zu verlassen, setzt der Bioarchitekt auf einen grünen Paravent, der das passende Mikroklima schafft und das Sonnenlicht mildert." Gemeinsam mit Botanikern befassten sich die Architekten mit der Begrünung; die Pflanzen wurden in einer Gärtnerei unter Bedingungen herangezogen, die denen auf den Türmen vergleichbar waren. Die Färbung des Laubs lässt im Lauf des Jahres die Türme immer wieder anders aussehen. Mit Gärten auf jeder Etage verändern diese Hochhäuser die urbane Dachlandschaft ganz eindeutig.

Réalisée dans le cadre d'un projet plus vaste de rénovation urbaine mené à bien par Hines à Milan, la Forêt verticale (Il Bosco Verticale) de Boeri Studio comprend deux tours hautes de 80 et 112 m et a été inaugurée en 2014. Conçues pour loger 460 habitants, les tours accueillent aussi 780 arbres, 5000 arbustes, 11 000 plantes vivaces et, apparemment, 1600 oiseaux et papillons. La mention des oiseaux et papillons fait référence aux réflexions de l'architecte selon lesquelles ce type de projet fait progresser la biodiversité. Boeri a notamment écrit : « L'architecte biologique mise sur un écran végétal pour créer un microclimat adapté et filtrer les rayons du soleil, il rejette l'approche purement technologique et mécanique de la durabilité environnementale. » Les architectes ont étudié la question de la végétation avec des botanistes et les plantes ont été cultivées en pépinière dans des conditions semblables à celles qui règnent sur les tours. Les couleurs changeantes du feuillage confèrent aux bâtiments une apparence différente selon les saisons. Avec leurs jardins à tous les étages, les tours transforment incontestablement le paysage des toits urbains.

The towers are heavily planted, right up to the uppermost level. In a sense the terraces are like a succession of planted rooftops, each hanging above the apartment below.

Die Türme sind bis zum obersten Stockwerk dicht begrünt. Die Terrassen sind begrünten Dächern vergleichbar, die jeweils das darunter-gelegene Apartment beschatten.

Les tours sont densément plantées jusqu'au dernier étage. Les terrasses sont comme une succession de toits végétalisés, chacun suspendu au-dessus de l'appartement d'en dessous.

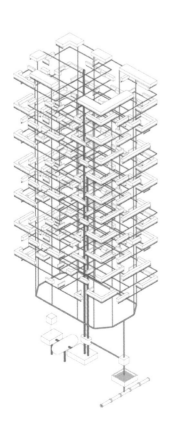

Below, a plan shows the relation
of the two buildings and the extent of
their green areas.

*Unten: Der Plan zeigt, wie die beiden
Gebäude ausgerichtet sind und über wie
viel Grünfläche sie verfügen.*

*Ci-dessous, un plan montre le rapport
entre les deux bâtiments et l'étendue de
leurs espaces verts.*

On the right page, the exceptional density
of the plantings is evident: if not a vertical
forest, then at very least they form a vertical garden.

*Rechts: Hier wird deutlich, wie außeror-
dentlich dicht die Begrünung ist – wenn
sie auch kein echter vertikaler Wald ist, so
doch auf jeden Fall ein vertikaler Garten.*

*Page de droite, la densité exceptionnelle de
la végétation saute aux yeux : elle forme,
sinon une forêt verticale, tout au moins un
jardin vertical.*

GHIORA AHARONI
New York [USA]
2008–09

West Village Penthouse

Address: not disclosed | Area: 139 m² indoor/outdoor
Client: not disclosed | Cost: not disclosed

This project involved the complete renovation of a pre-war apartment in a landmark building into a duplex penthouse. Roof space was added offering an additional indoor/outdoor living area. An intentional ambiguity between inside and out is maintained through such elements as the color scheme and wooden floors that continue outside. South-facing floor-to-ceiling folding glass doors open, creating a nine-meter-wide portal. A rotating interior fireplace warms both inside and out. The open-air living area includes an outdoor kitchen. In the evening, twin beams of light rise up from concealed coves inside the skylights. The designer writes: "The high parapet, punctured by four horizontal windows, and 24 birch trees planted along the roof edges create an outdoor room framed by the open sky."

Dieses Projekt beinhaltete die Komplettrenovierung einer aus Vorkriegszeiten stammenden Wohnung in einem denkmalgeschützten Bau zu einem Zwei-Parteien-Penthouse. Auf der neu erschlossenen Dachfläche entstand zusätzlicher Wohnraum, teils drinnen, teils draußen, wobei die Fortführung von Farbkonzept und Holzböden in den Außenraum die Abgrenzung der beiden Bereiche bewusst vage hält. Deckenhohe Glasfalttüren öffnen sich auf der Südseite zu einem 9 m breiten Portal. Ein schwenkbarer Innenkamin lässt seine Wärme bis nach draußen strahlen. Zum Außenbereich gehört unter anderem eine Freiluftküche. In Dachfensternischen untergebrachte verdeckte Strahler erhellen die Abende mit indirektem Licht. Der Designer kommentiert: „Die hohe, von vier waagerechten Fensterbändern durchbrochene Brüstung und 24 Birken an den Schmalseiten definieren ein Freiluftzimmer, über dem nichts als der weite Himmel steht."

Le projet comprend la rénovation totale d'un appartement d'avant-guerre dans un immeuble typique et sa transformation en un duplex de standing. Un espace sur le toit a été ajouté pour un séjour intérieur/extérieur supplémentaire. Certains éléments du décor, tels la gamme de couleurs et les planchers qui se prolongent au dehors, entretiennent délibérément une certaine ambiguïté entre intérieur et extérieur. Les portes pliantes vitrées du sol au plafond ouvrent au sud, créant un portail de 9 m de large. À l'intérieur, une cheminée rotative chauffe aussi l'extérieur. Le séjour en plein air comporte une cuisine. Le soir, des faisceaux lumineux jumeaux s'élèvent de recoins dissimulés dans les lucarnes. Le designer a écrit : « Le haut parapet percé de quatre fenêtres horizontales et les 24 bouleaux qui longent les avancées du toit créent une pièce extérieure encadrée par le vaste ciel. »

The warm wood employed for the outdoor terrace, together with plants, gives an enclosed comfort to the space which nonetheless reveals a typical Manhattan skyline in the distance.

Die warmen Holztöne und die Begrünung verleihen der Außenterrasse eine angenehme abgeschlossene Wohnlichkeit, ohne den Blick auf die typische Skyline von Manhattan in der Ferne zu verstellen.

La chaleur du bois utilisé pour la terrasse, avec les plantes, confère un confort clos à cet espace qui n'en révèle pas moins la silhouette caractéristique de Manhattan au loin.

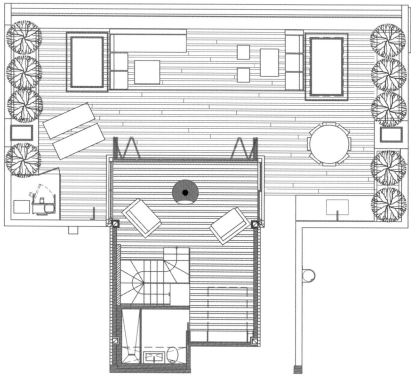

Left, a plan of the terrace areas. Large opening windows and a louvered canopy emphasize the intentional ambiguity between interior and exterior—at least in the warmer months.

Links: Grundriss der Terrassenfläche. Große, zu öffnende Fenster und ein Lamellenvordach unterstreichen die bewusst unklare Trennung von drinnen und draußen – zumindest in der wärmeren Jahreszeit.

À gauche, plan des terrasses. De vastes fenêtres et un auvent à claire-voie soulignent l'ambiguïté voulue entre l'intérieur et l'extérieur - au moins pendant les mois les plus chauds de l'année.

GHIORA AHARONI

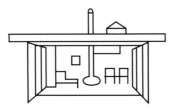

Ghiora Aharoni Design Studio
276 Fifth Avenue, Suite 1100
New York, NY 10001
USA

Tel: +1 212 255 1511
E-mail: info@ghiora-aharoni.com
Web: www.ghiora-aharoni.com

Ghiora Aharoni was born in Rehovot, Israel, in 1969, and has been a US resident since 1991. He holds an M.Arch degree from Yale (2001) and a B.Arch from the Spitzer School of Architecture (City College, New York, 1998). He founded his multidisciplinary studio in New York City in 2004, after working in several architectural firms, including Polshek Partnership (now called Ennead Architects) and Studio Daniel Libeskind, and was a member of the winning design competition team with Zaha Hadid and Arata Isozaki for the building and urban planning of the Fiera Convention Center (Milan, Italy, 2004). He has designed numerous architectural projects in New York, including the De Kooning residence; a duplex penthouse in the West Village (2008–09; see p. 366); the offices of an art law firm on 57th Street (2013); and a storefront studio/performance space in Williamsburg (2015). Aharoni's furniture designs are in a number of private collections. His artwork has been exhibited in New York and India, and is in private collections in the USA, India, and Europe. His solo museum exhibition, *Missives*, was seen at the Dr. Bhau Daji Lad Museum (formerly the Victoria and Albert Museum) in Mumbai (India, 2013).

SHIGERU BAN

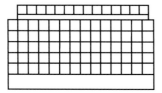

Shigeru Ban Architects
5-2-4 Matsubara
Setagaya-ku
Tokyo 156-0043
Japan

Tel: +81 3 3324 6760
Fax: +81 3 3324 6789
E-mail: tokyo@shigerubanarchitects.com
Web: www.shigerubanarchitects.com

Born in 1957 in Tokyo, Shigeru Ban studied at SCI-Arc from 1977 to 1980. He then attended the Cooper Union School of Architecture, where he studied under John Hejduk (1980–82), returning to graduate in 1984, after working in the office of Arata Isozaki for a year. He then founded his own firm in Tokyo in 1985. He designed the Japanese Pavilion at Expo 2000 in Hannover. His work includes the disaster relief Post-Tsunami Rehabilitation Houses (Kirinda, Hambantota, Sri Lanka, 2005); the Nicolas G. Hayek Center (Tokyo, Japan, 2007); Haesley Nine Bridges Golf Clubhouse (Yeoju, South Korea, 2009); the Paper Tube Tower (London, UK, 2009); and the Metal Shutter House on West 19th Street in New York (New York, USA, 2010). He installed his Paper Temporary Studio on top of the Centre Pompidou in Paris to work on the new Centre Pompidou-Metz (Metz, France, 2010). Recent work includes L'Aquila Temporary Concert Hall (L'Aquila, Italy, 2011); Container Temporary Housing, disaster relief project for the east Japan earthquake and tsunami (Miyagi, Japan, 2011); Tamedia (Zurich, Switzerland, 2011–13); the Cardboard Cathedral (Christchurch, New Zealand, 2013); Aspen Art Museum (Aspen, Colorado, USA, 2014); and Oita Prefectural Art Museum (Oita, Japan, 2015). Current work includes the Swatch Group Headquarters and Production Facility (Bienne, Switzerland, 2012–16); the Cast Iron House (New York, New York, USA, 2013–16; see p. 66); and the Cité Musicale (Île Seguin, Boulogne-Billancourt, France, 2016).

BIG

BIG-Bjarke Ingels Group
Kløverbladsgade 56
2500 Valby
Copenhagen
Denmark

Tel: +45 72 21 72 27
E-mail: big@big.dk
Web: www.big.dk

Bjarke Ingels was born in 1974 in Copenhagen, Denmark. He graduated from the Royal Academy of Arts School of Architecture (Copenhagen, 1999) and attended the ETSAB School of Architecture (Barcelona). He created his own office in 2005 under the name Bjarke Ingels Group (BIG), after having cofounded PLOT Architects in 2001 and collaborated with Rem Koolhaas at OMA (Rotterdam). Today, BIG is based in New York and Copenhagen, and has 12 partners and 17 associates, with an international team of 300 people. The Mountain (Copenhagen, Denmark, 2006–08; see p. 336), designed by BIG in collaboration with JDS Architects, received numerous awards, including the World Architecture Festival Housing Award, Forum Aid Award, and the MIPIM Residential Development Award. The firm has also designed the Danish Expo Pavilion (Shanghai, China, 2010); Superkilen Master Plan (Copenhagen, Denmark, 2011); the Maritime Museum of Denmark (Elsinore, Denmark, 2007–13); and the Gammel Hellerup Gymnasium (Copenhagen, Denmark, 2013). Current work includes Grove at Grand Bay (Miami, Florida, USA, 2013–16); W57 NY (New York, New York, USA, 2016); Shenzhen International Energy Mansion (Shenzhen, China, 2013–17); the Amager Bakke Resource Center (Copenhagen, Denmark, 2009–18); and Two World Trade Center (New York, New York, USA, 2021).

STEFANO BOERI

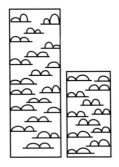

Stefano Boeri Architetti
Via G. Donizetti 4
Milan 20122
Italy

Tel: +39 02 55 01 41 01
Fax: +39 02 36 76 91 85
E-mail: studio@stefanoboeriarchitetti.net
Web: www.stefanoboeriarchitetti.net

Stefano Boeri was born in 1956, studied architecture in Milan, and in 1989 received his Ph.D. from the IUAV in Venice, Italy. Stefano Boeri has been the Editor-in-Chief of the magazines *Domus* (2004–07) and *Abitare* (2007–11), and was an architectural consultant for Expo 2015 in Milan. Boeri is Professor of Urban Design at the Milan Polytechnic Institute, and has taught as Visiting Professor at Harvard GSD, MIT, and at the Berlage Institute in Amsterdam among others. Boeri is the founder of Multiplicity, an international research network focused on the transformation of European urban areas. Stefano Boeri is the Principal and founder of Stefano Boeri Architetti (SBA), based in Milan, and with studios in Shanghai and Doha. The studio (called Boeri Studio until 2008) has completed projects including the refurbishment of Italy's oldest mall (Cinisello Balsamo, Milan, 2008); the renovation of the former Arsenale in La Maddalena (Sardinia, 2008–09); a housing project on the outskirts of Milan (Seregno, 2009); and the new RCS – Corriere della Sera Headquarters (Milan, 2003–11), all in Italy. Boeri's two "eco compatible" residential towers (Vertical Forest, 2008–14; see p. 358) were recently completed in Milan; and the "Villa Mediterranee," a multifunctional building for the PACA Region on the Marseille Waterfront (France) was also completed in 2014.

ALBERTO CAMPO BAEZA

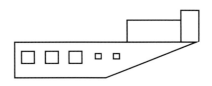

Estudio de Arquitectura Campo Baeza
C/ Almirante 4, 5ºB
28004 Madrid
Spain

Tel: +34 91 701 06 95
E-mail: estudio@campobaeza.com
Web: www.campobaeza.com

Born in Valladolid, Spain, in 1946, Alberto Campo Baeza studied in Madrid where he obtained his Ph.D. in 1982 (ETSAM). He has taught in Madrid, at the ETH in Zurich (1989-90), at Cornell University, at the University of Pennsylvania (1986 and 1999), and at ETSAM, where he has served as Head Professor of Design. His work includes the Fene Town Hall (1980); and the BIT Center in Mallorca (1998); as well as a number of private houses, such as the Belvedere, De Blas House (Sevilla de la Nueva, Madrid, 2000). In 2001, he completed what he considers his most representative building, the Headquarters of the Caja General de Ahorros de Granada. Other work includes the Montecarmelo Public School (Madrid, 2006); Olnik Spanu House (Garrison, New York, USA, 2005-07); Falla Square Housing (Cadiz, 2007); Centro de Interpretación Salinas de Janubio (Lanzarote, 2008); San Sebastián Castle (Cadiz, 2008); Between Two Cathedrals (Cadiz, 2009); and Offices for Benetton (Samara, Russia, 2009). More recently he finished Offices for the Junta de Castilla y León (Zamora, 2008-12); the House of the Infinite (VT House, Cadiz, 2014, see p. 136); and the Raumplan House (Madrid, 2015), all in Spain unless stated otherwise.

CETRARUDDY

CetraRuddy Architecture
584 Broadway Suite 401
New York, NY 10012
USA

Tel: +1 212 941 9801
E-mail: marketing@cetraruddy.com
Web: www.cetraruddy.com

John Cetra and Nancy Ruddy cofounded Cetra-Rudy in 1987. John Cetra received his B.Arch degree from the Spitzer School of Architecture of the City College of New York and his Master's degree in Architecture and Urban Design from the Harvard GSD. Nancy Ruddy received an undergraduate degree in Architectural History from New York University and a B.A. from the City College of New York. Branko Potocnik is a Senior Interior Designer at CetraRuddy and received his Bachelor's degree in Interior Architecture from the University of Arts (Belgrade, Serbia). Their recent work includes SushiSamba (London, UK, 2013; see p. 316); Lincoln Square Synagogue (New York, New York, USA, 2014); and the Galleria Hotel (Jeddah, Saudi Arabia, 2015). Ongoing projects include 242 West 53rd Street (New York, New York, USA, 2016); and the Choice School (Thiruvalla, India, 2018).

DELUGAN MEISSL

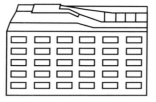

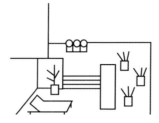

Delugan Meissl Associated Architects
Mittersteig 13/4
1040 Vienna
Austria

Tel: +43 1 585 36 90
Fax: +43 1 585 36 90 11
E-mail: communication@dmaa.at
Web: www.dmaa.at

Delugan-Meissl ZT GmbH was jointly founded by Elke Delugan-Meissl and Roman Delugan in 1993. In 2004, the firm expanded into a partnership and its name changed to Delugan Meissl Associated Architects. Elke Delugan-Meissl was born in Linz, Austria, and studied at the University of Technology in Innsbruck. She worked in several offices in Innsbruck and Vienna, before founding Delugan Meissl. Roman Delugan was born in Merano, Italy, and studied at the University of Applied Arts in Vienna. Dietmar Feistel was born in Bregenz, Austria, and studied at the Polytechnic in Vienna. He became a Partner at Delugan Meissl in 2004. Martin Josst was born in Hamburg, Germany, and studied at the Muthesius Academy of Art and Design in Kiel, Germany, before working in the office of Morphosis in Los Angeles and becoming a Partner at Delugan Meissl in 2004. They have completed the Porsche Museum (Stuttgart, Germany, 2006-08); the EYE Film Institute (Amsterdam, the Netherlands, 2009-11); the Festival Hall of the Tiroler Festspiele (Erl, Austria, 2010-13); and a number of residential projects in Vienna, including Ray 1 (2003) and TS 11 (2013), both published here, see pp. 240, 350. Current work includes the refurbishment and extension of the Badisches Staatstheater Karlsruhe (Karlsruhe, Germany, 2015-); and the Taiyuan Botanical Garden (Taiyuan, China, 2016-).

DILLER SCOFIDIO + RENFRO

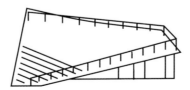

Diller Scofidio + Renfro
601 West 26th Street, Suite 1815
New York, NY 10001
USA

Tel: +1 212 260 7971
E-mail: disco@dsrny.com
Web: www.dsrny.com

Elizabeth Diller was born in Lodz, Poland, in 1954. She received her B.Arch degree from Cooper Union School of Arts in 1979 and is a Professor of Architecture at Princeton University. Ricardo Scofidio was born in New York in 1935. He graduated from Cooper Union School of Architecture and Columbia University, and is now Professor Emeritus of Architecture at Cooper Union. Charles Renfro was born in Baytown, Texas, in 1964. He graduated from Rice University and Columbia University. Diller+Scofidio was founded in 1979; Renfro became a Partner in 2004 and, most recently, Benjamin Gilmartin became a Partner in 2015. They completed the Blur Building (Expo '02, Yverdon-les-Bains, Switzerland, 2002); the Institute of Contemporary Art in Boston (Massachusetts, 2006); the Lincoln Center Redevelopment Project in New York, including the expansion of the Juilliard School of Music (2009), the renovation of Alice Tully Hall (2009), public spaces throughout the campus, and the Hypar Pavilion Lawn (2011; see p. 144). Other recent projects include the conversion of the High Line, a 2.4-kilometer stretch of elevated railroad, into a New York City park (Phase I, 2009; Phase II, 2011; Phase III, 2014); the McMurtry Building for the Department of Art and Art History at Stanford University (California, 2015); The Broad in downtown Los Angeles (California, 2015); and the Berkeley Art Museum and Pacific Film Archive (California, 2016), all in the USA unless stated otherwise.

VLADIMIR DJUROVIC

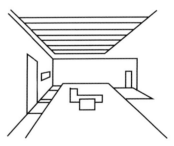

Vladimir Djurovic Landscape Architecture
(VDLA)
Broumana Main Road
Broumana
Lebanon

Tel: +961 4 86 2444/555
Fax: +961 4 86 2462
E-mail: info@vladimirdjurovic.com
Web: vladimirdjurovic.com

Vladimir Djurovic was born to a Montenegrin father and a Lebanese mother in 1967. He received a degree in Horticulture from Reading University in England in 1989 and his M.A. in Landscape Architecture from the University of Georgia in 1992, after having worked at EDAW in Atlanta. Vladimir Djurovic Landscape Architecture (VDLA) was created in 1995 in Beirut, Lebanon. The office has participated in and won several international competitions, such as Freedom Park South Africa (2003), King Hussein Memorial Jordan (2010), and King's Square Australia (2015). The firm won a 2008

Award of Excellence in the residential design category from the American Society of Landscape Architects (ASLA) for its Bassil Mountain Escape project in Faqra (Lebanon). The firm's work includes numerous private residences in Lebanon, including the F House (with Nabil Gholam; Dahr El Sawan, Lebanon, 2000-04); the Aga Khan award-winning Samir Kassir Square (Beirut, Lebanon, 2004); the Hariri Memorial Garden (Beirut, Lebanon, 2010); the SST Building Private Rooftop (Beirut, Lebanon, 2008-13; see p. 310); and the landscape architecture of the Wynford Drive site in Toronto (Canada) to accommodate the Aga Khan Museum by Fumihiko Maki and the Ismaili Center by Charles Correa (2015). Ongoing work includes 3 Beirut (Solidere, BCD, Lebanon, 2012-; architect Foster + Partners); Beirut Terraces (Solidere, BCD, Lebanon, 2013-; architect Herzog & de Meuron); the EDP Headquarters (Lisbon, Portugal; architect Manuel Aires Mateus); and the Mittal Residence (New Delhi, India, 2014-; architect Marcio Kogan).

DWP

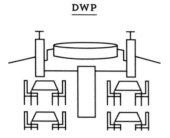

DWP
Design Worldwide Partnership
The Dusit Thani Building
946 Rama IV Road
Bangkok 10500 | Thailand

Tel: +66 2 267 3939
Fax: +66 2 267 3949
E-mail: thailand@dwp.com
Web: www.dwp.com

Scott Whittaker is the Group Executive Director, Creative Director, and founding Partner of DWP. He received his B.Arch in Australia and moved to Asia in 1994, together with business partners, founding DWP (Design Worldwide Partnership) in Thailand. Their work includes the Sirocco Restaurant & Skybar (Bangkok, 2004; see p. 280); Mezzaluna (Bangkok, 2004); 87 Plus at the Conrad (Bangkok, 2005); the Earth Spa at the Evason Hideaway (Hua Hin, 2005); and Distil and Breeze (Bangkok, 2006), all in Thailand. The firm also participates in DWP | WGC, which unites the architecture and interior design experience of DWP with the specialist audio visual and lighting design solutions of WGC International.

FLETCHER PRIEST

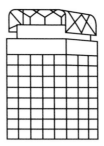

Fletcher Priest Architects
Middlesex House
34/42 Cleveland Street
London WIT 4JE
UK

Tel: +44 20 70 34 22 00
Fax: +44 207 37 53 47
E-mail: london@fletcherpriest.com
Web: www.fletcherpriest.com

Fletcher Priest is an international practice founded by Keith Priest and Michael Fletcher, with offices in London, Cologne, and Riga. Born in 1965 in Howarth, Yorkshire, Ed Williams is a Partner of Fletcher Priest and joined the firm in 1995. Sam Craig, born in 1967 in London, is a Senior Associate who joined the office in 2006. Mareike Langkitsch, born in 1980 in Lüdensheid, Germany, is an Associate, who studied at the Teschnische Hocschule Aachen (RWTH) and at La Sapienza University in Rome, before joining Fletcher Priest in 2007. Among completed work in the UK are 1 Angel Lane (London, 2007-09; see p. 30); and 6 Bevis Marks (London, 2012-14; see p. 38). Ongoing work includes Angel Court, City of London (2014-16); St. Anne's College Oxford (Oxford, 2014-16); 6 First Street Manchester (Manchester, 2016-17); Brunel Building (London, 2016-19); and Pinewood Studios (Buckinghamshire, 2014-).

FOSTER + PARTNERS

Foster + Partners
Riverside Three | 22 Hester Road
London SW11 4AN | UK

Tel: +44 20 77 38 04 55
Fax: +44 20 77 38 11 07
E-mail: info@fosterandpartners.com
Web: www.fosterandpartners.com

Born in Manchester, UK, in 1935, Norman Foster studied architecture and city planning at Manchester University (1961). He was awarded a Henry Fellowship to Yale University, where he received his M.Arch degree and met Richard Rogers, with whom he created Team 4. He received the RIBA Gold Medal for Architecture (1983). He was knighted in 1990 and honored with a Life Peerage in 1999. The American Institute of Architects granted him their Gold Medal for Architecture in 1994 and he was awarded the Pritzker Prize in 1999. Lord Norman Foster has notably built: the IBM Pilot Head Office (Cosham, UK, 1970-71); Sainsbury Center for Visual Arts and Crescent Wing, University of East Anglia (Norwich, UK, 1976-77; 1989-91); Hong Kong and Shanghai Banking Corporation Headquarters (Hong Kong, 1981-86); Stansted Airport (Stansted, UK, 1987-91); the Commerzbank Headquarters (Frankfurt, Germany, 1994-97); Chek Lap Kok Airport (Hong Kong, 1995-98); the new German Parliament, Reichstag (Berlin, Germany, 1995-99); British Museum Redevelopment (London, UK, 1997-2000); Millennium Bridge (London, UK, 1996-2002); Petronas University of Technology (Seri Iskandar, Malaysia, 1999-2004); Searcy's, 30 St. Mary Axe (London, UK, 2001-04; see p. 268); Millau Viaduct (Millau, France, 1993-2005); and Wembley Stadium (London, UK, 1996-2006). More recent work of the firm includes Beijing Airport (China, 2003-08); Faustino Winery (Ribera del Duero, Spain, 2007-10); Masdar Institute (Abu Dhabi, UAE, 2008-10); the Radio Rooftop Bar, ME London (London, UK, 2006-13); and Rooftop Garden, Crossrail Place (Canary Wharf, London, UK, 2015), both published here, see pp. 234, 262. Ongoing work includes the master plan for the West Kowloon Cultural District (Hong Kong, 2009-); and the new headquarters of Apple on a 71-hectare campus in Cupertino (California, USA) due for 2016 completion.

ANDREW FRANZ

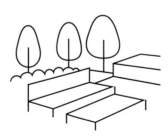

Andrew Franz Architect PLLC
135 West 26th Street, Suite 10B
New York, NY 10001 | USA

Tel: +1 212 505 1992
Fax: +1 212 505 1987
Web: www.andrewfranz.com

Andrew Franz was born in Hartford, Connecticut, in 1970. He attended Carnegie Mellon University (1988-90) and the University of Wisconsin (BS in

Architecture, 1993), creating his own firm in 2003. His work includes Dyckman Landing and La Marina (New York, New York, 2012); Lower Manhattan Loft (New York, New York, 2013; see p. 164); West Side Duplex (New York, New York, 2014); Maine Studio (Bristol, Maine, 2014); Beach House (Cape Cod, Massachusetts, 2016); an investment firm workplace (New York, New York, 2016); Fish Bar at North River Landing (New York, New York, 2016); and the Silo Ridge House (Amenia, New York, 2017), all in the USA. Andrew Franz also leads his firm's pro bono and charitable efforts, including work with Architecture for Humanity and desigNYC.

SOU FUJIMOTO

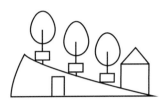

Sou Fujimoto Architects
6F Ichikawaseihon Building
10-3 Higashienoki-cho, Shinjuku
Tokyo 162-0807
Japan

Tel: +81 3 3513 5401
E-mail: media@sou-fujimoto.net
Web: www.sou-fujimoto.net

Sou Fujimoto was born in 1971. He received a B.Arch degree from the University of Tokyo, Faculty of Engineering, Department of Architecture (1990-94). He established his own firm, Sou Fujimoto Architects, in 2000. He is considered one of the most interesting rising Japanese architects, and his forms usually evade easy classification. His work includes the Seidai Hospital Occupational Therapy Ward (Hokkaido, 1996); Children's Center for Psychiatric Rehabilitation (Hokkaido, 2006); House O (Chiba, 2007); House N (Oita Prefecture, 2007-08); and the Final Wooden House (Kumamura, Kumamoto, 2007-08). Other recent work includes House H (Tokyo, 2008-09); the Musashino Art University Museum and Library (Tokyo, 2007-10); Tokyo Apartment (Tokyo, 2009-10); UNIQLO Shinsaibashi (Osaka, 2010); House NA (Tokyo, 2011); House K (Nishinomiya-shi, Hyogo, 2011-12; see p. 128); and the Serpentine Gallery Pavilion 2013 (Kensington Gardens, London, UK, 2013), all in Japan unless stated otherwise.

FRANK O. GEHRY

Gehry Partners, LLP
12541 Beatrice Street
Los Angeles, CA 90066 | USA

Tel: +1 310 482 3000
E-mail: info@foga.co m
Web: www.foga.com

Born in Toronto, Canada, in 1929, Frank O. Gehry studied at the University of Southern California, Los Angeles (1949-51), and at Harvard (1956-57). Principal of Frank O. Gehry and Associates, Inc., Los Angeles, since 1962, he received the Pritzker Prize in 1989, the Praemium Imperiale in 1992, and the Prince of Asturias Prize in 2014. His early work in California included the redesign of his own house, and the construction of a number of houses such as the Norton Residence (Venice, 1984) and the Schnabel Residence (Brentwood, 1989). His first foreign projects included Festival Disney (Marne-la-Vallée, France, 1989-92), and the Guggenheim Bilbao (Spain, 1991-97), which is felt by some to be one of the most significant buildings of the late 20th century. Other work includes the DG Bank Headquarters (Berlin, Germany, 2001); the Fisher Center for the Performing Arts at Bard College (Annandale-on-Hudson, New York, USA, 2003); and the Walt Disney Concert Hall (Los Angeles, California, USA, 2003). More recent work includes the Hotel at the Marques de Riscal winery (Elciego, Spain, 2003-07); his first New York building, the InterActiveCorp Headquarters (New York, New York, USA, 2003-07); an extension of the Art Gallery of Ontario (Toronto, Canada, 2005-08); and, again in New York, the Eight Spruce Street Tower (New York, New York, USA, 2007-11). He recently completed the Biodiversity Museum (Panama City, Panama, 2004-14); the Louis Vuitton Foundation for Creation in the Bois de Boulogne in Paris (France, 2008-14; see p. 156); and the Dr. Chau Chak Wing Building (Sydney, Australia, 2012-14).

GUNN LANDSCAPE ARCHITECTURE

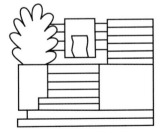

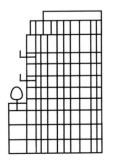

Gunn Landscape Architecture
345 Seventh Avenue, Suite 502
New York, NY 10001 | USA

Tel: +1 212 988 7065
E-mail: info@gunnlandscapes.com
Web: www.gunnlandscapes.com

Alec Gunn was born in Lawrence, Kansas, in 1969. He graduated from Cornell University with a Master's degree in Landscape Architecture (1996), having previously obtained a B.A. from Bates College. He founded Gunn Landscape Architecture in 2000, and is now its Managing Principal, and then cofounded Vert Gardens (2005) and founded Loam Landscape (2007). The work of the firm includes the Trump SoHo Spa (New York, New York, 2010); East Hampton Residence (New York, New York, 2012); New Canaan Residence (Connecticut, 2012); Hotel Lincoln, J Parker Rooftop Bar (Chicago, Illinois, 2013); and the Bridgehampton Estate (New York, New York, 2013). Current projects include the Printing House West Village Mews (New York, New York, 2016), all in the USA. Published here are Central Park West Residence (New York, New York, 2012-13); Tribeca Roof Terrace (New York, New York, 2013); and SoHo Roof Terrace (New York, New York, 2014), see pp. 74, 346, and 304.

GUSTAFSON PORTER

Gustafson Porter
1 Cobham Mews
London NW1 9SB | UK

Tel: +44 20 72 84 89 50
E-mail: enquiries@gustafson-porter.com
Web: www.gustafson-porter.com

Neil Porter was born in the UK in 1958. He attended Newcastle University School of Architecture (1977-80) and the Architectural Association (AA, London, 1981-83). He is a founding Partner and designer for Gustafson Porter. Mary Bowman was born in the US in 1958. She attended the University of Virginia (Charlottesville, Virginia, 1976-80), and the AA (London, 1984-88). She has been a Director of Gustafson Porter since 2002. Donncha O'Shea was born in Ireland in 1978 and joined the firm in 2008. He has been an Associate since 2013 and an Associate Partner since 2015. Work of the firm includes the Diana, Princess of Wales Memorial Fountain in Hyde Park (London, UK, 2003-04); the Cultuurpark Westergasfabriek (Amsterdam, the Netherlands, 2004); Old Market Square (Nottingham, UK, 2005-07); Towards Paradise (11th Venice Architecture Biennale, Venice, Italy, 2008); the Woolwich Squares (London, UK, 2006-11); New Ludgate (London, UK, 2013-15; see p. 190); Bay East, Gardens by the Bay (Singapore, 2006-, interim park since 2012); and Citylife Fiera Milano Park (Milan, Italy, 2011-).

ZAHA HADID

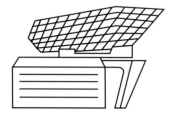

Zaha Hadid Architects
Studio 9
10 Bowling Green Lane
London EC1R 0BQ | UK

Tel: +44 20 72 53 51 47
E-mail: press@zaha-hadid.com
Web: www.zaha-hadid.com

Zaha Hadid (1950-2016) studied architecture at the Architectural Association (AA) in London, beginning in 1972, and was awarded the Diploma Prize in 1977. She then became a Partner of Rem Koolhaas in OMA and taught at the AA. She also taught at Harvard, the University of Chicago, in Hamburg, and at Columbia University in New York. In 2004, Zaha Hadid became the first woman to win the Pritzker Prize. As well as the exhibition design for "The Great Utopia" (Solomon R. Guggenheim Museum, New York, USA, 1992), her work includes the Vitra Fire Station (Weil am Rhein, Germany, 1990-94); the Lois & Richard Rosenthal Center for Contemporary Art (Cincinnati, Ohio, USA, 1999-2003); Phaeno Science Center (Wolfsburg, Germany, 2001-05); Ordrupgaard Museum Extension (Copenhagen, Denmark, 2001-05); the Central Building of the new BMW Assembly Plant in Leipzig (Germany, 2005); and the MAXXI, the National Museum of 21st Century Arts (Rome, Italy, 1998-2009). More recent projects include the Sheik Zayed Bridge (Abu Dhabi, UAE, 2003-10); the Guangzhou Opera House (Guangzhou, China, 2005-10); the Aquatics Center for the London 2012 Olympic Games (London, UK, 2005-11); the CMA CGM Tower (Marseille, France, 2008-11); the Heydar Aliyev Center (Baku, Azerbaijan, 2007-12); the Messner Mountain Museum Corones (Enneberg/Pieve di Marebbe, Italy, 2015); and the Port House (Antwerp, Belgium, 2009-; see p. 220).

HMWHITE

HMWhite
107 Grand St, 6th Floor,
New York, NY 10013 | USA

Tel: +1 212 868 9411
E-mail: info@hmwhitesa.com
Web: www.hmwhitesa.com

HMWhite was founded in 1992 by Hank White, "on the principle that the designed landscape is among the most powerful forms of cultural expression and environmental accountability." Born in 1957 in New Jersey, USA, he received his BA from Bucknell University and Master of Landscape Architecture from the Harvard GSD. The work of the firm includes the St. George Waterfront Park (with HOK Sport, Staten Island, New York, USA, 2001); The New York Times Building Lobby Garden (with Renzo Piano RPBW, New York, New York, 2006); the landscape design for the Morgan Library expansion (with Renzo Piano RPBW, New York, New York, 2007); Brooklyn Botanic Gardens Visitor Center garden (with Weiss Manfredi, Brooklyn, New York, 2012); the Penthouse Gardens (with Steve E. Blatz Architects, New York, New York, 2012; see p. 212); and the Midtown Manhattan Skygarden on the Western Publishing Company building (with Gertler & Wente, New York, New York, 2013), all in the USA.

TOYO ITO

Toyo Ito & Associates, Architects
Fujiya Building
1-19-4 Shibuya, Shibuya-ku
Tokyo 150-0002
Japan

Tel: +81 3 3409 5822
Web: www.toyo-ito.co.jp

Born in 1941 in Seoul, South Korea, Toyo Ito graduated from the University of Tokyo in 1965 and worked in the office of Kiyonori Kikutake until 1969. He created his own office, Urban Robot (URBOT), in Tokyo in 1971, assuming the name of Toyo Ito & Associates, Architects in 1979. He was awarded the Golden Lion for Lifetime Achievement from the 8th International Venice Architecture Biennale in 2002, the RIBA Gold Medal in 2006, and the Pritzker Prize in 2013. One of his most successful and widely published projects, Sendai Mediatheque, was completed in 2001, while in 2002 he designed the Serpentine Gallery Pavilion in London (UK). More recently, he has completed TOD'S Omotesando Building (Shibuya-ku, Tokyo, Japan, 2002-04); Tama Art University Library, Hachioji campus (Tokyo, Japan, 2004-07); ZA-KOENJI Public Theater (Tokyo, Japan, 2005-08); the Main Stadium for the World Games 2009 in Kaohsiung (Kaohsiung, Taiwan, Republic of China, 2006-09); Toyo Ito Museum of Architecture, Imabari (Ehime, Japan, 2008-11); CapitaGreen (Singapore, Singapore, 2012-14; see p. 52); and "Minna no Mori" Gifu Media Cosmos (Gifu, Japan, 2011-15). He is currently working on the National Taichung Theater (Taichung, Taiwan, Republic of China, 2005-).

JAG

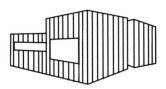

JAG Arquitectos
Rua Cidade de Lobito, 267, Loja A
1800-0088 Lisbon
Portugal

Tel: +351 21 854 91 22
Fax: +351 21 854 91 22
E-mail: jag_arquitectos@sapo.pt
Web: www.jagarquitectos.pt

João Alexandre Gois was born in Lisbon, Portugal, in 1972. He received his degree in Architecture from the Lusiada University in Lisbon in 1999. From 2001 to 2006, he worked with the architect Gonçalo Byrne. In 2006, he worked with Francisco Mangado on the Congress Center in Palma de Majorca, and then created his own firm, JAG Arquitectos, in Lisbon. His work includes a spa in Estoi (Estoi, 2009); the renovation of a building on Largo de São Paulo (Lisbon, 2011); renovation of the Citadel of Cascais (Cascais, 2011); and the Roofbuildinghouse (Lisbon, 2015; see p. 256), all in Portugal.

JAKOB + MACFARLANE

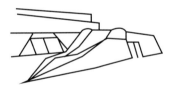

Jakob + MacFarlane
sarl d'Architecture
13-15 Rue des Petites Écuries
75010 Paris
France

Tel: +33 1 44 79 05 72
E-mail: info@jakobmacfarlane.com
Web: www.jakobmacfarlane.com

Dominique Jakob was born in 1966 and holds a degree in Art History from the Université de Paris I (1990) and a degree in Architecture from the École d'Architecture Paris-Villemin (1991). Born in New Zealand in 1961, Brendan MacFarlane received his B.Arch at SCI-Arc, Los Angeles (1984), and his M.Arch degree at the Harvard GSD (1990). From 1995 to 1997, MacFarlane was an architecture critic at the Architectural Association (AA) in London. They founded their own agency in 1992 in Paris, and were also cofounders with E. Marin-Trottin and D. Trottin of the exhibition and conference organizer Periphériques (1996-98). Their main projects include the T House (La-Garenne-Colombes, 1994, 1998); Georges Restaurant (Georges Pompidou Center, Paris, 1999-2000); the restructuring of the Maxime Gorki Theater (Petit-Quevilly, 1999-2000); and the Renault International Communication Center (Boulogne, 2004). Recent and current work includes the City of Fashion and Design (Paris,

2007-08); another dock project, the Orange Cube (Lyon, 2010); The Docks Rooftop Terrace (City of Fashion and Design, Paris, 2012; see p. 322); Les Turbulences, the FRAC Contemporary Art and Architecture Center in Orléans (2013); Green Pavilion, Lyon Confluence, Euronews Headquarters (Lyon, 2013); Maison S (Boulogne-Billancourt, 2014); Gaumont Parnasse Cinema (Paris, 2015); and Boerenboom Square (Knokke-Heist, Belgium, 2015), all in France unless stated otherwise.

JDS

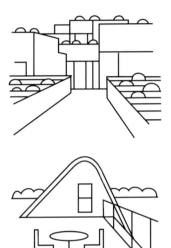

JDS Architects
Rue de la Senne 34B
1000 Brussels
Belgium

Tel: +32 2 289 00 00
E-mail: office@jdsa.eu
Web: www.jdsa.eu

Julien De Smedt, born in Brussels (Belgium) in 1975, is the founder and Director of JDS Architects based in Brussels, Copenhagen, and Shanghai. He obtained diplomas in Architecture from the St. Luc Architecture Institute (Brussels, 1995), the Superior Architecture Institute of the French Community (La Cambre, Brussels, 1995-96), and the Architecture School at Paris-Belleville (1996-97). From 1997 to 1998, he worked in the office of OMA/Rem Koolhaas in Rotterdam. He then went on to further studies at SCI-Arc in Los Angeles (1999) and at the Bartlett (London, 1998-2000), before again joining OMA in Rotterdam (2000-01). He cofounded the architecture firm PLOT with Bjarke Ingels in Copenhagen (2001), before creating JDS in 2005. Work by the firm published here are the Mountain (with BIG; Copenhagen, Denmark, 2006-08; see p. 336); the Holmenkollen Ski Jump (Oslo, Norway, 2011); and Hedonistic Rooftop Penthouses (Copenhagen, Denmark, 2011; see p. 122). Other work includes the Faaborg Harbor Bath (Faaborg, Denmark, 2013); the Iceberg (Aarhus, Denmark, 2013); Gangnam Bogeumjari District Officetel (Seoul, South Korea, 2014); Entrepots Macdonald S4 and N4 (Paris, France, 2015); Qingdao Marine Biotechnology Center (Qingdao, China, 2015); Hangzhou Open Gateway (Hangzhou, China, 2015); and Maison Stéphane Hessel (Lille, France, 2016).

LOT-EK

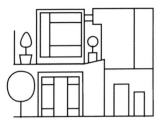

LOT-EK
181 Chrystie Street #2
New York, NY 10002
USA

Tel: +1 212 255 9326
Fax: +1 212 255 2988
E-mail: info@lot-ek.com
Web: www.lot-ek.com

Ada Tolla was born in 1964 in Potenza, Italy. She received her M.Arch from the Architecture Faculty of the "Federico II" University (Naples, 1982-89) and did postgraduate studies at Columbia University (New York, 1990-91). She is one of the two founding Partners of LOT-EK, created in Naples, Italy, in 1993 and in New York in 1995. The other cofounder is Giuseppe Lignano, who was born in Naples, Italy, in 1963. He also received his M.Arch degree from the "Federico II" University (1982-89) and did postgraduate studies at Columbia at the same time as Ada Tolla. Their work includes the Guzman Penthouse (New York, New York, 1996; see p. 116); UNIQLO Container Stores (New York, 2006); Theater for One (Princeton University, Princeton, New Jersey, 2007); PUMACity (Alicante, Spain, and Boston, Massachusetts, 2008); Weiner Townhouse (New York, New York, 2008); PUMA DDSU (South Street Seaport, New York, New York, 2010); APAP Open-School (Anyang, South Korea, 2010); and Van Alen Books (New York, New York, 2011). More recent projects include the Whitney Studio (New York, New York, 2012); Pier 57 (New York, New York, 2011-13); and Band of Outsiders (Tokyo, Japan, 2012-13). Their current work includes Drivelines, residential building (Maboneng, Johannesburg, South Africa, 2014-16); Qiyun Mountain Camp, entry pavilion, retail, service and activity facilities (Qiyun, China, 2015-17); and the West Collection, art and retail center (Philadelphia, Pennsylvania), all in the USA unless stated otherwise.

FRANCOIS DE MENIL

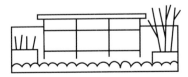

FdM: Arch Francois de Menil Architect, PC
270 Lafayette Street
New York, NY 10012
USA
Tel: +1 212 779 3400
Fax: +1 212 779 3414
E-mail: info@fdmarch.com
Web: www.fdmarch.com

Francois de Menil was born in Houston, Texas, in 1945. He obtained his B.Arch degree from the Cooper Union (1983-87), having previously attended Columbia University (1965-66). He was an independent filmmaker (1966-83), before working in the offices of Richard Meier (1985) and Kohn Pedersen Fox (1987-89). He founded his own firm in 1991. His completed work includes the Byzantine Fresco Chapel Museum (Houston, Texas, 1996); Bottega Veneta Retail Shops (various locations, Japan and USA, 1996-98); Carriage House Renovation (New York, New York, 2000); the Museum Tower Roof Garden (New York, New York, 2004-05; see p. 184); Amagansett House (Amagansett, New York, 2010); and the Seneca Art and Culture Center at Ganondagan (Victor, New York, 2015), all in the USA.

ERIC OWEN MOSS

Eric Owen Moss Architects
8557 Higuera Street
Culver City, CA 90232
USA

Tel: +1 310 839 1199
Fax: +1 310 839 7922
E-mail: mail@ericowenmoss.com
Web: www.ericowenmoss.com

Born in Los Angeles, California, in 1943, Eric Owen Moss received his B.A. degree from UCLA in 1965 and his M.Arch from UC Berkeley in 1968. He also received an M.Arch degree at Harvard in 1972. He has been a Professor of Design at the Southern California Institute of Architecture since 1974 and has served as Director for the past eight years. He opened his own firm in Culver City in 1973. His built work includes the Lindblade Tower (Culver City, 1987-89); Paramount Laundry (Culver City, 1987-89); I.R.S. Building (Culver City, 1993-94); Samitaur (Culver City, 1994-96); Stealth (Culver City, California, 2002); 3555 Hayden (Culver City, 2007); and the Samitaur Tower (Culver City, 2007-10). Recent and ongoing work includes Pterodactyl (Culver City, 2013-14; see p. 226); Waffle (Culver City, 2015); Warner (Culver City, 2017); and (W)rapper (Los Angeles, 2017), all in California, USA.

RYUE NISHIZAWA

Office of Ryue Nishizawa
1-5-27 Tatsumi
Koto-ku
Tokyo 135-0053
Japan

Tel: +81 3 5534 0117
E-mail: office@ryuenishizawa.com
Web: www.ryuenishizawa.com

Ryue Nishizawa was born in Tokyo in 1966. He graduated from Yokohama National University with an M.Arch in 1990, and joined the office of Kazuyo Sejima & Associates in Tokyo the same year. In 1995, he established SANAA with Kazuyo Sejima, and two years later his own practice, the Office of Ryue Nishizawa. SANAA won the 2010 Pritzker Prize. Nishizawa has worked on all the significant projects of SANAA, featured in a recent Museum of Modern Art exhibition in New York ("Japanese Constellation," 2016). His work outside SANAA includes a Weekend House (Gunma, 1998); the N Museum (Kagawa, 2005); Moriyama House (Tokyo, 2006); House A (East Japan, 2006); Towada Art Center (Aomori, 2006-08); the Teshima Museum (Teshima, Kagawa, 2009-10); Garden & House (Tokyo, 2010-11; see p. 108); the Hiroshi Senju Museum (Karuizawa, Nagano, 2011); and Fukita Pavilion in Shodoshima (Shodoshima-cho, Kagawa, 2013), all in Japan.

JEAN NOUVEL

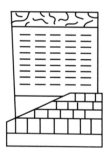

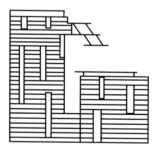

Ateliers Jean Nouvel
10 Cité d'Angoulême
75011 Paris
France

Tel: +33 1 49 23 83 83
Fax: +33 1 43 14 81 10
E-mail: info@jeannouvel.fr
Web: www.jeannouvel.com

Jean Nouvel was born in 1945 in Fumel, France. He studied in Bordeaux and then at the École des Beaux-Arts (Paris, 1964-72). From 1967 to 1970, he was an assistant of the architects Claude Parent and Paul Virilio. He created his first office with François Seigneur in Paris in 1970. Jean Nou-

vel received the RIBA Gold Medal in 2001 and the Pritzker Prize in 2008. His first widely noted projects were the Institut du Monde Arabe (Paris, France, 1981-87, with Architecture Studio) and the Fondation Cartier (Paris, France, 1991-94). Major projects since 2000 are the Music and Conference Center (Lucerne, Switzerland, 1998-2000); the Agbar Tower (Barcelona, Spain, 1999-2005); an extension of the Reina Sofia Museum (Madrid, Spain, 1999-2005); the Quai Branly Museum (Paris, France, 1999-2006); the Guthrie Theater (Minneapolis, Minnesota, USA, 2001-06); "40 Mercer" apartment building in SoHo (New York, New York, USA, 2005-08); the Danish Radio Concert House (Copenhagen, Denmark, 2003-09); Le Loft Restaurant, Hotel Stephansdom (Vienna, Austria, 2007-10; see p. 150); the City Hall in Montpellier (France, 2003-11; the Doha Tower (Qatar, 2007-11); Jane's Carousel, Brooklyn Bridge Park (Brooklyn, New York, USA, 2011); "Las Boas" and "Patio Blanco" apartment buildings in Ibiza (Spain, 2006-12); the Renaissance Barcelona Fira Hotel (Barcelona, Spain, 2008-12); One Central Park (Sydney, Australia, 2010-14; see p. 204); and the new Philharmonic Hall in Paris (France, 2007-15). Current work includes the Louvre Abu Dhabi (UAE, 2007-under construction); 53W53 Tour de Verre in New York (New York, USA, 2007-under construction); and the National Museum of Qatar (Doha, Qatar, 2008-under construction). Jean Nouvel is the architect in charge of the coordination of the Seguin Island urban renewal project in Boulogne-Billancourt (Paris, France, 2009-23).

MOSHE SAFDIE

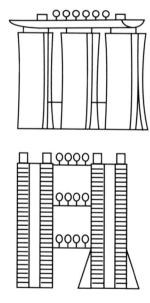

Safdie Architects, LLC
100 Properzi Way
Somerville, MA 02143
USA

Tel: +1 617 629 2100
Fax: +1 617 629 2406
E-mail: boston@msafdie.com
Web: www.msafdie.com

Born in Haifa, Israel, in 1938, Moshe Safdie moved with his family to Canada in 1953. He received his degree in Architecture from McGill University (Montreal, 1961). He worked as an apprentice in the

office of Louis Kahn in Philadelphia, and, in 1964, he created his own firm to realize Habitat '67 at the 1967 World Exhibition in Montreal. Safdie is a winner of the Gold Medal of the American Institute of Architects (2015) and the Royal Architectural Institute of Canada (1995). Other significant projects include the National Gallery of Canada (Ottawa, Canada, 1983-88); Salt Lake City Public Library (Salt Lake City, Utah, USA, 1999-2003); Yad Vashem Holocaust History Museum (Jerusalem, Israel, 1997-2005); Khalsa Heritage Center (Anandpur Sahib, Punjab, India, 1998-2011); Kauffman Center for the Performing Arts (Kansas City, Missouri, USA, 2000-11); United States Institute of Peace Headquarters (Washington, D.C., USA, 2001-11); Crystal Bridges Museum of American Art (Bentonville, Arkansas, USA, 2005-11); Skypark, Marina Bay Sands Integrated Resort (Singapore, Singapore, 2005-11; see p. 296); the Skirball Cultural Center (Los Angeles, California, USA, 1986-2013); and SkyHabitat (Bishan, Singapore, 2012-15; see p. 286).

ANNABELLE SELLDORF

Selldorf Architects
860 Broadway, 2nd floor
New York, NY 10003
USA

Tel: +1 212 219 9571
E-mail: info@selldorf.com
Web: www.selldorf.com

Annabelle Selldorf was born in 1960 in Cologne, Germany. She received her B.Arch degree from the Pratt Institute (New York) and an M.Arch from Syracuse University (Florence, Italy). She founded Selldorf Architects in New York in 1988 and the firm currently employs 65 people. She has been responsible for the design of a number of the most visible contemporary art galleries in Manhattan, including spaces for David Zwirner, Hauser & Wirth, Gladstone Gallery, and the Michael Werner Gallery. She also renovated the Neue Gallery, a private museum for Austrian and German art located at 1048 5th Avenue (New York, New York, 2001) and has worked on a number of new buildings, such as a 19-story residential tower at 200 11th Avenue (New York, New York, 2011); and another new residential building at 21 East 12th Street (New York, New York, 2013-18; see p. 44), all in the USA unless stated otherwise. Her current work includes an expansion of the Museum of Contemporary Art San Diego (California, 2015-18); and Luma Arles (Arles, France, 2013-18), a contemporary art center sponsored by Maja Hoffmann and located in a former rail depot to the south of the French city. Selldorf Architects is participating in this project with other architects, including Frank O. Gehry and Bas Smets.

KEN SMITH

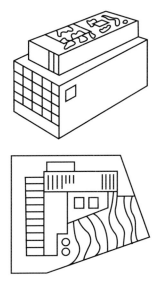

WORKSHOP: Ken Smith Landscape Architect
450 West 31st Street, Fifth Floor
New York, NY 10001 | USA

Tel: +1 212 791 3595
Fax: +1 212 732 1793
E-mail: info@kensmithworkshop.com
Web: www.kensmithworkshop.com

Ken Smith was born in 1953, and graduated from Iowa State University with a B.S. in Landscape Architecture (Ames, Iowa, 1975). He attended Harvard GSD (Master of Landscape Architecture program, 1986). He worked as a Landscape Architect for the State Conservation Commission in Iowa (1979-84), as a consultant for the Department of Environmental Management (Massachusetts, 1984-86), in the office of Peter Walker and Martha Schwartz (New York, San Francisco, 1986-89), and with Martha Schwartz Ken Smith David Meyer Inc (San Francisco, 1990-92), before creating his present firm, Ken Smith Landscape Architect, in New York. His current and recent landscape work includes Lever House Landscape Restoration (New York, New York, 2000); the Museum of Modern Art Roof Garden (New York, New York, 2004-05; see p. 178); 7 World Trade Center, Triangle Park (New York, New York, 2002-06); 40 Central Park South, Courtyard Garden (New York, New York, 2006); H-12 Office Complex (Hyderabad, India, 2007); Santa Fe Railyard Park and Plaza (Santa Fe, New Mexico, 2008); 17 State Street Plaza (New York, New York, 2008); Orange County Great Park (Irvine, California, 2007-11); Conrad Hotel (New York, New York, 2011-12; see p. 80); Brooklyn Academy of Music Cultural District Public Space and Streetscape (Brooklyn, New York, 2006-13); and the Croton Water Treatment Plant (Bronx, New York, 2015). Ongoing work includes the East River Waterfront (New York, New York, 2006-), all in the USA unless stated otherwise.

JOSÉ ANTONIO SOSA + MAGÜI GONZÁLEZ

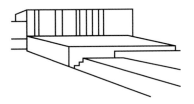

Magüi González + José Antonio Sosa.
nred arquitectos
Muro, 2ª planta, oficina 2 / Sor Ana 1, Monte Lentiscal | 35002 Las Palmas / 35310 Las Palmas
Spain

Tel: +34 928 36 34 62 / +34 928 43 05 30
E-mail: maguiglez@arquired.es / jasds@arquired.es
Web: www.nred-arquitectos.eu

José Antonio Sosa was born in Las Palmas de Gran Canaria (Spain, 1957). He obtained his B.Arch from the Technical University of Madrid and a Doctorate in Architecture from the University of Las Palmas de Gran Canaria. Magüi González was also born in Las Palmas de Gran Canaria (1953). She obtained her B.Arch degree from the Technical University of Las Palmas de Gran Canaria and, like, José Antonio Sosa, is a Professor of Architectural Projects at the University of Las Palmas de Gran Canaria. Their work includes a plaza and underground areas at Calle Venegas (Las Palmas, 2006); the Old City Hall Renovation (Las Palmas de Gran Canaria, Spain, 2009; see p. 196); and the new headquarters of the Judiciary in Las Palmas (2004-13).

SPONGE / IOU

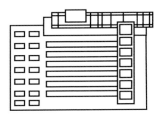

SPONGE Architects
Neveritaweg 15 N12 | 1033 WB Amsterdam
The Netherlands

Tel: +31 20 422 37 11
E-mail: mail@sponge.nl
Web: www.sponge.nl

IOU Architecture
Herengracht 247
1016 BH Amsterdam | The Netherlands

Tel: +31 20 427 77 45 | E-mail: mail@i-o-u.nl
Web: www.i-o-u.nl

Björn van Rheenen was born in 1975 in Düsseldorf, Germany. He studied architecture at the University of Kaiserslautern (1994-2001), and at the University of Delft (1997-98). He worked for Koen van Velsen (Hilversum, 1998-2002), and Sluijmer & van Leeuwen (Utrecht, 2002-03), before founding SPONGE in Amsterdam in 2003. In 2008, he created SCOPE & SPONGE as a real estate development venture. He has worked on projects such as the Gooise Warande Restaurant (Bussum, 2011); and a temporary corporate building for MX3D (Amsterdam, 2015), both in the Netherlands. Roland Pouw was born in 1969 in Utrecht, the Netherlands. He graduated from the Academy of Architecture, Amsterdam School of the Arts, in 2006. He also studied at the Hogeschool van Utrecht, Department of Building Industry, as an engineer. He worked with Rienks Architecten (Breda, Amersfoort, 1996-98),

OPL Architecten (Utrecht, 1998-2001), and then with Sluijmer & van Leeuwen (Utrecht, 2001-03), before founding IOU in Amsterdam. He has worked on such projects as the remodeling of a canal house on Nieuwe Achtergacht (Amsterdam, 2013); the remodeling of the top floor of a former flour factory into a loft (De Weichsel, 2015); and City Beach Amstelveen, a floating swimming pool and pavilion (Amstelveen, 2016). Together, they completed the Ronald McDonald VU-Kinderstad (Amsterdam, the Netherlands, 2006-07; see p. 240).

TSAO & MCKOWN

Tsao & McKown Architects
242 Third Street
Brooklyn, NY 11215 | USA

Tel: +1 212 337 3800
E-mail: info@tsao-mckown.com
Web: tsao-mckown.com

Calvin Tsao graduated in 1974 from the University of California at Berkeley with a B.Arch degree. He obtained his M.Arch degree from the Harvard GSD in 1978. Tsao has served as the Eliot Noyes Visiting Design Critic in Architecture at Harvard University, and also taught at Cooper Union, Syracuse University, and Parsons The New School for Design. He served as Director of the Storefront for Art and Architecture (New York, 2002-05). Zack McKown graduated from the University of South Carolina's Honors College in 1974 and obtained his M.Arch degree from the Harvard GSD in 1979. Their work includes the Nai Lert Park Hotel (Bangkok, Thailand, 2004); Riverlofts Condominiums (New York, New York, USA, 2002-05); Piedmont House (Piedmont, California, USA, 2003-06); the Cipriani Residences and Club (New York, New York, USA, 2006); the SEVVA Restaurant (Hong Kong, China, 2008; see p. 274); and the Berkshire Mountain House (Alford, Massachusetts, USA, 2010). More recent work includes the Agora Tower (Qingdao, China, 2012); Bhutan Elder Sangha Sanctuary (Punakha, Bhutan, 2015); the Octave Living Room (Shanghai, China, 2015); and Sangha, a "community for learning, wellness, and living" (Suzhou, China, 2016).

MICHAEL VAN VALKENBURGH

Michael Van Valkenburgh Associates, Inc.,
Landscape Architects, PC
16 Court Street, 11th Floor
Brooklyn, NY 11241
USA

Tel: +1 718 243 2044
Fax: +1 718 243 1293
E-mail: mvva_ny@mvvainc.com
Web: www.mvvainc.com

Michael Van Valkenburgh received a B.S. degree from the Cornell University College of Agriculture (Ithaca, New York, 1973) and a Master of Fine Arts in Landscape Architecture from the University of Illinois (Champaign/Urbana, 1977). He oversees both the New York and Cambridge (Massachusetts) offices of the firm he founded in 1982—Michael Van Valkenburgh Associates, Inc. (MVVA)—and is involved in some way in every project. Other firm Principals are Matthew Urbanski, who is a lead designer for many of the firm's public projects, and Laura Solano, who is a specialist in landscape technology. Matthew Urbanski joined MVVA in 1989 after receiving a Master of Landscape Architecture degree from Harvard in 1989. Paul Seck was born in 1973 in the US Virgin Islands. He received a B.S. in Landscape Architecture from Ohio State University in 1996, and joined MVVA in 1996. Their work includes Tahari Courtyards (Millburn, New Jersey, 2002-03); Alumnae Valley Landscape Restoration, Wellesley College (Wellesley, Massachusetts, 2001-05); the Connecticut Water Treatment Facility (with Steven Holl; New Haven, Connecticut, 2001-05); Teardrop Park (New York, New York, 1999-2006); Harvard Yard Restoration (Cambridge, Massachusetts, 1993-2009); the George W. Bush Presidential Center (Dallas, Texas, 2013); and Maggie Daley Park (Chicago, Illinois, 2002-15; see p. 172). Ongoing work of the firm includes Brooklyn Bridge Park (Brooklyn, New York, 2003-16); Brooklyn Botanic Garden (New York, 2010-16); and City Arch River 2015 (St. Louis, Missouri, 2010-), all in the USA.

VERDE-GARTENGESTALTUNG

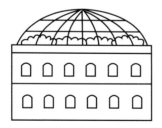

verde-gartengestaltung
Am Grossen Wannsee 67
14109 Berlin
Germany

Tel/Fax: +49 30 805 93 17
E-mail: verde-garten@t-online.de
Web: www.verde-gartengestaltung.de

Dagmar Heitmann was born in 1960 in Rahden, Germany. She studied biology at the FU-Berlin (1980-87). She completed her Ph.D. in Molecular Genetics in 1993, and studied landscape architecture at the Technical University in Berlin with a focus on Japanese gardens (1993-2003). She worked in the office of Ingenbleek Architekten from 1993 to 2005 and created her own firm in 2005. She has placed an emphasis on creating rooftop gardens and backyard gardens in Berlin, often with Japanese design elements incorporated in the completed gardens. Her work includes a private garden at Prinz-Handjery-Strasse (Berlin, 2005); front gardens and a loft house garden at Fichestrasse 12 (Berlin, 2009), next to the Fichtebunker published here (Berlin, 2008-09; see p. 96); House of the Magicians (Berlin, 2014); and the Silent Green Kulturquartier, a patio and garden of an old crematorium, now used as a cultural center (Berlin, 2015), all in Germany.

RAFAEL VIÑOLY

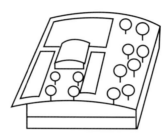

Rafael Viñoly Architects
50 Vandam Street
New York, NY 10013
USA

Tel: +1 212 924 5060
E-mail: alamberti@rvapc.com
Web: www.rvapc.com

Rafael Viñoly was born in Montevideo, Uruguay, in 1944. Twenty years later he was a founding partner of Estudio de Arquitectura, which would become one of the largest design studios in Latin America. It was after that date that he received his Diploma in Architecture (1968) and an M.Arch (1969), both at the University of Buenos Aires. He moved to the United States in 1978, founding Rafael Viñoly Architects PC in New York in 1983. His most significant projects include the Tokyo International Forum (Tokyo, Japan, 1996); Kimmel Center for the Performing Arts (Philadelphia, Pennsylvania, 2001); Boston Convention and Exhibition Center (Boston, Massachusetts, 2004); University of Oxford Master Plan and Mathematics Institute (Oxford, UK, 2013); Cleveland Museum of Art expansion (Cleveland, Ohio, 2013); and 432 Park Avenue, a 432-meter residential skyscraper at 57th Street (New York, New York, 2015). Current work includes the New Stanford Hospital (Stanford, California, 2015-18); the Manchester City Football Club Etihad Campus (Manchester, UK, 2012-18); and The Hills at Vallco (Cupertino, California, 2015-23; see p. 328), all in the USA unless stated otherwise.

WORK ARCHITECTURE COMPANY

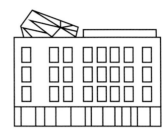

WORK Architecture Company
156 Ludlow Street, 3rd Floor
New York, NY 10002
USA

Tel: +1 212 228 1333
E-mail: office@work.ac
Web: www.work.ac

Born in Beirut, Lebanon, Amale Andraos received her B.Arch at McGill University (1996) and her Master's degree from Harvard University (1999). She worked with Rem Koolhaas/OMA (Rotterdam, 1999-2003), before founding WORK AC in New York in 2003. She is currently Dean of Columbia University's Graduate School of Architecture, Planning and Preservation. Dan Wood, born in Rhode Island, received his Bachelor's degree (in Film Theory) from the University of Pennsylvania (1989) and his M.Arch from Columbia University (1992). He lived in Paris and the Netherlands, before moving to New York in 2002. He worked with Rem Koolhaas/OMA (Rotterdam, 1994-2000) and was President and founder of AMO, Inc. in New York (2000-03) and a Partner with Rem Koolhaas/OMA in New York (2000-03), before cofounding WORK AC with Amale Andraos. Their work includes the Diane von Furstenberg Studio Headquarters (New York, New York, 2005-07; see p. 86); Public Farm 1 (Long Island City, New York, 2008); Wild West Side (New York, New York, 2008); designs for the Shenzhen Metro Tower (Shenzhen, China, 2010); Wuhan University Library (Wuhan, China, 2010); Kew Gardens Hills Library (Queens, New York, 2011); Children's Museum of the Arts (New York, New York, 2011); and Edible Schoolyard, PS 216 (Brooklyn, New York, 2011), all in the USA unless stated otherwise.

Boyoun Kim was born in Korea and studied illustration at the School of Visual Arts in New York. Her work has been showcased by the American Illustration society, the Society of Illustrators, and has featured in a number of publications including *The New York Times*, *The New Yorker*, and *The Washington Post*.

Illustrations: Boyoun Kim, New York
Design: Benjamin Wolbergs, Berlin
Project management: Inga Hallsson and Florian Kobler, Berlin
Collaboration: Harriet Graham, Turin
Production: Ute Wachendorf, Cologne
German translation: Claudia Arlinghaus, Münster
French translation: Claire Debard, Freiburg

Cover: HMWhite, Penthouse Gardens, New York, New York, USA

Printed in Slovakia

ISBN 978-3-8365-6375-8

© 2016 TASCHEN GmbH
Hohenzollernring 53
D-50672 Cologne
www.taschen.com

EACH AND EVERY TASCHEN BOOK PLANTS A SEED!
TASCHEN is a carbon neutral publisher. Each year, we offset our annual carbon emissions with carbon credits at the Instituto Terra, a reforestation program in Minas Gerais, Brazil, founded by Lélia and Sebastião Salgado. To find out more about this ecological partnership, please check: www.taschen.com/zerocarbon
Inspiration: unlimited. Carbon footprint: zero.

To stay informed about TASCHEN and our upcoming titles, please subscribe to our free magazine at www.taschen.com/magazine, follow us on Twitter, Instagram, and Facebook, or e-mail your questions to contact@taschen.com.